HOLINESS AND POLITICS

HOLINESS AND POLITICS

PETER HINCHLIFF

Darton, Longman and Todd
London

First published in Great Britain in 1982 by
Darton, Longman & Todd Ltd
89 Lillie Road
London SW6 1UD

ISBN 0 232 51502 6

British Library Cataloguing in Publication Data

Hinchliff, Peter
Holiness and politics.
1. Christianity and politics
I. Title
261.7 BR115.P7

ISBN 0-232-51502-6

Printed in Great Britain by The Anchor Press Ltd
and bound by Wm Brendon & Son Ltd
both of Tiptree, Essex

For the members of the 'lunch-time discussion group' at Balliol between 1972 and 1982

CONTENTS

ACKNOWLEDGEMENT

The Scripture quotations in this publication are from the Revised Standard Version of the Bible, copyrighted 1971 and 1952 by the Division of Christian Education of the National Council of the Churches of Christ in the USA.

INTRODUCTORY NOTE

I have come to realize that the fact that this book was originally a series of lectures has imposed a somewhat curious structure upon it. The eight Bampton Lectures have to be delivered at irregular and sometimes lengthy intervals, spread over a period of about five months. No individual lecture can last for more than forty minutes. This means that the lecturer can make only a very limited number of points in each lecture and cannot rely on his audience – even if it were to contain the same people each time – being able to remember a point between one lecture and the next. The effect of these restraints has been to give the book a cyclical character. A problem has to be expounded at one point and the proposed answer at another, giving an appearance of contradicting as well as repeating what has been said earlier. There seemed no way of avoiding this effect. I hope I have not really contradicted myself. What I intended to do was to expand a point each time I returned to it, by feeding into the discussion other points raised along the way, thus gradually building up a fuller and more complete picture.

I have to thank Dr Haddon Willmer, the Reverend Dr Edward Yarnold, S.J., David Young and Michael Banner for reading the manuscript, in whole or in part, at various stages, and for their valuable comments and criticisms. Any faults that remain are my own. I am also extremely grateful to my wife for typing the greater part of it, twice over, once as lectures and once as the book, which must have been a very frustrating thing to have to do.

1

THE IMPOSSIBILITY OF POLITICS

Ambition, ruthlessness, and the pursuit of fame are among the *essential* characteristics of the successful politician listed by James Margach in *The Anatomy of Power*. 'A great leader must never be squeamish at the sight of blood, other people's blood. . .'[1] Meekness, mercy and humility are the characteristics Jesus is said to have listed as *essential* to the Christian. It is little wonder, then, that politics and Christianity are thought of as being about as compatible as oil and water. Margaret Thatcher, no doubt with complete sincerity, quoted the so-called prayer of St Francis on the night of her election victory in 1979, asserting a desire to bring pardon where there had been injury, hope where there had been despair. The only effect of such a claim was to make the prayer unusable for its original purpose.

The disconsance of Christianity with politics is now almost welcomed with delight. The optimism of the tradition associated with William Temple, which took it for granted that faith required social as well as personal expression, has disappeared. The reasons for this are complex. Life is obviously less comfortable for Christians if they put their beliefs into practice in terms of political action. But, equally, substituting political programmes for more specifically religious goals, or identifying Christianity with particular and extreme political movements, offends many because it seems to contradict the values which Jesus himself embodied. By the 1970s there was a widespread feeling that there was far too much politics in religion. A private piety, detached from social and political issues, had become very fashionable.

There are pressures, nevertheless, which prevent the fashion from sweeping the board entirely. The very people who care most about personal piety are deeply disturbed by what they think of as the decay of morals in society. Though they are most worried by contemporary sexual mores, attempts to prevent any further deterioration necessitate the use of political means – lobbying, pressure groups, acts of parliament, mobilising the churches. The seventies were also a decade of rather obvious public corruption, of which Watergate was the most spectacular example. Public morality has become an issue. There has also been a growing awareness of the fragility of human societies. Pollution, the exhaustion of natural resources, over-population and consequent starvation, pandemic disease or nuclear war could all destroy us within the foreseeable future. These are, therefore, all seen as moral issues. And they are not issues which private piety and morality can cope with. They are political issues with a moral dimension upon which, therefore, religious beliefs have a bearing. In many countries, moreover, the churches are directly involved in political crises. Even those who believe that this is undesirable have to face the fact that it is happening and are compelled therefore to articulate their reasons for disapproving of it.

For these reasons, and in spite of the current fashion for trying to separate Christianity and politics, the relationship between the two continually attracts public interest. The debate goes on in the press all the time. It attracts a great deal of attention. It is always news. Yet the main issue itself and the complex problems through which it is repeatedly raised seem to come no nearer a solution.

This book is based on the Bampton Lectures delivered in the University of Oxford in 1982. The trust from which the lectures are endowed requires the lecturer either to defend certain specified Christian beliefs or to take a clause of the creeds as his theme. Because the relationship between Christianity and politics is of such current practical importance and raises so many difficult moral problems, it seemed a topic worth considering. I have dealt with it under the clause of the Nicene creed which reads, 'I believe one, holy, catholic and apostolic Church'. This is not simply an artificial device to enable the lectures to be brought within the terms of the trust. It is obvious that, at bottom, politics is about human nature. Theologically speaking, it is the doctrine of man which one is discussing. To use the categories of classical theology, this means that original sin (the only empirically verifiable doctrine) is basic to any Christian consideration of politics. And in the scheme of Christian theology the Church is the mirror-image of humanity. Human society is fallen man: the Church is redeemed man. To return to the language with which this chapter started, if the problem is that the essential characteristics of a successful politician are precisely the opposites of the essential characteristics of a good Christian, one seems to be saying that the morality required by politics is incompatible with the holiness of the Church. To examine the whole question of Christianity and politics in the light of the idea of 'the holy Church' is, therefore, not just a device for satisfying

John Bampton's trust. It is the appropriate framework for the debate.

Those who wish to stress the incompatibility of Christianity and politics usually do so in one of three ways. One of these is simply – but often unconsciously – prejudiced and not very honest. It assumes that one's own politics is not politics and is, therefore, perfectly compatible with Christianity. It is only other kinds of politics that are incompatible. This attitude is very neatly illustrated by a letter written by the churchwardens of a vacant parish, describing the kind of incumbent whom they hoped would be appointed. They said, in effect, that they would like a sound Tory because '. . . our experience and reports we have heard of politically active clergy in this part of the country compel us to believe that such a ministry would be neither beneficial nor fruitful'. What is interesting is the implied assumption that to be a supporter of the Conservative Party is not to be 'politically active'.

The second attitude may be illustrated by an extract from an article about the Pope's visit to Nagasaki and Hiroshima in March 1981. 'Ever since the Founder advised a Roman centurion that there was no Divine objection to giving to Caesar the things that belong to the State, such as military service, Christians have wrestled with the problem of war without much success.'[2] It is difficult to imagine a piece of journalism with more howlers to the column inch. Where did the centurion come from? Who mentioned military service? Nevertheless, this sentence reflects a common understanding of the saying, 'Render to Caesar the things that are Caesar's and to God the things that are God's'. [3] It is taken to mean that there are two entirely separate sphere's, God's and Caesar's. Each reigns supreme in his own sphere and is entitled to receive whatever properly belongs to that sphere. Politics belongs to the State, and the State is entitled to demand what it deems necessary for the maintenance of the political. God has no objection to this, so long as he receives what is his proper due in his own sphere, of religion. In the article quoted, moreover, there is a hint that this separation is what has made political life possible for Christians. Politics would be impossible if it had to be played according to God's rules. Politics requires ruthlessness: God requires mercy. But there is no 'Divine objection' to Christians playing the political game according to the political rules.

If taken seriously this would be an unbearably hypocritical and cynical attitude. It is the morality of the Nazi concentration camp commandant singing Christmas carols with his family round the piano. And yet it is this assumption of the two separate spheres, each with its own autonomous set of standards, which often underlies the assertion that the Church should keep out of politics. And it is understandable, because the disconsonance between the two sets of values is so great that there seems to be no way of reconciling them.

The third way (though mistaken) is the only *respectable* argument for separating Christanity and politics.

> At his baptism in the River Jordan, Jesus initiated a ministry that was characterized by a call to personal redemption, to the renunciation of sin, and a departure from the world's values. It was also a rejection of the politicized official religion of his day. Time was short: eternity pressed near.[4]

This is a quotation from E. R. Norman's Reith Lectures which, though they were not entirely free from the other two kinds of argument,[5] concentrated chiefly upon asserting that Christianity was essentially an other-worldly religion which ought not to allow political goals to become its chief concerns.

There is, however, an entirely different way of understanding the words, 'Render to Caesar the things that are Caesar's. and to God the things that are God's'. They are attributed to Christ as part of an argument about the payment of taxes. He asks the question, about the actual coinage with which the tax is to be paid, 'Whose image and superscription is this?' The answer is that it is Caesar's and so, because it bears Caesar's image, it belongs to him and can properly be given to him. But we are to give to God what belongs to God. There is, therefore, an implied parallel series of questions and answers. 'What do we give to God?' 'Why, that which bears *his* image'. 'And what does bear God's image?' 'Man, of course, as the book of Genesis tells us.'

The implication of this interpretation is that there is no separation of spheres. The whole of a man bears God's image. The whole of himself is owing to God, including his political life. What he owes to Caesar is a small part of what he is worth. God claims the whole and, therefore, God reigns supreme even over the political sphere.

This may sound like the trendy political theologizing of the twentieth century but it has an ancestry that goes back to Tertullian and the end of the second century. In at least five of his works[6] Tertullian interprets the saying in this sense and, in doing so, can take it for granted that this is what it means. 'While you give money to Caesar', he says, 'you give yourself to God.'[7]

Tertullian uses this interpretation of the text to advance an argument for martyrdom. 'If I owe God the [whole] man, and my blood, and am at the point where I am asked to pay what I owe to God, then indeed I cheat God if I act in such a way that I fail to pay what I owe.'[8] In the context in which Tertullian wrote, the assertion that God's claim was upon the whole man had become almost an argument that Caesar had no claim at all.

Tertullian wrote, of course, in the context of persecution. Belonging to the rigorist North African tradition which treated martyrdom as if it were a hardly exceptional part of Christian spirituality, he was arguing against any attempt to escape from martyrdom. Moreover all the passages probably belong to the period when Tertullian's rigorism, and his devotion to martyrdom, had taken him into Montanism.[9] Nevertheless, no part of his argument would be valid if he were not able to assert that one's duty to God is overwhelming and all-embracing and that all other duties, even to Caesar, are subordinate to that. And that is a theological proposition which must be beyond question. Whatever else 'Render to Caesar the things that are Caesar's and to God the things that are God's' may mean, it cannot mean that there are two separate spheres, parallel, autonomous and having equal claim upon the Christian – religion and politics.

Yet there is a sense in which the position into which Tertullian's argument leads him is not so very different from that of those who interpret Christ's saying to mean that there *are* two separate spheres. He consistently takes a stand against any sort of compromise and – at any rate in a pagan and potentially persecuting state – that means a kind of separation from the secular world. Though he denies that Christians lack a concern for the welfare of emperor and empire, he asserts that their real loyalty is elsewhere. Their hope is that they will attain the eternal promises of God: their fear is that they will be punished if they live otherwise than God has commanded.[10]

This is not unlike the point made by E. R. Norman but it is quite different from the other two – and much more widespread – kinds of disapproval of the intermingling of religion and politics. Indeed it is sometimes far from clear whether the popular distaste is an expression of a fear that religion will be contaminated by politics, or politics by religion. 'Keep religion out of politics' is often said in exactly the same tone of voice as 'Keep politics out of sport' and, in the second case, it is perfectly clear in which direction the contamination works. With the example of Northern Ireland in people's minds it is, perhaps, not surprising that religion is thought of as a debasing influence in politics.

There is also a strong tradition in this country that it is *party* politics with which Christianity should not seek to involve itself. Any attempt to express Christian opinion in practical political terms provokes an immediate rejoinder that it is taking sides. On 9 March

1981 *The Times* reported that the Anglican, Methodist and Roman Catholic departments concerned with social responsibility had called for a day of Lenten prayer and fasting for justice in public expenditure. Two days later the same newspaper published a letter from a Jesuit priest saying, 'I hasten to dissociate myself from what must be classified as an outrageous example of partisan politics, excusable only in terms of what appears as the invincible ignorance of its promoters.'[11]

It has to be said that the religious correspondent of *The Times* had given the call for a Lenten fast a more partisan character than it need have had by linking it with an address given a few days before in the church of St Lawrence Jewry by Mrs Thatcher, the prime minister. But, in a sense, that merely underlines the point. For Mrs Thatcher was quoted as saying that, if the churches took sides on practical issues, 'this can only weaken the influence and independence of the church, whose members ideally should help the thinking of all political parties.' This seems to be saying that the churches can be very influential as long as they do not actually try and influence anything.

One suspects, of course, that complaints about political partisanship come chiefly from those whose party is under attack at the time, but there is a sense in which Christians would do well to beware of allying themselves with any one political organization or regime. There are a good many instances in the history of modern Europe of churches identifying themselves so closely with a party (usually of the right) as to deprive them of any claim to speak without prejudice on social questions.

What is unfortunate – though perhaps inevitable – is that those who ask for Christian neutrality in party politics usually seem to be asking for a neutrality modelled on that of the civil service. This, too, is understandable. A politically neutral civil service is very desirable. In Britain, and in countries whose traditions have been influenced by Britain, it is regarded as vital. But the model is an unfortunate one for the churches to adopt, in spite of its attractions, and it seems to have been the model Mrs Thatcher had in mind in using the phrase 'help the thinking of all political parties'.

Having spent most of my life in South Africa, it is inevitable that I should draw many of my examples from events in that country. The strength of the neutral civil service tradition there was very clearly illustrated during the so-called 'Muldergate' scandal in South Africa in the late 1970s which led to the resignation of the prime minister (later president), B. J. Vorster. It was alleged that prominent civil servants had used public funds for private purposes. It also emerged that civil servants had been using a variety of secret and more or less devious methods to influence public opinion abroad in South Africa's favour. To do this they had been using funds authorised by cabinet ministers who denied that they had done so. To many people it seemed incredible that civil servants and politicians should be reviled for doing everything possible, however deviously, to gain allies abroad for a policy which the vast majority of the electorate enthusiastically supported. But what was regarded as really scandalous, in South Africa itself, was the fact that members of the government had authorised civil servants to use public funds to gain control of a *South African* newspaper which supported the ruling party. The public service had ceased to pretend to be neutral.

This model of political neutrality, where what is thought to matter is not the moral quality of the government's policies nor the integrity of the methods used to put them into practice, but that one should never be *seen* to be taking sides under any circumstances whatever, is an unfortunate one for the churches to be expected to adopt. For one thing, it is perfectly possible to be neutral in an entirely different sense – as a judge is neutral. To criticize or even condemn the policies of one party is not the same thing as being partisan. It is perfectly possible to argue that the government's programme is unjust, without necessarily implying that the opposition's programme is perfect. Even in very practical and detailed criticisms, such as Mrs Thatcher was referring to, one can be completely neutral in the sense that one can be reserving the right to be equally critical of programmes of other subsequent administrations. But the civil service model of neutrality tends to suggest that one ought to act as if one were *advising* the government, even-handedly reviewing the possible options and pointing out the pros and cons of each. And this is the approach the churches have all too often adopted, saying, on the one hand, this about capitalism and, on the other, that about the welfare state. This merely makes them seem bland and ineffective.

Worse still, the civil service model of neutrality is dangerous because it suggests that the churches, like civil servants, ought to be servants of the government. This is an easy posture to adopt because there is a genuinely Christian tradition which stresses the duty of obedience, a theme which will be looked at again in a later chapter. It is, perhaps, a particularly tempting pattern for English Christians to follow for historical reasons connected with the establishment and the pressures it has created even for non-conformists. In a country where religious dissent has often been equated with political unreliability, this must be the case. But in other countries, too, political neutrality is only too easily confused with support for the *status quo*. To take South Africa as an example again, in spite of the fact that most of the leaders of the Dutch Reformed Church have supported the policies of the Nationalist administrations, accusations of 'interfering in politics' are levelled only at those who *criticise* the government. Much the same could be said of America during the Vietnam war. People were horrified by clergymen who criticised the war and encouraged young men to dodge the draft. Eminent evangelists who backed the administration and spoke in support of the war were accused of many things but not of interfering in politics.

In the end, however, there is this to be said for those who object to Christian support for partisan politics. The churches need to be able to stand aside from *all* political programmes in order to examine them critically. It is this which, in spite of the support it tends to draw from prejudiced and simplistic opinion, gives weight to the more self-consciously theological version of the argument. Like Tertullian, its proponents maintain that Christianity is 'about' eternal salvation and, therefore, about obedience to God's commands and the attainment of perfection. There can, in consequence, be no compromise between that ideal and the realities of politics.

The very words 'eternal salvation' would now be regarded as begging the crucial question. Not only have Christians been accused of diverting attention from social problems by offering an other-worldly salvation but the whole concept of an 'other world' is seriously questioned by some theologians for reasons which have nothing to do with political or social issues. Analytical philosophy has made it difficult to describe or defend an existence which is 'spiritual' and 'supernatural' and wholly outside time and space. Therefore theologians have attempted to give accounts of Christianity which do not rely on such concepts. Whether God's 'kingdom' and his purpose for the universe are eternal and supernatural or whether they are to be conceived of as falling entirely within the realities of time and space and history is itself a matter for debate among even a-political theologians. But obviously if one does reject 'other-worldly' views it is much easier to reconcile one's understanding of Christianity with a Marxist analysis of society and its belief that history is moving towards the resolution of social and economic injustices. It is this that makes it possible for Dr Norman to argue that the abandonment of traditional orthodoxy leads to a politicized and left-wing Christianity.

It seems to me that this is an altogether too simple view. Not every theologian who finds it necessary to abandon traditional supernatural categories, moves into the realm of political theology. Those who hold a very traditional and orthodox belief may, on the basis of an argument which Tertullian would have accepted, find themselves insisting upon the importance of the political and the historical. In any case the Christian world is not neatly divided into those who accept a traditional and supernaturalist understanding and those who insist that this world is all there is. There are a great many positions in between.

There are also a great many problematical or disputed areas. The authority of the biblical writings, the way in which they are to be interpreted, the theological conclusions to be drawn from them, as well as the validity of those theological conclusions in terms of contemporary philosophy, are all questions to which different answers are given by Christian scholars. It simply is not possible to produce a complex and, at the same time, agreed account of a complete theological system. And an approach to politics which is dependent upon a complex, disputed and problematical construction is not of much practical use. It merely poses, more sharply than ever, the question whether Christianity has anything to say which has a bearing on what is actually happening.

Moreover, there appear to be moral difficulties about a position which rejects everything other than the historical, just as there are about a position which insists that Christianity is about that which is eternal. It would seem to follow logically from the latter view that one ought to have nothing to do with the realities of politics since a concern for perfection ought to exclude the art of the possible altogether. But that, in practice, all too often means the acceptance of a *status quo* which is full of compromise and, sometimes, even injustice. On the other hand, if the goal of history is political rather than eternal, then all those generations which precede the final emergence of the just society are, in a sense, dehumanized. Their sufferings and their struggles are merely stepping stones towards the goal. Yet those who advance a political theology claim to be moved by the very sufferings of those who exist now.

It seems to me, therefore, that the moral issue is a possible starting point. For every Christian accepts that what they believe makes a claim upon them in terms of the way in which they behave. They also believe that that claim is absolute. Those who believe in the eternal share *that* with those who do not. My argument is chiefly directed to the former, for my own beliefs are closer to theirs, and therefore I shall chiefly be concerned with the question: Are politics and Christianity incompatible because of the demands of Christian morality? But it seems to me that the same question needs to be asked of those who are concerned with the doing of political theology – though I recognize that the question will sound completely different to them: Does Christianity impose *any* moral restraints upon political action?

The problem I wish to examine is not a matter of practice, whether politicians are sometimes personally corrupt. It is not, after all, a *necessity* of politics that politicians should accept bribes. Nor am I concerned with the question whether certain specific political philosophies or programmes are compatible with Christianity. The problem I wish to examine is what is the proper interface between politics and personal Christian moral standards, given that Christianity makes demands of an absolute kind. After all, unless it can be shown that there is a proper interface, it would seem to follow that moral considerations can be treated as irrelevant in either one's personal life or in political action – or both.

I shall not be considering rival moralities or attempting to defend Christian ideas of morality against the views of secular moral philosophers. The question is not whether Christian morality is right but whether it is compatible with the practicalities of politics. It would be nicer, and much simpler, if one could ignore the views of moral philosophers altogether but this has turned out to be impossible. Nevertheless I hope to limit what I have to say, in this area, to those points where what is said by *some* philosophers (one could not consider them all) falls into one of three categories:

(1) where they themselves are arguing that morality and politics are incompatible or where they draw attention to the problems inherent in trying to apply morality to politics;

(2) where they, without necessarily implying that Christianity and its morality are wrong, seem to question certain assumptions about the very nature of moral issues which are integral to a correct understanding of the methods of Christian moral theology; and

(3) where the ways in which they have posed moral issues seem particularly illuminating.

I have used practising politicians in much the same way except that, fortunately, politicians have not written so much on the subject of the relationship between politics and morality as philosophers have.

The problem is, then, whether Christian morality and political reality can be reconciled at all. The difficulties inherent in attempting to do so can be simply demonstrated. The works of Reinhold Niebuhr provide what is almost a paradigm of the Christian's dilemma in relating the ideal to the political.[12]

His first book, *Does Civilization Need Religion*, was published in 1927 when capitalist America seemed to be a society not merely demonic but on the verge of collapse. Then Niebuhr argued for something very like a social gospel, maintaining that reality could be made gradually to approach the ideal and that a depersonalised society had to be redeemed by the political and economic embodying of Christian and therefore truly human values. Five years later, in *Moral Man and Immoral Society*, he had become rather more specific about the means and, perhaps for that reason, rather less idealistic. If good men wished to help to create a better world they might have to be prepared to use what lay to hand to achieve it, means which they (as good men) would not immediately have chosen. Thus the essentially selfish class interests of the proletariat might have to be harnessed to achieve social justice.

The implicit tension here between an individual morality of love and the corruptness of society capable of no more than justice, at best, moved Niebuhr to a new attitude. In *Reflections on the End of an Era* of 1934, he was still insisting upon the inevitability of the triumph of the proletariat in the interests of a juster society. But the book ended with a chapter on grace, a theological emphasis which made his argument vulnerable to the charge that he was not finally concerned with real solutions to real political problems. In the following year *An Interpretation of Christian Ethics* appeared, in which original sin is the key theme, necessarily requiring an explicit recognition that nothing human could be perfect. It is no longer society as opposed to the individual which is the source of corruption but the reality of human nature itself. And so, in *Beyond Tragedy* of 1937, with Hitler's Germany threatening Europe, Niebuhr argued that all evil is a result of the attempt to make the finite infinite, to make human goals ultimate goals. Three years later, for all that he believed that America *must* enter the war, he was asking, in *Christianity and Power Politics*, what the good man was to do in a bad world. And he was asking the question in a tone of voice that implied that there was no answer. The defeat of Nazi Germany would not automatically mean the emergence of a new and redeemed Europe. The political necessity was merely a negative one. And so, in 1943 with the war at its height, he wrote his greatest work, *The Nature and Destiny of Man*. Man's nature is fallen: his destiny is elsewhere.

A summary of this kind can only be a caricature. Niebuhr was never finally either disillusioned or detached in his attitude to society for after the war he played a large part in developing what was called Christian Realism. But he had come to see the problem as very much more complex and as, in a positive sense, insoluble – that is to say, not negatively insoluble as if there *were no solution to be found*, but almost as if it were not *meant* to *have* a solution. Man, product of nature and set in a context of history, is nevertheless a spirit which is outside nature, life, history, outside himself and his reason, outside the world, that is to say 'in God'. The problem for Niebuhr at every turn was that to engage with the realities of politics is to compromise the eternal values: to assert those values uncompromisingly is to disengage from the actual needs of human society.

The caricature, however unfair and therefore improper, is worth considering simply because it delineates the problem so neatly. It is difficult for a Christian seriously to adopt the separate-spheres view of religion and politics, simply because God's claim upon man is, as Tertullian saw, total – a claim upon the whole of life. If God is irrelevant to politics, which is an important part of life and one which raises serious moral issues, what validity has his claim? If society is immoral, if some political acts (like injustice, oppression and exploitation) are wrong, Christians simply cannot stand aside and regard them as outside the range of religion. And concern for the casualties of immoral politics will move Christians to protest. Protest and criticism may not be enough: there may have to be active opposition. Nor can criticism, as Niebuhr saw, content itself with being 'timeless' and general. It has to be specific and practical, which is to say that it has to be political.

This point has been very well put, as follows:

> Those who have a well worked out idea of the ultimate purposes of life and the intriguing ways of Providence do have to have some dealings with less than ultimate purposes as a means to the end. To preach of Justice and Truth in general must involve preaching justice and truth in each particular time and place, which is how politics and theology must encounter each other, disdainfully or otherwise.[13]

J. W. de Gruchy has shown with admirable clarity how, again and again, the South African churches set out to preach Justice and Truth and found themselves dealing with justice and truth in very particular contexts.[14] The specific issue of 'politicizing' he deals with most clearly of all in his account of the *Message to the People of South Africa* published by the South African Council of Churches in 1968.[15] The *Message* was a six-page document which attacked *apartheid* and separate development on theological grounds, arguing that 'this doctrine of separation has become, for many, a false faith, a novel gospel which offers happiness and peace for the community and for the individual'.[16] It claimed, in other words, that Christians who supported separation were falling into the trap of politicising the gospel, in E. R. Norman's sense of substituting temporal goals for eternal ones.

There were, nevertheless, Christians who regarded racialism as unjust and immoral but who thought the *Message* placed too much emphasis on political ideas. The Baptist Union issued a critique of the *Message*, saying: 'The views and attitudes of an individual in racial matters do not enter into the realm of his being justified by faith.'[17] This is an extreme form of the argument that politics and theology have nothing to do with each other, and it raises all sorts of questions. Would the views and attitudes of an individual in sexual matters, or any other area in which moral issues are raised, not enter into the realm of his being justified by faith? If one was not prepared to follow the Baptist Union along this road, the only logical basis upon which to reject the *Message* was by a defence of separate development on theological grounds. That is to say, one would have to attempt to show that it was a legitimate political programme which did not necessarily involve injustice or other forms of immorality and that it was not a substitution of temporal and political goals for eternal salvation.

In the actual situation, however, there was pressure upon the Council of Churches to advance beyond the theological statement rather than upon its opponents to produce a counter-theology. There is an inevitable logic in a context of this kind. Politicians, faced with theological criticism of particular policies, inevitably demand that their critics propose a viable (that is, a practical) alternative. If the theological critics refuse to do so, they appear to be saying, 'We haven't got any answers and you shouldn't have any either'. It seems as though belief in God and in the eternal destiny of man is simply a device for evading the real problems of an actual society. The Council of Churches, and even more the Christian Institute of Southern Africa, therefore became involved in a study project (called Spro-cas I) and a programme to follow it up with action (Spro-cas II), which would work out, and attempt to work towards, quite specific socio-economic alternatives to *apartheid*. As a result there developed close links between the Christian Institute and the 'black consciousness' movement which led eventually to the banning of the Institute in 1977.[18] It now appeared that it was the critics of *apartheid* who were the politicizers.

It is very significant that E. R. Norman's survey of the political alternatives suggested by Christian opponents of *apartheid*, [19] contents itself with pointing out that they are equally open to criticism, from a Christian point of view, on moral or theological grounds. It is significant, not because criticism of the critics can possibly count as a defence of *apartheid* (and Norman himself dislikes *apartheid*), but because it underlines the fact that no political programme is above reproach. As soon as Christians attempt to advance practical solutions to political problems there is a danger that they may embrace solutions which are wrong – morally wrong or simply unworkable.

The classic case of the latter sort is the way in which some members of the Christendom group in England in the 1930s enthusiastically embraced the social credit economics of Major C. H. Douglas.[20] They appear to have done so because his criticisms of a capitalist system, supposedly about to collapse under its own weight, appealed to their theological (and possibly romantic) preconceptions of what society ought to be like. They lacked the expertise to assess Douglas's theory and, therefore, accepted what is now seen to be faulty economics for reasons which had nothing to do with economics at all. Their naivety in this field undermined genuine theology and exposed it to ridicule.

In the same period some of Niebuhr's American contemporaries like Sherwood Eddy and H. F. Ward, accepted the social gospel with a whole-heartedness which Niebuhr himself never exhibited. Disgusted by the harsh and selfish (and therefore immoral) consequences of free enterprise capitalism revealed in the economic crises of the twenties and thirties, some Christian thinkers became whole-hearted supporters of communism. This led to the destruction of the very presuppositions from which they had begun. An initial concern for human beings and the brotherhood of man ended in commitment to a system in which human beings had little value over against society.[21] The politicising of theology destroyed the theological foundation of the political position itself.

Both the Christendom group and Ward's League for Peace and Democracy accepted analyses of capitalism which maintained, though in very different ways, that it was breaking down under pressure from its own processes. One failed because it lacked the expertise to propose a viable alternative and the other because of its own inconsistencies. But, in fact, it was neither the weak economics of the Christendom group nor the inconsistent theology of the League which really put an end to the attempts to find a Christian answer to the economic problems of the twenties and thirties. It was political reality, not theology or economic theory, which did so. The events leading up to the outbreak of the second world war, and to America's participation in it, created a different order of priorities. Older loyalties cut across social concerns. International politics took precedence over economics and necessitated a restructuring of the economy. In spite of the Christian attractiveness of pacifism, most Christians accepted the political necessity of war. The impossibility of reconciling morality and politics seemed to have been proved.

With hindsight it is possible to ask whether it is really fair to make fun of theologians for not understanding economics. In our own day we are coming to realize that even the economists do not seem to understand the economy. Indeed the economy appears to be almost as incomprehensible as the mysteries which are the subject matter of theology. There are as many schools of thought, as much odium, and as few certain answers among economists as has traditionally been the case with theologians.

To say this is not merely to give oneself the pleasure of pulling the legs of the economists acd certainly not to excuse Christians from the necessity of taking trouble to understand the complex and technical realities we live with. There is a serious point. It may be that there *are* no long-term certainties in economics. Keynes, after all, was a far better economist than Major Douglas. For an entire generation his was the dominant, almost the unchallenged, orthodoxy. A very great many people, who would otherwise have been unemployed, had reason to be grateful for the 'success' of his theories. Yet we are often now told, apparently authoritatively, that though he 'was an exceptional economist while he lived . . . [he] has become a malevolent myth since he died'.[22] If that is the case, then one may be forgiven for adopting a cynical attitude to economic theories in general. One might conclude that there are no permanent solutions to the problems of society. The only possible course in politics seems to be one of extemporised, provisional management, limited to the short-term pragmatic future. And if that, in turn, is the case, the contrast between eternal values and the ephemeral political *now* becomes even sharper. One might legitimately contend that political and economic programmes are a matter of mere fashion and that the Christian had better stand aside from them – though with a hostile and critical attitude. The compromises of principle which the practicalities of politics appear to require are simply not worth it, if we cannot even be sure that they will produce answers. We seem to be forced back on to the two-spheres view. After all there is no absolute necessity for us to become engaged in the large issues to which there seem to be no solutions. We might as well go for holiness.

Unfortunately such an attitude seems equally impossible, at least for severely practical reasons. Tertullian's rigorism can be dismissed as a response to persecution, and we are not persecuted. If the pagan state had left him and his fellow Christians alone he might never have expressed such vigorous views about the claims of God. But, in fact, so long as we are part of human society, the state cannot leave *us* alone either. Theoretically, we might each retire to a remote and isolated hut and grow our own food and make our own clothes (while being careful not to earn enough money to come within the range of income tax demands – for that, after all, is how most people support government). Short of drastic action of that kind we remain trapped in the dilemma.

This was brought home very clearly by the notorious A.B.C. trial of a few years ago. The case, so called because of the initial letters of the surnames of the three defendants, was a prosecution under the Official Secrets Act of two journalists and a former soldier. During his service with the army, this man had worked with equipment which, he believed, was being used to an immoral end. And he felt compelled to reveal what was happening.

It appears from reports of the case[23] that, in sentencing the accused, the judge said that he *had* to be punished because he knew full well that he was breaking not only the law *but his solemn undertaking as well.* There was no point in adding that second phrase – for to break his undertaking *was* to break the law – unless the judge intended to invoke some sort of moral sanction to strengthen the claim of the law. One can see why he should wish to do so. There is in any case a close similarity in the kinds of argument used in law and in morality, since both are concerned with behaviour in relation to obligations. Moreover moral concepts such as natural justice are sometimes used in law. But here one suspects – from other remarks the judge was reported to have made[24] – that the prime motive was rather different. The truth is that in matters of this kind the state is powerless to protect itself by the law alone. For the law can only punish after the event when the damage has been done. And in cases of this sort the damage is irreparable. If the punishment is not a sufficient deterrent then the state must make quasi-moral claims to prevent such things happening again.

I do not know whether the accused was a Christian but let us suppose that he was. He could say to himself that God's claim upon him was absolute. If he believed that what was happening was, in Christian terms, immoral, then he was right to try and stop it. He would be obliged to say that crime and sin are the not the same thing. Some sins are not crimes. Sometimes the demands of morality may *require* one to break the law, as Tertullian knew. If he was very brave and very convinced, not even the death penalty would be an effective deterrent against such a man. That seems the clear, simple statement of Christian duty, however unpalatable.

But there is a counter-case – one which the judge was implicitly invoking. Any person who has given his solemn undertaking ought to be bound by it. And that holds for Christians, too. It simply is not moral to promise something one does not intend to fulful. So a Christian who has signed the Official Secrets Act ought not to reveal the secrets he thus obtains access to. The trouble is that, in the nature of the case, one cannot know the secrets till one has given the promise. There would be a case for arguing that the promise could not be binding – as the marriage vows are sometimes held not to be binding where one party cannot understand them or is ignorant of something that might have prevented consent. But in the case of the Official Secrets Act the ignorance is quite explicitly accepted by the signatory and it is very difficult for a Christian to give such an undertaking unless he makes its conditional character perfectly clear – 'I am giving this undertaking on the understanding that, if I find I am required to keep immoral secrets, I shall break it.' And then he would not get the job.

There seems every reason to believe that the Christian, because of God's claim upon him, should not take the kind of job which requires that degree of obedience to the state. After all Hippolytus, a contemporary of Tertullian's, was very clear that there were many jobs that were totally incompatible with the Christian profession.[25] Along with such obviously immoral things as soothsaying and prostitution, he included the service of the state, both civil and military. The trouble is that this interface between religion and politics is neither small nor remote. Every undergraduate doing a vacation job as a porter at Broadmoor or as a clerk in the local office of the Department of Employment, has to sign the Official Secrets Act. Even at so trivial a level – to earn some pocket-money – one has to accept an open-ended moral obligation intolerable for a Christian unless treated as a formality. And it is clear that senior civil servants, whether Christian or not, are acutely aware of this dilemma.[26]

The Official Secrets Act may seem to be a special case. But the truth is that the state and its activities pervade our lives. It employs a great many of us – or at least contributes to our incomes. A large part of our income, in turn, goes to maintain its activities, good and bad. It plays a part in many of the most ordinary aspects of everyday life. Despite the fashionable tendency to complain about collectivism, bureaucracy and overmanning, we would lose a great deal if it were not so. And, in any case, it is so. As society has become secular and pluralist and the state has become neutral in matters of religion – so that, superficially, it might seem less likely to make claims upon the conscience – it has also extended its activities into more and more aspects of our lives. Its claims upon us have become more extensive, in consequence, and the private realm where the individual conscience can remain insulated has become smaller.

It can be very cogently argued that in England the extension of the welfare state, the secularisation of society and the growth of government have gone together. In pre-industrial England religion was regarded as a perfectly proper area for state intervention. Dissent carried penalties and disadvantages. At the same time, vast areas which are now thought of as almost inevitably part of the state's responsibility – education, health, employment, the police, even sewage – were not so regarded though, in theory at least, the established church and the morally responsible landowner might be thought of as supplying some of these services. But penalising dissent politically could not be defended for ever. Secularisation would be an inevitable outcome of removing from the established church many of the privileges it possessed. Equally inevitably, what would follow would not be a society of Christian men and women, free to live according to their own consciences unimpeded by either ecclesiastical or secular authority. It would involve the acceptance of a kind of collectivism in which the state would shoulder the moral responsibility for a wider and wider range of activities which were necessary for the creation of a 'good' society.

> The secularization of the State is a process based on the principle that what are believed to be wholly secular objectives are the only possible results of organized public endeavour. The achievement of these ends is, however, deemed to be so important, and the organization required to attain them so all-embracing and powerful, that it presumes a concentration of authority. . . If the State was to achieve these secular objectives which it became increasingly clear it must achieve, if it was to educate the people, supply a healthy environment . . . and regulate the conditions under which they worked, then it must take to itself sufficient authority to achieve these ends, and it could not allow its purposes to be impeded by the vagaries of the individual conscience or the eccentricities of private opinion.[27]

It is sheer romanticism to hanker after the revival of a religious state in the seventeenth-century sense. There seems no way in which the process of secularisation could be undone. Anyone, moreover, who has lived in a society where education, health or employment are not regarded as proper areas for government intervention, is unlikely to desire such a state of affairs in Britain. But, if one accepts that the state is to have these concerns, then one has also to accept that the state will insist that one pays one's taxes (even if one regards as immoral some of the purposes to which they will be put). If the state is required to achieve certain purposes, then it *will* take to itself the authority necessary to compel obedience.

The upshot is that while we may no longer be threatened by overtly religious pressures from the state, its claims upon us – claims which are likely to raise moral issues – are very extensive. To opt out of involvement with the larger issues of public policy does not absolve us from the obligation to respond to those claims. Nor does the avoidance of certain jobs. We all rightly owe a measure of loyalty to society and, sooner rather than later, society will ask for it. Merely to be a member of society is to be entrapped in the dilemma. We cannot disengage from the political: but to be engaged seems to require a potential betrayal of Christian moral standards at some point or other.

This is not a simple problem, for it presents itself at both a practical and a theoretical level. I have just been saying that we cannot disengage from the political and, at that moment, I was thinking of the sheer practical impossibility of opting out of the complex, collectivist structure of modern society. Earlier, when I was talking of Niebuhr, I spoke of the way a Christian can be *driven* to wrestle with the moral issues that arise for a member of society. This is a different sense in which it is impossible to be detached and neutral. It is not just that, at a practical level, there is no possibility of escape. It is that, in principle, there is a moral compulsion to care about the condition of other human beings – of society, that is. Yet, because man is fallen and imperfectible, no political solution to society's problems will ever be perfect. The very moral principles which compel us to pronounce upon the character of society seem to become compromised if they are translated into political programmes. That is, again, a matter of both practicality and principle. Either we may have debased the moral principles for which we stand. Or we may be demanding a politically impractical programme. Theological as well as practical considerations compel us to be involved in society. Theological and practical difficulties seem to drive us out again into the hermit's cave.

Looked at from the point of view of Christianity, then, politics is easily criticised. Human society cannot be perfect because man is imperfectible and humanity in the aggregate is fallen humanity. The difficulty arises because criticism always implies a hypothetical standard against which society is being judged. That standard cannot comfortably be allowed to remain a mere implication: there will always be pressure for it to be stated explicitly. And this is where the difficulty arises. For to state the preferable alternative will be to lay oneself open to one of two charges. Either the alternative will be itself imperfect in practice (for the same reason, that man is imperfectible) or, if perfect, will be impractical. Neither naive economics nor deliberate corruption is a necessity, but when we look at the range of *possible* options with which political events present us the perfect, ideal or wholly moral seldom seem to be among them.

Admittedly, as this book progresses, I shall be wanting to redefine the problem somewhat. I shall argue that part of the difficulty is eased by fuller understanding of what morality means. But the problem will not vanish because the terms are redefined. The Christian's dilemma may present itself in a different way but it will not disappear. The mere fact that the characteristics of *successful* politics are so far removed from typical Christian virtues suggests that the morally desirable and the politically desirable are likely to be incompatible.

Notes

1. J. Margach, *The Anatomy of Power*, W. H. Allen 1979, pp. 1f.
2. Murray Sayle, 'A Pope for Nearly All Seasons' in *The Spectator*, 7 March 1981.
3. Matthew 22:21; Mark 12:17; Luke 20:25.
4. E. R. Norman, *Christianity and the World Order*, O.U.P. 1979, p. 78.
5. See my criticisms of Norman's lectures in H. Willmer (ed.), *Christian Faith and Political Hopes*, Epworth Press 1979, pp. 17f.
6. *Adversus Marcionem*, IV.38.2; *De Corona*, 12.4; *Scorpiace*, 14.2; *De Idolatria*, 15.3; *De Fuga*, 12.10. I am indebted to Professor R. D. Sider for help in locating these passages.
7. *De Idolatria, loc. cit.*.
8. *de Fuga, loc. cit.*
9. But see T. D. Barnes, *Tertullian*, O.U.P. 1971, pp. 30ff. for a detailed and meticulous attempt to date Tertullian's writings. Barnes does not, for example, accept the usual view that *Scorpiace* belongs to Tertullian's Montanist period (p. 172).
10. *Ad Scapulam*, 1 and 2.
11. The Reverend Paul Crane, S.J., in the correspondence columns of *The Times*, 11 March 1981.
12. I am much indebted for my understanding of Niebuhr's writings to Donald B. Meyer, *The Protestant Search for Political Realism*, Greenwood Press (reprint) 1973, particularly pp. 217ff.
13. Clifford Longley. 'Marx, Benn and Other Political Theologists', *The Times*, 28 April 1980.
14. J. W. de Gruchy, *The Church Struggle in South Africa*, S.P.C.K. 1979.
15. de Gruchy, *op cit.*, pp. 108f. and 117ff.
16. *Ibid.*, p. 120.
17. *Ibid.*, p. 121.
18. *Ibid.*, pp. 109f.
19. E. R. Norman, *op.cit.*, pp. 64ff. Norman's later and more detailed consideration of Christianity and politics in South Africa (*Christianity in the Southern Hemisphere*, O.U.P. 1981, pp. 96–188) effectively stops short in the 1950s when Christian critics of *apartheid* had not really begun to develop alternatives. Norman makes generalized comments on black consciousness, which had hardly been heard of in his period, but does not back them with precise facts.
20. See R. H. Preston, *Religion and the Persistence of Capitalism*, S.C.M. 1979, p. 16 and, for more detail, P. Mayhew, *The Christendom Group*, Oxford University B. Litt. thesis 1977, pp. 78ff., 91 and 102ff.
21. D. B. Meyer, *op.cit.*, pp. 200ff.

22. See e.g. E. S. and H. G. Johnson, *The Shadow of Keynes*, Basil Blackwell 1978, p. 226.
23. *The Times*, 18 November 1978.
24. *Ibid.*, 'We will not tolerate defectors or whistle-blowers from our intelligence services who seek the assistance of the press or other media to publicize secrets, whatever the motive.'
25. *Apostolic Tradition*, II.16.
26. See report of Royal Institute of Public Administration Conference in *The Times*, 13 April 1981.
27. G. Kitson Clark, *Churchmen and the Condition of England*, Methuen 1973, p. 332.

2

THE UNDESIRABILITY OF MORALS

If there are real problems, from the Christian point of view, in relating morality to politics, there seem to be equally difficult problems from the point of view of the practical politician. Pilate's famous question to Jesus (in John 18:38), 'What is truth?' epitomises those problems. Pilate may not have been jesting: nor is the question attributed to him necessarily a cynical one. The passage may be interpreted in a quite different way. Pilate has been trying to get Jesus to reply to the charge brought against him. He is concerned with the facts and their political implications. He wants to know whether Jesus had actually claimed to be a king and, if so, whether his claim was of a kind which constituted a threat to Roman authority. Jesus is not able to give a simple factual answer to the kind of questions Pilate is asking because, within the moral and theological framework upon which his teaching is based, they are misconceived. Of course he is a king, in the sense that his authority over his followers claims to be absolute. Of course his teaching threatens Roman authority, in the sense that it threatens all temporal authority. But he is not a king in the sense that would lead his followers to fight against Rome. His authority is that he bears witness to the truth.

But Pilate, who is a politician as well as a judge, is concerned with practical realities not with the abstractions of moral philosophy. He has to deal in hard, intractable facts. 'What is truth?' is neither humorous nor cynical but impatient.

It is possible to sympathise with Pilate. There is some evidence to suggest that the trial narratives of the gospels formed the basis of a tradition about the proper way in which Christian martyrs ought to behave before judicial and political authorities. The tradition, moreover, seems to have exaggerated the element of cross-purposes which the Johannine narrative contains. Just as Jesus and Pilate were talking about different things, so martyrs seem to have been almost encouraged to answer questions at their trials in a way that could be misunderstood. Anyone reading the account of the trial of Justin Martyr is bound to feel a great deal of sympathy with the prefect Rusticus, trying to keep order in his court, while Christians leapt up and down insisting on their right to be martyred and giving theological answers even to questions about their parentage. 'Our true father is Christ, and our mother is our faith in Him.'[1] The same kind of thing, in a less extreme form is found in the first trial of St Cyprian in 257. Given an opportunity by the proconsul to change his mind and recant, Cyprian replied, 'A good mind, which knows God, it is not possible to change.'[2] This answer, with its overtones of metaphysical questions about perfection and change, might well have provoked a tried rejoinder of the same order as 'What is truth?'

It is, of course, impossible to tell how accurate these accounts of the trials of the martyrs are, how soon after the event they were written or whether the narrator actually knew what had happened at the trial. But it is fairly safe to assume that, even if they are not based on fact, they reflect the Christian opinion of the way in which a faithful disciple ought to behave. One was expected to take one's stand on moral and theological absolutes and not get embroiled in a discussion of practicalities. It reflects the same sort of concern as Tertullian's view, quoted in the previous chapter, that Christians dare not live otherwise than God has commanded. That meant that they could not trim their behaviour to meet the demands of circumstances. And sometimes, no doubt, as the accounts of their trials seem to suggest, they went out of their way to exaggerate the contrast between the absolutes implied by eternal truth and the temporising required by temporal circumstances.

It is not surprising that Roman officials found their patience strained by some of these attitudes. Those concerned with the practicalities of politics are often impatient with talk of the absolutes of morality amid the hard facts of reality. For instance, one of the arguments regularly used against open government is that civil servants would be less willing to express their opinions honestly.[3] What this amounts to is the assertion that, if public servants were made more accountable to the public, they would almost certainly wish to be untruthful. The conclusion drawn is not that that would be immoral. The blame is not laid at the door of those who might behave less honestly. It is implied, rather, that the realities of life and of human nature are such that it would be bound to happen. The fault would lie, not with the deceivers, but with those who were so naive as to wish for a more honest and open system.

This is not a clash of principle between the extremes on either side, the heirs of the martyrs over against the heirs of the anti-Christian Roman politicians. It would be entirely understandable if atheist and amoral politicians were critical of the foolishly exaggerated stance of those who courted martyrdom. But some of those who insist most strongly that Christians ought not to depart from the eternal and absolute seem also to claim that the very professional business of political tactics is not an area in which the absolute standards of Christian morality can easily be applied.[4] And politicians sympathetic towards Christianity have been as impatient as agnostics about attempts to apply moral absolutes to the practical problems of politics.

Edmund Burke was a practical politician, as well as a political thinker, and a very devoted Christian. Anthony Quinton, writing about the religious as well as the political roots of English conservatism, has said of him that he believed 'that the peremptory demands of morality should be kept at a pacifying distance from the circumstantial expediencies of politics'.[5] He then quotes directly from Burke himself on the subject of those who seek by political action to enforce absolute principles, such as the equality of all men, upon the rest of society whether it shares their conviction or not.

> On the scheme of this barbarous philosophy . . . laws are to be supported only by their own terrors, and the concern which each individual may find in them from his own private speculations, or can spare to them from his own private interests. In the groves of their academy, at the end of every vista, you see nothing but the gallows.[6]

Burke was, of course, writing about the revolutionaries in France. I am not quite sure, frankly, that the actual passage quoted is a particularly good illustration of the point made in Quinton's splendid paraphrase. As I read it, Burke's passage is actually an attack upon those who insist on applying doctrinaire *political* principles in spite of their obviously *immoral* consequences.

Burke's view of society has been described as:

> . . . flexible, pragmatic, slow moving, highly political. Politics is a computing principle. 'All government, indeed every human benefit and enjoyment, every virtue, and every prudent act, is founded on compromise and barter . . .' He opposed another view of politics which was the imposition of an abstract view upon society. This view, usually traced to the philosopher John Locke, is a vision of individual rights with an existence independent of society. It is moral, principled, legalistic, authoritarian, weak on pragmatism, strong on theory.[7]

In this sense Quinton's paraphrase about the peremptory demands of morality fits Burke at one remove, so to speak. Burke's remarks quoted by Quinton were originally directed at Englishmen, nonconformist ministers and Whig politicians – 'political theologians and theological politicians' Burke calls them[8] – who applauded what was happening in France. In their conviction that 'democracy' and the social contract were right, they were condoning regicide. And there are plenty of other passages in the same work which make it very clear that Burke did not approve the intermingling of religion and politics.

> No sound ought to be heard in the Church but the healing voice of Christian charity. The cause of civil liberty and civil government gains as little as that of religion by this confusion of duties. Those who quit their proper character, to assume what does not belong to them, are, for the greater part, ignorant both of the character they leave, and of the character they assume. Wholly unacquainted with the world in which they are so fond of meddling and inexperienced in all its affairs, on which they pronounce with so much confidence, they have nothing of politics but the passions they excite.[9]

Moreover, it is very important to realise that Burke '. . . does not deny that there is a universal moral order. As a sincere and professing Christian such a denial would be impossible for him. What he does deny is the direct political applicability of universal moral truths. The politically right is not unequivocally determined by the morally right.'[10]

Thinking of this kind will awaken a sympathetic reaction in many of us. We would agree that one cannot leap in some direct and simple fashion from the belief that God creates all men and loves them all, to the principle that men should be treated with justice and equality, to a political programme aimed at establishing an egalitarian society by revolution, to chopping off the heads of those who are more equal than others. Nor is Burke's argument one for expedience, pure and simple. It is just because a mechanical (and false) reasoning from absolute moral principle to direct political action is itself productive of immorality, that it is wrong. So to oppose expediency and morality in a simple way is to encourage argument at cross purposes. And Christian politicians and theologians have been among those who have argued most strongly that expediency is often *right* – and by 'right' they have meant 'morally right'. The most influential theologian of Burke's own day was William Paley, famous for his two apologetic works *Evidences of Christianity* and *Natural Theology*. And his very first book, *Principles of Moral and Political Philosophy*, is a defence of expediency. He, too, would have said that he was moved in this defence by *moral* considerations.

Burke's was, at least in religion, a relatively homogeneous society. The religious establishment, he believed, proclaimed England's Christian character and consecrated the state. 'All persons possessing any portion of power ought to be strongly and awfully impressed with an idea that they act in trust: and that they are to account for their conduct in that trust to the one great Master, Author and Founder of society.'[11] However much, then, Burke believed in tempering, for moral reasons, the absolutes of morality to the shorn lamb of political expediency, he was able to appeal to a standard of values, commonly accepted and themselves serving as the yardstick for arguing the claims of expediency. Convention, a broad, often unexpressed agreement about certain large issues, provided a framework within which one might act with common sense and a sense of continuity. The exercise of moral judgement took place within that framework.[12]

Quinton would, I think, dissent from this view in that he would argue that there was 'something straightforwardly objective and historical' which acted as the 'restraining agent'. And that, he would argue, was the constitution.[13] But the British constitution is not quite so objective, unchanging and precise as that suggests. It is interesting that Quinton's book, which contains this study of Burke, ends with a consideration of Michael Oakeshott whom he regards as perhaps the one certainly conservative contemporary thinker in the tradition of Hooker and Burke. But Quinton believes that Oakeshott differs from them in substituting the vaguer 'tradition' for the more objective 'constitution' and that to define tradition as Oakeshott does is to indulge in 'nostalgic illusion'. Even if one were to feel that Quinton distinguishes the British constitution from convention and tradition far too sharply, as though it were not the unwritten, flexible thing that it is, his criticism of Oakeshott is cogent. Oakeshott's famous inaugural lecture delivered in 1951 at the London School of Economics[14] is really an argument for 'a traditional manner of behaviour' as the proper guide in political decision and action. And it is often pointed out that a corollary of Oakeshott's view is that something like Westminster democracy cannot be exported since the traditional manner of behaviour cannot be exported with it. Indeed Oakeshott himself says that the traditional manner of behaviour can become disrupted, diverted, restricted, arrested, dried up or rendered incoherent by outside influences.[15]

The question then arises whether in a secular – and therefore neutral – and pluralistic society such restraining traditions can grow naturally. They might have to be positively created. And I do not know whether one *can create traditions*. A friend of mine, when he was proctor used to attempt to alleviate the tedium of ceremonial university occasions by inventing 'ancient Oxford customs', like removing his cap whenever the name of the Vice-Chancellor's college was mentioned. Even if he had got that custom to 'take', he could hardly have claimed to have been behaving like a conservative, for he was innovating not conserving.

One does occasionally come across attempts to argue that the necessary framework of traditions can continue to be created even in contemporary pluralist Britain. Significantly, many of these attempts look to religion to serve as a basis for such traditions and some are mere nostalgic expressions of a desire for the return of the alliance between constitution and established church which underlay the attitudes and arguments of Hooker and Burke. More cogently it had been argued that the survival of a pluralist society depends upon some deeper underlying unity,[16] for the only hope for a pluralist society is in tolerance. Tolerance is not, however, a self-existent moral quality. It is the product of a system of values and dependent on a residual sense of things that hold the country together. It is argued that the only way to make an open declaration that the country stands by certain moral values is by having an established religion linked with the monarchy, as almost the only effective symbol of national unity.

Attractive as such an attempt, realistic rather than nostalgic, to restate a throne-and-altar view of society may be, it is unlikely to convince many. It may be true that in Britain Christianity is the only religion which could possibly make a bid to act as the symbol of national tolerance. But one of the features of modern British pluralism is the existence of other religions. Islam has, for instance, more adherents in Britain than in most other nations save the traditionally Islamic ones. It is difficult to see how Christianity can provide a basis for creating common national traditions of behaviour for British Moslems. Much more convincing, at an immediate level at any rate, is the argument that in a pluralist society workable principles of action and convincing ethical pronouncements only grow out of small, close-knit sub-groupings.[17]

This is not to say, of course, that Christians are wrong to believe in universal ethical values but that is not really the issue at this point. The question is whether a whole society, of a widely varied kind such as modern Britain, can create or recreate common ethical standards to provide a framework within which common sense can make practical judgements based on expediency and yet keep expediency within some kind of moral limits. If a fragmented society is unlikely to throw up common traditions, and if traditions cannot be artificially created, is there some alternative way of establishing values which will serve as the standards by which expediency is to be judged? There is, of course, a persisting hope that somehow or other, on a purely rational basis, it may be possible to arrive at a view of justice and the common good which will embody values and yet not do violence to the hard facts of political experience.[18] Justice, it can be argued, for instance, is to be sought not because it is a moral absolute but because it is plainly desirable for reasons of utility. The greatest happiness of the greatest number is served in a just society. And there have been other attempts to adumbrate a concept of a rational society which is also a good society. To some of these we shall have to return, but let me simply say at this point that it seems to me that the difficulty that they present to the Christian is this – morality is essentially a matter of values which it is difficult to quantify, or even to argue about in empirical terms. Most of the attempts to argue on a purely rational basis for a just or good society cope fairly easily at the level of material 'goods'. What they find much more difficult to insist on is that, less easily defined or measured, set of human needs which are not concerned with money, food, shelter or clothing but which are about human worth. The need to be more than 'hands', to have a sense of usefulness and dignity, to have a contribution to make even if one is old or semi-invalid or not outstandingly intelligent – needs of this kind are difficult to bring within the scope of a 'good because rational society'.

If one is concerned with what can be defended on purely rational grounds, one seems edged towards saying that the hard realities of political *fact* themselves must provide the sole basis for determining what *ought* to be done. Keith Joseph and Jonathan Sumption have written a book called *Equality*. Like the preacher whose sermon was 'about sin', they are against it. They argue that the belief that all men ought to be equal is merely an assertion while the arguments against equality can be bolstered by solid fact. The whole economy of a whole society, they say, can be considerably improved by a little *in*equality.[19]

This is, in fact, little more than a particularised, but disguised, version of the argument that moral principles cannot be shown to be true in the way that applies to matters of fact, and are, therefore, more like matters of taste. But apparently Joseph and Sumption think that moral principles can be shown to be *false* by the use of factual evidence and so their argument becomes an argument for expediency and against moral principle. Even though, as I shall attempt to show later, some Christian ethicists have moved in this direction, it seems a curiously inconsistent view. For if one stated the principle the other way round and said that human beings *ought* to be quite *un*equal, one could find facts to support the proposition that a little more equality would improve the state of society. Moreover, if a general principle which cannot be proved from factual evidence is to be described as 'merely an assertion', then all moral principles could presumably be dismissed in this way. They are in the last resort, as Joseph and Sumption say, beliefs. That the law should not discriminate against anyone because of his race or religion is merely an assertion, for instance. And it could very easily be shown that the South African economy would not be as buoyant as it is if a black man had the same legal rights there as a white man does. On the argument of Joseph and Sumption discriminatory legislation is positively desirable.

The real problem raised by arguments for expediency unrestricted by the limitations of a traditional framework of morality, is that it is difficult to see why one should ever cease to use them. If facts are to count as evidence against moral principles, then any kind of consequentialist reasoning – anything which points to material benefit – will do. Not only does this raise the difficulty, already referred to, that less easily quantifiable 'goods' may be lost sight of, but there is also the problem of whose benefit one is to bear in mind other than one's own. An unequal society may possess a booming economy, advantageous to the rich, the successful, the clever and the unscrupulous. It could even be said that society as a whole benefits from economic expansion. but how is one to take account of the casualties of inequality, themselves as much a fact as anything else? Even the application of the principle of utility provides no simple solution. At what point does the pain of how large a proportion of the population outweigh the pleasure of those who benefit?

Moreover, all consequentialist arguments based on expediency alone can be justified by precisely the same impatience with idealistic morality no matter how extreme the action. G. Gordon Liddy, convicted of complicity in the Watergate burglary in 1972, is said to have become something of a cult figure as the apostle of expediency and realism. Insisting that reality is that 'the big fish always eat up the little fish' he is reported as justifying Watergate as a simple act of political intelligence-gathering and the possible assassination of investigative journalists as a 'preventive thing'.[20] Not many people, including apparently Liddy's own employers in the Watergate affair, would be willing to take the argument as far as to justify assassination. But it is difficult, unless one invokes moral principles, to see why. Sir William Rees-Mogg, writing about Nixon and Watergate, though not specifically about Liddy's attitude to realism, has said, 'I wonder how many men of power would have seen the moral issue of Watergate in a different way? Confronted with a situation in which a subordinate had committed a relatively minor act of criminal folly, how many would, *for moral reasons*, have done other than try to limit the political damage?'[21] The question is whether, confronted with a situation in which a subordinate had committed a *major* act of criminal folly, a man of power would not still have done all he could to limit the political damage, unless restrained *by moral reasons*? Fear of being discovered, perhaps – certainly nothing in the philosophy of 'realism' alone – might restrain him.

Even if one assumes that it is motivated by the best possible intentions – security and the national interest, which is what is usually invoked to demonstrate the impracticability of morality – there are considerable problems in the use of consequentialist arguments from expediency alone. It is not clear, even, that a consequentialist approach is very practical. The whole basis of the supposedly realistic view is that one can foresee the consequences of all possible courses of actions and that one can then choose the one which will produce the preferred result. Someone tells an official lie and justifies it by saying that otherwise the consequences for the country would have been too terrible. The implication is that he can actually assess the importance both of what did happen and of what might have happened – not only immediately but in a year or two's time. That sounds, at first sight, a reasonable claim. If I want something badly and cannot afford to buy it, I can borrow the money and that will allow me to have it. I have produced the consequence I desired and predicted. But, in practice, consequentialism has to confine itself to the immediate results of an action. We simply do not know what the long-term consequences may be. This is partly because we are simply not able to predict and partly because all the consequences are not in principle predictable. I may borrow the money to buy the thing I want and find that it doesn't bring me the satisfaction I expected. Or I may find that, when the time comes to repay the loan, I have lost my job or the rate of income tax has increased and I am no longer in a position to find the money.

The more complex the situation I am trying to interpret, the more difficult it will be to predict the consequences – and political situations tend to be more complex than personal ones. Even our ability to use computers to set up models to assist in predicting the consequences of various courses of action does not enable us to say that there is more than a probability of being right. Determining which course of action will produce the *desired* result – and which consequence *is* the desirable one – remains a matter for human judgement.

To will the end is to will the means. This is a truism of moral philosophy. The problem is, however, that talk of ends – though we indulge in it all the time – is misleading. History has no ends, as it has no beginnings. Or, perhaps, one ought to say that it has only one end, the final one. And the same is true of human life. Therefore the 'end' one wills will turn out to be a beginning of, or part of the means towards, another end. Moreover we do not really understand what causation in history is. Attempts to define precisely in what sense event A is the cause or explanation of event B run into great difficulties. Causation in history is different from causation in natural science. There is no simple equation that will assure us that A produces B. It may all, as Schopenhauer remarked, be a vast confusion of *post hoc* with *propter hoc*. In the end we are reduced to saying that it is a matter of common sense that certain events were the result of certain other events or factors which, in retrospect, can be seen to be significant.[22] But, in part, the significance we attribute to them derives from the belief that they helped to cause the events which followed them. The interpretation of history and the explanation of what happened is itself a matter of judgement not calculation.

We can see this very clearly when we look at what we call the 'ifs' of history. What would have happened if Wellington had not defeated Napoleon at Waterloo? Those who ask such questions usually imply that the whole course of modern European history would have been different. Undoubtedly, in one sense, that is true. *How* different it might have been is, however, a matter of speculation. Wellington might have regrouped his forces and defeated Napoleon in the outskirts of Brussels a few days later. The course of history would have been different but the consequences might have been much the same. Or Waterloo might have led to the beginning of a new Napoleonic empire and the creation of a single and better European community a hundred years ago. It is no wonder that historians are so scathing about attempts to speculate.

What can be seen so clearly in relation to history ought to be just as clear in terms of consequentialist arguments from expediency when applied to either political or personal decisions. Those arguments *for* expediency and *against* moral principle which assume that expediency is realistic, imply that the consequences of a course of action are obvious and sensible. Liddy, again, is quoted as saying scathingly: 'There is nothing wrong in talking to God. It is when God starts talking back and tells you how to run the country that you have a problem, especially if he tells you one thing one day and something else the next.'[23] The implication is that, provided one does not drag religion or moral principle into the picture, it is easy to design a practical and consistent programme which will achieve the desired effect.

In fact, however, this is not the case. One may choose a course of action only to find that it does not produce the desired consequence, either because one has been wrong in judging the effect or because no one could have foreseen the full consequences. Or, though the desired consequence materialises and does indeed turn out to be as desirable as one thought, it may have side-effects which are not at all desirable. Or, while one's chosen course of action is actually in train, new factors can enter the situation which makes one's original goal no longer so desirable. Or, since 'ends' are not in fact final, one may discover that the goal one had set oneself has become the beginning of a new and undesirable situation. My own generation can remember very well the temptation to cynicism when World War II brought the end of Nazi Germany but the beginning of Communist domination of eastern Europe and the cold war. One was almost bound to ask oneself whether Hitler had been right to insist that the real priority ought to have been the defeat of Bolshevism. And even as one rejected that nightmarish thought one found oneself asking whether all the expedients devised to bring about the defeat of Germany had been as clearly desirable as one had thought at the time. It is so easy to justify immoral actions on the grounds that expediency requires them. It is so very difficult to be certain that the 'ends' which are used to justify them are, in fact, the consequences which will actually follow.

There is a further difficulty about expediency. It is possible to state two quite different, theoretical positions. One is: there are three courses of action open to me at this moment – A, B and C. It is likely that the consequence of A will be X, of B will be Y, and of C will be Z. Because Y is clearly and obviously preferable to X or Z, I must choose to do B, even though its morality is somewhat doubtful. (Of course, it is seldom the case that the choice will be as simple or the consequences so obvious as that). That is the kind of situation that the realists usually assume and they appear to have a strong case for arguing consequentially against moral principle and for expediency. The other position can be stated thus: in the present situation the consequence I should like best is N, so what ought I to do or what story ought I to tell in order to produce N? This assumes an apparently quite different set of circumstances, where N is not, so to speak, a consequence of one of a set of choices which arise 'naturally' out of the situation as X, Y and Z were. One goes out of one's way, by the creation of a false 'scenario', to produce an 'ideal' consequence. Many realists who would accept the validity of the first position, would be unhappy with the second.

The trouble is that the distinction is chiefly verbal. The difference between the two positions is simply a matter of how one phrases them. Was Watergate the result of saying, 'In order to defeat the Democrats there are a number of possible options, one of which is a simple piece of political intelligence gathering which, though illegal and unethical, would enable us to discredit and outmanoeuvre them'? Or was it the result of saying, 'The most desirable possible situation is one in which the Democrats are outmanoeuvred and discredited. What can we do, however illegal and unethical, which would achieve that?' There is, perhaps, a difference of motive or intention implicit in the way in which the two positions are formulated but that is not a difference which the pure realist such as Mr Liddy would be willing to take seriously. The only expedient argument against the false scenario is that the necessity to pile lie on lie increases the risk of exposure.

For those who are concerned about morality perhaps the most immoral aspect of pure expediency is that it may demand that people be sacrificed to preserve falsehood. This is the kind of thing that we are familiar with in the context of war – the commander who sacrifices some of his troops in a feint designed to draw attention from the real attack – where we accept it as part of the necessity of a life-and-death struggle. Outside that context we find it less palatable and in the nature of the case we are seldom told about it when it happens. At the time of the publication of the Bingham report on the breaking of Rhodesian oil sanctions it was widely said that the stationing of British warships off the east coast of Africa was a smokescreen deliberately set up by successive British governments, anxious not to lose the friendship of, and trade with, black African states, though they knew perfectly well that the blockade was ineffective and that British firms were implicated in the supply of oil overland from South Africa to Rhodesia. Speaking in the House of Commons on 7 July 1978 Dr David Owen, then Foreign Secretary, denied this and said that the naval patrol had helped to cut off supplies by the quickest and cheapest route, that the British government had always openly acknowledged that supplies were reaching Rhodesia by land and that force would have been the only way to prevent that happening.[24] There is no reason to suppose that his explanation was untrue.

But if, for the sake of argument, we take the rumour, and not Dr Owen's statement, to have been true then we should have a hypothetical case of the kind I have been referring to. It could be argued that the prolongation of the Rhodesian civil war was the result of

Britain's action in condoning the involvement of British companies in breaking the sanctions and that the charade of the naval patrol was designed to preserve a respectable image for successive governments. It could then be said that an act, justifiable on consequentialist grounds, but wholly cynical since it was intended to deceive the government's own nation and its allies rather than an 'enemy', was undertaken at the expense of those who continued to die in Rhodesia and of those who were deceived, to no purpose other than to save the reputation of those who perpetrated it. What is unacceptable in such a case is that the cost of the untrue scenario achieves nothing but the maintenance of the untruth itself. Circumstances may change. New circumstances may dictate a different course of action. Indeed the exposure of the scenario may necessitate disowning the original plan. Those sacrificed have then been sacrificed not even in order to achieve the desired *end* but to sustain an unnecessary *means*. Whereas an action performed for principle can be openly acknowledged and defended, this kind of sacrifice can not. It is no comfort, of course, to be killed for a principle – particularly if one does not know that this is what is happening – but it may be preferable to being killed because someone has made a bad guess about consequences or for the sake of maintaining a charade.

It is difficult, then, to defend expediency pure and simple. There are very good reasons for arguing that it needs, at least, to be confined within some framework of accepted morality. For while a case can be made by the realists for using expediency to justify *exceptional* actions, which cannot be justified ethically, expediency alone carries no surer guarantee of practicality than principle does. The problem is still that of discovering where the proper restraining framework of accepted morality is to be found in a secular and pluralist society. The Christian, like every other citizen, seems to be driven back on his own moral values in the absence of some morality acceptable to all which might be derived either from the traditions of the society or from a consensus based upon rationality. In other words the problem is not simply that it is difficult to apply absolute moral standards, *any* absolute moral standards, to politics. There is the added difficulty that the standards are private and individual and are therefore difficult to apply to the actions performed on behalf of society corporately, which does not accept a corporate morality. Any possible standards appear to derive from what Burke called one's private speculations. The only possibility for consensus seems to be about the demands of what is expedient. And, in spite of what I have just been saying, it often seems to be the case that the moral consequences of so-called private speculations do seem to be impractical, even to sympathetic observers. In 1980, when the Campaign for Nuclear Disarmament was being revived, Robert Nowell wrote in *The Times*[25] about the inability of the Churches to say anything helpful 'in a field they tend to regard as peculiarly their own, that of practical morality'. In the political field morality just does not seem to provide practical and positive guidelines.

The obvious answer, when one is presented with so sharp a cleavage, is to suppose that some sort of compromise might be devised. David Owen, when he was Foreign Secretary, wrote a book called *Human Rights*, which set out to show how he believed it possible to reconcile his Christian commitment and his political loyalties. Significantly he began that book with a defence of compromise. Inflexible, uncompromising principle, he maintained, is impossible in politics and often ends up by achieving less of what is morally desirable than compromise does.[26] For all that Owen comes from a very different political tradition from that of Burke, there seem to be some echoes of Burke here. Like Burke, Owen is not always talking about inflexible moral principles, so much as about doctrinaire political principles which claim the sanction of morality. In that context it is easy to see that a policy which moves in the right direction can be morally desirable even if it does not go as far as one would like. The trouble is that a defence of compromise *in that sense*, very easily becomes a justification of compromise *for its own sake*. And Owen has not avoided that trap.

Moreover, as a device for solving moral dilemmas compromise has severe limitations. When an arbitration commission sits to consider a trades union claim for a 10 per cent wage increase and an employer's offer of 5 per cent, one always anticipates an award of something like 7½ per cent. There may be no very great harm in that, save for the cynicism engendered by the implication that it had taken days of evidence and argument followed by days of reflection before the commission was able to work out the simple arithmetical sum. But the really important political compromises are not arithmetical ones. One cannot begin from the assumption that the poles between which compromise has to be reached are both of equal value. And here we are talking of compromise between moral principles, on the one hand, and the demands of expediency, on the other, and the problem is that, even if there could be a calculable mean in such a case as that, it would still be something that was less than moral.

Inevitably, then, there have been attempts to discover whether there is a different *kind* of morality which applies to political as opposed to private life. If there were, then it would be possible to say that the demands made by the political realities had themselves a moral quality. Sir Stuart Hampshire has argued that there is

> . . . such a 'different' morality – not 'different' in the sense that different sets of prescriptions are to be applied in private and in public life as if these were self-contained spheres of activity. The claim is rather that the assumption of a political role, and of powers to change men's lives on a large scale, carry with them not only new responsibilities, but a new kind of responsibility, which entails, first, accountability to one's followers, secondly, policies that are to be justified by their eventual consequences, and, thirdly, a withholding of some of the scruples that in private life would prohibit one from using people as a means to an end and also from using force and deceit.[27]

If this simply means that the circumstances which have to be taken into account in deciding what is morally right are more complex and difficult in the political sphere, then there is no great problem – as I shall hope to show later. But it seems to mean rather more than that, at least in the third characteristic listed by Hampshire. In spite of his disclaimer, it does seem that a willingness to use deceit, for instance, implies a different set of prescriptions applicable in public as opposed to private life. Or, at the very least, it is not clear how the morality of one's private life is to be held together with this 'different' morality. Politics does seem to require a willingness – even among those who, like Hampshire himself, believe passionately in the *im*morality of some political actions[28] – to regard moral scruples as a luxury which public life simply cannot afford.

It may be, however, that what is being suggested is that when one acts in a representative character one is bound to act, not as one would wish to act oneself, but as one is required to act by the role one is performing. This is a reasonable supposition. Everyone plays a number of roles and most of us have experience of what it is like to act in a *defined* capacity, which may be an official one even if it is not precisely a public or political one. One may be a civil servant, a soldier or a policeman, a lawyer, a doctor, an educator or a clergyman, a businessman, a trades unionist or a member of a student organisation, and in each of these roles one may behave in a way in which one would not behave privately. Everyone, moreover, tends to separate his public from his private *persona* and to behave in one role as he would not in the other.

This happens in different ways. A student body may mandate its representatives to demand certain concessions from university authorities, even though the representatives do not agree with the case they have to present. Similarly a diplomat may be required to say what his government wishes him to say, right or wrong. There is nothing dishonest about acting as a mouthpiece for someone else, even if one holds different views oneself. Nor is it necessarily immoral to advocate a course of action which one believes to be wrong in principle. The head of an institution or corporation may have to argue vigorously for a course of action which he believes to be wrong because any other course would irretrievably divide the community for which he is responsible. His role requires this action. The difficulty arises when one is required to tell what one knows to be a lie, on someone else's behalf, or to advocate a course of action which may have immoral consequences. The difference is a clear one. In the first case one could say quite openly, 'I don't happen to agree with what I have been told to do but the case is nevertheless a cogent one.' And one could argue it, quite happily on its merits. In the second case one cannot make an analogous statement and carry out one's task effectively at the same time. To say, 'I know that this is a lie but I am required to tell it, nevertheless', will destroy one's chances of being able to do what one has been sent to do.

Nevertheless we all tend to behave as though immoral official actions are not as bad as private ones.[29] A doctor or a clergyman may feel obliged to withold the truth from someone who is dying. In such a case there may be differences of opinion about whether he was right or wrong to do so but the difference will usually be expressed in terms of expediency – was the dying person able to cope with the knowledge? – rather than in terms of moral principle. Yet a kind of restraining framework of morality is implied in the concern felt for the dying person. What seems to be happening is that the doctor or the cleryman is saying to himself that his professional role requires him to tell this lie even though, privately, he is an intensely honest person. The role requires him to have a concern for the well-being of the dying person which may supersede other moral considerations.

Sometimes, however, the differences in moral standard as between private and official behaviour seem to be merely a matter of professional convention. A barrister is expected to argue his case with vigour and conviction, regardless of his private opinion as to client's guilt or innocence. That seems perfectly reasonable. The situation is the same as that of the representative speaking on behalf of someone else. But he is also free to hector and harass a witness, destroy his credibility and therefore his character, without being regarded as immoral.[30] He is only doing his job. Yet one is bound to ask whether behaviour of this kind is essential to the doing of the job. Is it actually required by the adversarial character of the British judicial system or is it something immoral which professional conventions have come to accept as normal? When one reads accounts of murder trials dating from the days before capital punishment was abolished one is sometimes appalled by the supposedly witty repartee bandied back and forth between bench and bar. The same kind of 'wit' if displayed by officers of the Gestapo before the execution of their victims would be regarded as evidence of an obscene depravity. Showing off the brilliance of a debating society sense of humour at the expense of someone whose life is at stake, who cannot really answer back, and who does not share one's professional need to relieve the boredom of the job, is hardly morally commendable. It is fairly clear that mere professional conventions about what constitutes acceptable behaviour are not a sufficient guide to the 'different' morality appropriate to defined roles.

It is possible, then, to make some sort of analysis of the distinction between the morality of official and of private action but neither expediency nor morality by itself is enough to establish the distinction. If the framework of restraint within which expediency operates is prescribed by mere convention then it is easy to accept standards of behaviour, recognisably immoral and not strictly essential, simply because they are customary. The representative character of some roles do seem to require one to act differently from ways in which one would act privately but the difference is not always one that can be expressed simply in moral terms. In some cases the morality of such a 'different' action seems neutral, in some cases questionable and in some uncertain. This suggests that there is not so much a sudden 'threshold' which is crossed when one acts officially, as that allowances are, in practice, made for those who shoulder certain responsibilities because of the complexity of the problems they face and the larger number of factors that they have to take into account when making their decisions.

The question remains how one is to relate one's private morality and the 'different' morality of public or official action when society has no agreed system of moral values. It is sometimes supposed that natural law, independent of any specific set of religious beliefs, may provide a way of bridging the gap. When theologians define natural law as 'the law implanted in nature by the Creator which rational creatures can discern by the light of natural reason',[31] it looks as if they are talking about an objective and discernible system. Unfortunately, behind this apparently innocuous definition there lurk a great many problems. What looks like an inevitable concomitant of any theistic belief proves surprisingly difficult to work with. When the Pope asserts, for instance, that contraception is contrary to natural law it sounds as though he is appealing to moral standards reflected in creation – that he is saying, in fact, that it is against nature. Some of Richard Hooker's statements in the *Laws of Ecclesiastical Polity* also seem, at least on the surface, to speak of a law revealed in nature (which has a specific content) and which ought to be detectable, on the one hand, and consonant with the moral law revealed by religion, on the other. But any attempt to argue against a papal pronouncement on the ground that, in fact, there is no evidence in biology to back it up, very quickly brings the explanation that natural law and the scientifically discoverable laws of nature have very little to do with one another.

Natural law, one will be told, is really that which will tend to the doing of good and the avoidance of evil, and which might be perceived by a man of good will, by rational argument alone and without reliance upon revealed truth. In that sense natural law is about the argument employed rather than the *content* of the law. It is undoubtedly attractive because it suggests that there might be a purely rational way of arriving at moral values, which would have an autonomy of its own and not be dependent upon Christian standards of morality, and yet would be consonant with Christian beliefs. Such natural law arguments could be based upon utility or even self-interest. The snag is that at this point it begins to sound as though natural law means that which most people would accept as right. But that is not what its proponents intend.

The problem lies in the phrase 'man of good will'. It is open to the natural-law theologian to say that those who remain unconvinced by the 'rational' arguments are being perverse and are not men of good will – they do not choose to be convinced. That raises two further difficulties. In the first place it makes it clear that natural-law arguments are really attempts to convince others of the rightness of a morality arrived at for religious reasons without requiring the acceptance *of* the religious reasons. Secondly, it reminds us that theologians themselves disagree fundamentally about whether the reason of fallen man is ever reliable even when illuminated by good will. Every believer may agree that the creator will necessarily impress something of his own character upon his creatures. Whether fallen man, entrapped in original sin, retains enough of the divine image to be a sufficiently faithful reflection of what is good, or possesses sufficient light to be able to discern it, is a hotly debated issue.

Natural law continues to be used by some lawyers as a way of integrating ethics, social theory, political philosophy and the law. It performs for them, in other words, precisely the function we have been talking about – of bridging the gap, or attempting to do so, between ethical theory, on the one hand, and the real needs and behaviour of society, on the other.[32] One can see, of course, why some lawyers should wish to operate with some such concept even when they do not wish to give it an overtly religious character. Without something of this kind it is impossible to distinguish between 'good' law which one has a moral obligation to obey, and 'bad' law which one has not. That is a distinction that has often been made, though it is equally true that some lawyers insist that the whole question of moral obligation is irrelevant.[33] Whether there is such a thing as 'natural' law is disputed.

Natural law is therefore a very difficult concept to work with, partly because it is used in so many different contexts and partly because it is not really intended as a means of reaching consensus. I do not think it answers our present problem though I shall return later to consider its value in other ways. Secular moral philosophers have no need of it. Very few Christian moral theologians attempt to use it any longer – at least in the field of political morality.

One other device for gap-bridging is, perhaps, important to take note of and that is what is called the 'middle axiom'. Middle axioms are, in Ronald Preston's words, 'half way between general principles which are easily accepted because they have no empirical content, and detailed policies, which depend on so many empirical factors that a consensus is unlikely'.[34] They can be the basis for agreed action. Because there is a tacit agreement to *treat* them as axiomatic, they can actually be accepted for a variety of reasons or even for no particular reason at all. The famous medieval definition of a just war, for example, could be held to satisfy Preston's description of a middle axiom. One could agree to accept those defining conditions without necessarily agreeing with the arguments or the moral attitudes which led the medieval moralists to arrive at them. Some people might accept them simply because they reacted sympathetically to them at an emotional or instinctive level. This seems, in a sense, rather more realistic as a basis for consensus than the hypothetical rational arguments that might be held to convince the man of good will in the notion of natural law. But it would depend on, rather than actually create, agreement and I do not know whether it would have any appeal for those who rely upon expediency pure and simple. Joseph and Sumption could dismiss middle axioms as 'merely assertions' and middle axioms are, by their very nature, particularly vulnerable to this charge.

The more one examines the matter, then, the more it seems that there is no way for Christians to arrive at a broad view of their own morality in which the whole of a modern, pluralist society can share. This may not distress us very greatly in terms of our private lives, since a plural society, secular and neutral in its attitude to religion, will allow us to go each on his or her own way. But it does matter to anyone who believes morality to be important when he or she comes to consider the political sphere because this is precisely the point at which the whole of society is involved and where the application of morality to society counts.

Moreover, there is one sense in which anyone concerned with morality is specially bound to take account of political morality and that is as it concerns people in public life. In John's narrative of Jesus' trial, from which this chapter began, Jesus says to Pilate, 'You would have no power over me unless it had been given you from above' (John 19:11). That is, in part, a recognition of the providential character of government which recurs in other parts of the New Testament and to which I shall have to return. But the other half of the sentence attributed to Jesus has complex implications – 'therefore he who delivered me to you has the greater sin'. This seems to suggest that, in a sense, Pilate is there (very nearly impersonally) to administer justice – as if he were running a machine. The moral questions are to be asked primarily about those who fed Jesus into the machine. But not quite. For, although the *greater* sin lies with them, the use of the comparative implies that moral questions are also to be asked about Pilate's conduct. The providential character of government and the apparent impersonality of the administrative machine, do not mean that the person exercising authority is excused from moral responsibility for his actions.

This, as it seems to me, is a vital point. For it is easy, when we are discussing public morality, to forget that the reason why the issues are moral issues is because they involve people. If we were discussing the impersonal administrative machine we might be concerned for the maintenance of abstract principles, but the real difficulties of the moral problems raised are derived from the human beings caught up in them. And those who exercise authority are themselves people, which makes it more than ever difficult to maintain that public or political morality is somehow of a different order from private morality.

One might say, for instance, that the difference, the 'threshold', between public and private morality was very well illustrated by the statement, 'As Home Secretary he was prepared to authorise methods of interrogation which he would not have countenanced as a private individual'. One knows what the statement means and can at least respond sympathetically to the moral attitude implied by it. But it remains a haunting fact that the Home Secretary has no existence independent of the human being who occupies the office. Taking repeated decisions to permit torture may have a quite desperately brutalising effect. And it will not be some impersonal public office which is brutalised by the process: it will be the human person occupying the office.

It will not do, therefore, to discuss issues of political morality simply as though they were to do with impersonal processes. Nor ought the discussion to be primarily about the maintaining of absolute moral principles. The *truth* to which Jesus says that he has come into the world to bear witness, provoking Pilate's famous question, is not so much a categorical imperative as a gospel concerned with the redemption of *people*. It would be appallingly immoral for a Christian to say to himself that he was not prepared to soil his hands with the necessary deceptions and brutalities of politics but was content for the Home Secretary to do it on his behalf.

This is the more important because it does seem as though people are the one bridge that does, in fact, span the gap between public and private morality. For all sorts of reasons one may deplore the fact that this is so. It is a symptom perhaps, of the excessively individualistic character of modern Western society. It may be the result of a disastrous privatising of religion and morality. But it seems to be the case. The application of absolute morality to politics seems both undesirable and impossible, because impractical. Yet pure expediency appears no more desirable and not much more practical. What seems to be required is a restraining framework of moral values within which expedient decisions can be taken, abrogating the absolutes of morality where necessary. And, in actual fact, society seems willing to make all sorts of allowances for people holding public office because of the complexity of the problems they face. Because there is no agreed system of public morality, however, it is left to the individual to determine not simply the proper and expedient judgement to be made in terms of the circumstances but also the moral framework within which to make them. It is already clear that this is a demanding task and, if Christians corporately have any concern at all for bringing morality to bear upon the political structures of society, they need to be willing to accept a high degree of responsibility for those directly involved in political action.[35]

It is important to perceive that this argument – which asserts that human beings seem to be the one bridge over the gap between Christian morality and political necessity – is not an argument for a private and individual religion. Political theology (theology mediated through what is public or social) is, in part, a protest against the tendency to restrict the relevance of religion and morality to the private lives of individuals. What I have said here is not intended to counter such a protest. Indeed, the first chapter of this book ought to have made it clear that I regard a private Christianity as not only a distortion but also, in fact, an impossibility. What I wish to argue is that, though religion and theology *have* to possess a public dimension, it is through *people* and their actions that this has to come. In a pluralistic society it is no longer possible to look for a corporate moral framework which will limit expediency. Neither 'rationality' nor the sheer facts of a situation can serve as a substitute. In effect, a reliance on the supposedly factual is largely responsible for the removal of the religious from the public to the private domain. But no one wishes to surrender the freedom that pluralism has brought and it is only through the engagement of Christians in what is social and public that they, and others who have an equal concern for morality, can hope to bring their concern to bear upon society as a whole. This sounds trite, of course. But there is all too often an assumption made by some Christians that the only way for society to become moral is for everyone to accept the private moral standards of those Christians. Alternatively, those Christians who are engaged in political activity often tend to assume that they can accept the general moral assumptions of society and work within them. The reality of the situation seems, in fact, to be that there is no public moral framework. That makes the role of the Christian in society very much more difficult and one which he or she ought not to be expected to perform in isolation. Yet, in practical politics, the Christian is often most alone when he or she faces the moral issues. And the crux of the problem is this: is the 'right' thing to do, in politics, the principled thing, or the thing that actually achieves what is aimed at. And that is as true, as I shall hope to show, for our hypothetical Home Secretary as for a revolutionary guerrilla.

Notes

1. *Acta SS Justini et soc.*: translation in J. Stevenson, *A New Eusebius*, S.P.C.K. 1957, pp. 28ff.
2. *Acta Proconcularia S. Cypriani*, I; and see P. Hinchliff, *Cyprian of Carthage*, Geoffrey Chapman 1974, p. 121.
3. See e.g. *The Times*, 13 March 1980, for an account of a report on open government prepared for the Association of First Division Civil Servants.
4. E.g. E. R. Norman, *Christianity and the World Order*, O.U.P. 1979, p. 18.
5. A. Quinton, *The Politics of Imperfection*, Faber 1978, p. 96.
6. *The Works of Edmund Burke* (Bohn's Standard Library) George Bell & Sons 1882, vol. II, p. 350.

7. *M. Jackson,* 'British Theology and the Universal Church', *Theology*, LXXXII, p. 248.
8. *Works of Edmund Burke*, vol. II, p. 285.
9. *Ibid.*, p. 286.
10. Quinton, *op.cit*, p. 61.
11. *Works of Edmund Burke*, vol. II p. 365.
12. M. Jackson, *loc. cit.*
13. Quinton, *op. cit.*, p. 96.
14. 'Political Education', in P. Laslett (ed.), *Philosophy, Politics and Society* (First Series), Basil Blackwell (paperback edn) 1975, pp. 1ff.
15. *Ibid.*, p. 15.
16. The Bishop of Durham in an appeal to his diocese on behalf of the 'Projects Fund' – see report in *The Times* for 22 September 1980.
17. E.g. P. Laslett, 'The Face to Face Society' in P. Laslett (ed.) *op.cit.*, n.b. p. 164.
18. The best known such work is probably J. Rawls, *A Theory of Justice,* O.U.P., 1972. It has been the centre of a continuing and lively discussion but has not commanded universal agreement – see N. Daniels (ed.), *Reading Rawls*, Basil Blackwell (reprint) 1978, and J. R. Lucas, *On Justice*, O.U.P. 1980, pp. 185ff.
19. K. Joseph and J. Sumption, *Equality*, John Murray 1979, pp. 3, 23 and 123f.
20. Michael Leapman, 'New York Diary' in *The Times*, 15 December 1980. Liddy's autobiography, *Will*, is published by Sphere Books, 1980.
21. Reviewing Lord Longford's *Nixon: A Study in Extremes of Fortune*, in *The Times*, 13 October 1980. The italics are mine.
22. See e. g. A. Donagan, 'Historical Explanation: the Popper-Hempel Theory Reconsidered,' *History & Theory*, IV, pp. 3ff. and n.b. pp. 24f.
23. Michael Leapman, *loc. cit.*
24. *The Times* parliamentary report, 8 November 1978.
25. *The Times*, 10 November 1980.
26. D. Owen, *Human Rights*, Jonathan Cape 1978, pp. 2f.
27. S. Hampshire (ed.), *Public and Private Morality*, Cambridge University Press 1978, p. 52.
28. *Ibid.*, p. 51, where Hampshire is outspoken about the moral infamies of American activities in Vietnam.
29. S. Bok, *Lying*, Harvester Press 1978, pp. xvi ff.
30. B. Williams, 'Politics and Moral Character' in S. Hampshire (ed.), *op.cit.*, p. 65.
31. F. L. Cross (ed.), *Oxford Dictionary of the Christian Church*, O.U.P. (2nd edn) 1974, 'Natural Law'.
32. See e. g. J. Finnis, *Natural Law and Natural Rights*, O.U.P. 1980, n.b. p. 18.
33. E.g. J. Raz, 'The Obligation to Obey the Law', in *The Authority of Law*, O.U.P. 1979, pp. 233ff.
34. In *Theology*, LXXXI, p. 441.
35. D. Jenkins, 'Faith and Politics in Britain Today', in H. Willmer (ed.), *Christian Faith and Political Hopes*, Epworth Press 1979, p. 76.

3

MORALITY AND POWER

Thus far I have said very little about what Christian morality is or about why it should be at odds with practical necessity[1] – except to suggest that it is because humanity is fallen and sinful that no society can be perfect. It is time to set out an account of that morality and to consider how far it really is impossible to reconcile it with the needs of society. It has to be said, however, that there is no single view of Christian morality. There have always been different schools of thought and different emphases. There simply is not the time to set them all out and attempt a critical assessment of them. I must content myself with saying how I understand the ethical demands which Christianity makes and hope that I am not wildly unrepresentative.

Even within the New Testament itself there are different accounts of what is essential Christian morality. One of the best known is Matthew's so-called Sermon on the Mount. A part of that 'sermon' (Matthew 5:43–8) reads:

> You have heard that it was said, 'You shall love your neighbour and hate your enemy.' But I say to you, Love your enemies and pray for those who persecute you, so that you may be sons of your Father who is in heaven; for he makes his sun rise on the evil and on the good, and sends rain on the just and on the unjust. For if you love those who love you, what reward have you? Do not even the tax collectors do the same? And if you salute only your brethren, what more are you doing than others? Do not even the Gentiles do the same? You, therefore, must be perfect, as your heavenly Father is perfect.

One could hardly wish for a starker statement of the absolute claims of Christian morality. To be perfect as God is perfect is not only an absolute but an impossible command. And, as if to underline the impossibility of it all – perhaps particularly in the political context which is our special concern – there is that terrible example of what it means to be perfect: 'Love your enemies and pray for those who persecute you.' Not only absolute, not only impossible, but also typical of precisely the kind of thing that makes the practical man say that religion must be kept out of politics at all costs.

I am not competent to get into arguments about which source this passage comes from or whether Matthew has preserved the original sense better than the equivalent passage in Luke (where the crucial verse (Luke 6:36) is 'Be *merciful*, even as your Father is merciful') or whether Luke has read and expanded on Matthew. It does seem almost impossible, however, to think that those verses are simply, in Matthew, a chance arrangement. There is such an obvious thread of argument running through the six verses that it is difficult to believe that the evangelist did not put them in that order on purpose. And the argument is that perfection consists of a love which is unwaveringly directed at everyone regardless of *their* behaviour. Love, that is, is a condition of the lover not of the beloved – a truth which anyone who has ever been in love knows only too well. I love because of something in *me* – essentially and in the last resort – and not because of whatever it is about the other person. Of course 'being in love' is not at all the same thing as loving in the Christian sense. But they share this characteristic among others, that one can still love when the love is neither desired, nor deserved, nor responded to. 'Love' describes the person from whom it comes and not the person to whom it goes. The obligation laid upon the Christian by this passage in Matthew is that he or she is to be constantly loving because that is what God is like.

It is, in any case, the sequential emphasis, rather than source criticism or even the nature of Christian love, which is my main concern. 'You must be perfect *just as* your heavenly Father is perfect.' You must be like this *because* that is what God is like. So the really important question is, 'Why should a morality follow upon religious belief?' A great many people, particularly those who have no religious commitment, think of it simply as a kind of package. Adultery is out for Christians just as alcohol is out for Muslims. It just is so. But that is, of course, a very inadequate account, and the very fact that morality differs from religion to religion makes that plain. A particular morality follows upon a particular understanding of God.

Christianity has always insisted that morality is the imperative which follows upon faith in God. Even the so-called 'new morality' of the fifties and sixties contrasted its 'situational' approach to the rules and regulations of the 'old morality' not by arguing that there were *no* imperatives, but by arguing that there was only one single imperative, one commandment – to love. Though it will already be apparent that I am sympathetic to a view which stresses the primacy of love, the 'new morality' seems to me to be too simplistic. The connection between belief and morals is complex because Christian faith is rich rather than simple and its richness is reflected in the life that flows from it.

If one holds that morality follows upon belief one may argue one's case in three developing stages:

(1) I believe in God and he has commanded certain things (e.g. 'Thou shalt not steal'), therefore I am obliged to obey and need ask no further questions.

(2) I must obey God as a response to what he has done. For example, God has created me and set me in a good world and in gratitude I ought to worship and obey him. What God requires of me no longer has to be defined simply as an arbitrary command. It can be seen rather as logically related to what he has done and, therefore, to what he is like. In the case of the example given, for instance, I can say, that everything has been made by God and must be treated accordingly.

(3) I believe that God has revealed himself in Christ, and in doing so has shown me what he is like and what man *ought* to be like. The logical connection between belief and morality is even stronger. I ought to model myself upon Christ: *Imitatio Christi* becomes the basis of morality. The obligation upon me is to see that my actions in relation to everyone and everything else are modelled upon those of Christ so that they are consonant with the nature of God himself.

The first of these ways of looking at the connection between belief and morality is the one which people usually have in mind when they talk about absolute morality and its incompatibility with the realities of politics. The third way is, however, the one which I believe to be a fuller and better statement of the connection. To understand Christian morality, then, one has to understand Christian faith.

It must, of course, be very naive in this day and age to assume that one can make a brief and uncontroversial summary of the Christian position. Any attempt to do so will be challenged at almost every point, not only by those who wish to argue about *whether* it is true, but also by those who wish to argue about *in what sense* it is true. Nevertheless it must be attempted because otherwise it is not possible to talk about morality at all.[2]

That which is personal, that is to say God, is both primal and ultimate in relation to the universe. My own personalness reflects it. Therefore the personal dimension of my own life – loving my wife and children, doing a satisfying job, creating something worthwhile – is more important than the mere maintenance of myself as a physio-chemical existent. Moreover, belief in the Christian revelation includes the belief that the personalness of God is focused, embodied and specified in the human being called Jesus of Nazareth. He is the means of knowing what kind of person the God is, whose universe this is, and thus provides the clue for making sense of our existence within the universe.

If this *is* the proper way to understand reality two things follow. First: Christ demonstrates the kind of human life which 'fits' with the nature of God and, therefore, with all creation. And secondly: to live like that is to be, at least in some degree, a vehicle for God's activity. For if God is the loving, creative and personal for which all the physical universe is the vehicle, then we also possess the potential to be the vehicle of his love and creativity. And if God is expressed in all creation and especially through human beings, then how we treat creation and other people has to be seen as part of the way we treat God.

And if all *this* is true, then the 'moral imperatives' are not merely a set of arbitrary decisions on God's part – a declaration that he has whimsically decided to reward some actions and punish others. They are, rather, the way in which we realize the potential of which we are capable, the way in which we come to be at one within ourselves and with each other, with the whole of existence and with God. Morality is not peripheral and secondary. It is the way in which we express faith. If the Christian conjecture is true then a Christ-like life is the proper life, the life that 'fits'.

Unfortunately we not only find ourselves unable, by an act of will, to *be* good when we want to, we often do not want to. And, even worse, other people create situations in which it is difficult even to *know* what is good, let alone do it or even want to do it. If everything else exactly and harmoniously reflected the will and the being of God, then at least we might see clearly how we ought to be, in order to fit in. If one has a clear and beautiful mosaic which lacks one piece, one may easily see what the missing piece *ought* to be like and one may relatively easily make a piece like that. But if the whole mosaic has been dropped and scattered it may be almost impossible to know what sort of piece is needed. If the whole of creation is out of kilter, one cannot know what sort of person one ought to be. And even if one did know, and became that sort of person, one would still be at odds with a great deal of the rest.

A doctrine of original sin – of a creation which is not what it ought to be – therefore demands a concept of morality very different from a simple assertion that each individual human being need only obey the known commands of God. It requires the recognition that the individual is part of a context which will not, itself, perfectly reflect the nature or the will of God. Morality will also have to concern itself with how a human being copes with that context. Christ has to be seen not just as the pattern for one's own life but as the restorer of the harmony of all things. This is what it means to say that God was in Christ reconciling the world to himself. He is the source of the grace needed if one is to live by the pattern. He is also the source of the forgiveness needed when one fails to live by the pattern.

What, then, are the basic moral values[3] to be perceived in the life of Christ, as revealing the nature of God, and – therefore – telling us what kind of human life runs with, and not against, the grain of true reality? In a sense the answer to this question must be somewhat subjective, for we may each evaluate the characteristics of Christ in a different order. For me the distinctive thing about him is his integrity.

'Integrity' has two meanings. It means 'wholeness'; and Jesus appears in the gospels as the supremely whole man. He is whole in the sense that we intend when we speak of an *integrated* personality. He fits together, is not frustrated by being at odds with himself. He is free to achieve what he sets out to achieve because he is *whole*-hearted. He does not will one thing and slip into doing another. He is whole, therefore liberated, therefore transcending the fragmented, disintegrated, conflicting desires, ambitions, drives and motives which limit our own lives.

Indeed, this wholeness is the very thing he offers us. The word 'salvation' means health and healing, wholeness. Atonement – at-one-ment – speaks for itself. Healing men's brokenness, within themselves, from each other and from God, is what Christ's life is about.

But he is also the example of integrity in the other sense – honesty and truth. 'I *am* the Truth.' We see him, again and again, remaining painfully true and honest at enormous cost. In the end he dies on the gallows because he will not compromise his integrity. He will not soft pedal his shocking proclamation that God is our intimate, is unconcerned with conventional piety, and cares for human beings, even sinners, as they are, in the thick of everyday life. Nor would he minimise the total obedience which this down-to-earth Father demands. Caring for the broken and despised ruined his reputation among the pious and respectable. His flouting of official, professional religiosity and of political expediency brought him to his death so that we, and millions like us, might know and experience the truth about God.

The salvation, wholeness and integrity which Christ offers us is, therefore, uncomfortable. It is not a safe seat in an ethereal heaven so much as a demand that we shall be whole, entire and uncompromising in a world which has clearly decided that integrity is an unnecessary piece of lumber or an expensive luxury.

There is at present rather a vogue for saying that we seldom have a real choice between good and evil. There is seldom a clear-cut black and white, we are always having to choose between shades of grey, having to look for the lesser of two evils.

Of course we all know that moral decisions are not always easy, simple or cut-and-dried. There are times when the choice is agonisingly difficult and there does not seem to be a wholly right course of action. This is an inevitable consequence of the fact that creation is out of kilter, that not just the individual but the context is imperfect. But to say *that* (as I shall be saying repeatedly in this book) is not at all the same thing as saying that we seldom if ever are able to make clear-cut decisions. We do often have a clear choice between good and evil. But also, far too often, we comfort ourselves with the *thought* that we have to choose between two evils. Sometimes we simply don't look hard enough. The two evils may not be the only possible choices: there may be a third, fourth, fifth, sixth or even seventh course of action which might be good, but we have given up too easily. Or it may be that we are in a position where we only *seem* to have a choice between evils: one of them may be so remote a possibility that it ought not to weigh against the real and obvious damage of the other. Or, perhaps, we have put ourselves in the position of having to make this difficult choice through some wrong action in the first place. If we analyse the situation, and go back to the roots of it – how we got there – we may find that there is a way of untangling it which is quite different from the choice which seems to confront us. Or the analysis may enable us to see that one of the choices rests upon a prior or deeper commitment than the other. And sometimes one of the 'evils' is not an evil at all: it is simply something that we do not want to have to do or that society would not like.

The Christian, therefore, is called to an uncompromising integrity; to be true to himself, to truth and reality, and to Christ, no matter what other people may think or what society may want him to do.

Integrity – being true to himself – is *the* great characteristic of God in the Old Testament. It is called the 'faithfulness' of God and it is epitomised in the whole idea of covenant – God binding himself by his own unchanging nature. 'I have sworn by *myself*.' It underpins the constancy of nature, of time, of history, of all existence. And, as the book of Hosea shows, it underpins God's love for his people. God's love is covenant-love, like the love of a man for an erring wife, taking her back again and again in spite of her faithlessness. So God's love is never to be understood or measured in terms of the deserving qualities of those he loves – their nobility, beauty, strength, success or moral qualities. It is only to be understood as a measure of his *own* nature. God loves man, not for any reason that has to do with what man is like, but for reasons to do with what God is like. It is an expression of his faithfulness, his integrity, his wholeness. And that is why the Old Testament does not see any conflict between the justice and the wrath of God, on the one hand, and his love on the other.

And so we come to the next great characteristic of Christ, which is love. This love is not an excuse for selfishness, self-gratification, possessiveness, sentimentality or indulgence. And that is why I began with integrity rather than love, for love, like everything else, has to possess integrity.

Jesus does, indeed, say that love is the greatest commandment but notice how, in the summary of the law, we are told that we are to love other human beings *as* ourselves. Is it a little surprising, as an atheist colleague once said to me, that Christians are not told to love their neighbour *more* than themselves? I do not think so. It simply is not, in this context, a question of who is to be put first. It is that there are no real distinctions between 'me' and 'them'. I am to care for them with the same simple, unquestioning, wholeheartedness with which I care for myself. Love is, again, being defined in terms of the lover not of the person who is loved.

The command to love, then, is a command to love as God loves and this enables us to define love in terms of the behaviour of Christ, who reveals God. It is not embodied in rules or formulae, but in a person. Eternal and absolute moral truths are not so much abstract principles as ideals expressed in a particular life.

This love is, first and foremost, faithful – never shaken or diminished by the faithlessness of others. It is, therefore, a matter of the will, of determination. It is disciplined, not self-indulgent. It is loyal. It possesses integrity. It is true to itself and its own standards and it does not lower them in order to win affection cheaply. Jesus loved the rich young ruler but he let him go when the young man could not meet the demands of Jesus' standards. There was neither possessiveness nor a willingness to indulge, to 'spoil'. But there was integrity.

But if love is a matter of the will, it is also a matter of the emotions and that is something that Christian moralists have dodged too often, talking as if one could love with the will alone, by a great gritting of one's teeth. Christ's love is, indeed, an emotion, a yearning and a longing, which he himself compares with a mother hen's desire to gather her chickens under her wings. It is not a desire to possess the beautiful, the admirable and the esteemed. It is a longing to protect and comfort the weak, the loveless, the despised, the poor and the unlovely; those who are hurt by life: however much of a burden and a liability they may be. And that is one of the most difficult lessons of love, which the supposedly strong and successful have to learn – that they have to *become* weak, vulnerable, and caring. For it *is* possible to learn to love, however strange that may sound. It can be done by sympathy and sensitive imagination, putting yourself in someone else's shoes and trying to understand what it is that they are going through.

Does it have to be said that such a love has to be directed towards people? Surprisingly, perhaps, I think it does – and in two connections. First: Christian love is quite different from a sort of generalized good will. It is easier to endow charities, invent new sources of protein, direct government health services, do all sorts of good in the abstract, than to cope with and try to understand the needs of a single human being who is poor, dirty, unrespectable or unloved. The other things *have* to be done, but they should only be done out of a quite specific care for the needs of real people whom one actually knows. Otherwise one is always in danger of becoming self-important and patronising, convinced that one knows what is good for other people.

The most moving part of St John's passion narrative is the moment on the cross when Jesus dying, as we say, for the whole human race, concerns himself with the welfare of the two actual people whom he loves most – his mother and his best friend. The general becomes specific.

Love also includes the willingness to suffer. No one can look at the cross and be oblivious of that fact. But it is also something within our own everyday experience. We know that we are vulnerable to, can be hurt by, and suffer most for those whom we love. Their unkindness, ingratitude or anger can hurt us as no one else's can. When they suffer pain or sorrow it hurts us. When they reject our love, it breaks our hearts. Yet if we say to ourselves that we can stand no more pain but will become tough and insensitive – or if we are tough and insensitive, anyway – we will not be able to love. For love means being thin-skinned, willing to suffer, to care *for* and *about* people so much that one is exposed to them and therefore open to being hurt. That is why Love was 'despised, rejected, a man of sorrows and acquainted with grief'.

A true understanding of Christian morality omits neither the awfulness of sin nor the inexhaustibility of forgiveness. Sin is always horrible – no matter how much we may tell ourselves that what we have done did not greatly matter – because sin is to block the manifestation of God's love in the world and to distort or pervert the potential of which man is capable. Yet it remains gloriously true that no sin is so bad as to be beyond the reach of forgiveness – provided I recognize my failure.

Forgiveness is, in fact, experienced in repentance. This is far more than mere pallid regret for lost opportunities. It is the realisation of how great the damage is that we may have done to other people, to the whole shape of existence, to the goal to which life ought to move, and so to God himself.

And forgiveness is not pallid or shallow either. It is not at all a matter of pretending that the sin has not happened. If our sins did not matter, that would mean that we were of no importance to God, either. Because part of existence is in *our* hands, what we do does matter and when we damage it, the cost and the consequence all too often falls elsewhere. What we call the atonement is God's acceptance of the ultimate responsibility for that. All the hatred of Christ's enemies was flung at him, was gathered up and held to himself, not passed on in hurting others, but formed into a great creative and self-giving act of love.

It is this kind of forgiveness that we ourselves also have to learn. It is not the mere offering and accepting of *apologies*. But a change in attitude on the one hand and a willingness to bear the hurt and to try to find some way of making it creative rather than destructive, on the other. Moreover, repentance involves not merely the determination to do what I can to redeem and alleviate the consequences of my own sin, but also to learn the meaning of forgiveness by bearing willingly the consequences of other people's failures, individually and collectively. To learn to forgive and to learn to be forgiven are equally hard. They go together and they cannot be had separately.

What one is saying, as a Christian, then, is that Christ is *at least* the way to understand what a human life is like when it is faithful to the divine; the cross is the focal point of that life because that is where Christ's integrity takes him: the cross also asserts the centrality of self-sacrificing and forgiving love; the Church is the community that flows from the cross and is committed to the person whose integrity and love were expressed upon it. What seem like comfortably abstract theological formulations – christology, soteriology and ecclesiology – contain uncomfortable and immediate moral implications. Morality is not an arbitrary package; not even a second stage logical deduction from doctrinal premises. It seems to be very much more organically and immediately involved in the very affirmations of faith themselves. To believe in God revealed in

Christ is already to be committed to such things as integrity, love and community.

I wish there were some other terminology which would enable me to say this without reawakening the embarrassing associations which these words have acquired as bits of modern quasi-theological jargon. That the coinage has become debased, however, does not relieve one of the necessity of shopping with it. I have already argued that love is the most demanding, costly, self-sacrificing 'commandment' that could possibly be laid upon us, requiring a degree of faithfulness and self-discipline and a willingness to suffer which none of us finds easy to accept. In the same sort of way 'community' has to be understood properly. It has recently become an in-word, used as if 'togetherness' were an end in itself, without any need to define its value or proper limits. This is not only sloppy and sentimental but absurd.[4] An intensely 'together' Ku Klux Klan dinner party, to celebrate their one hundredth lynching, would then qualify as an example of a good community. Christian community is as difficult a concept as Christian love since it has both to express quite specific values and yet be without the sharply defined in-group frontiers that make most communities viable. William Temple is supposed to have said that the Church was the only community which existed for the benefit of those who were not its members. If he did say that – and I have never been able to trace it to its source – it isn't even strictly true. There are other institutions that could claim to qualify. But the idea which that dictum tries to express, does represent a truth about Christian community which is an essential part of the gospel and makes it impossible for Christian morality to be other than social.

To be a member of the Church, then, is to be a member of a community which flows from, and is committed to, a self-sacrificing love whose hall-mark is integrity and faithfulness. It is not just any sort of community. Being together is not its only characteristic or purpose. Not only is it committed to being a certain kind of community but it is a community whose purpose is outside itself. If the Church is intended to be an alternative, a redeemed humanity, then it ought also to be a paradigm of what all human communities ought to be and it ought to be concerned not just to set an example but to influence human communities.

This last paragraph reveals one of the great difficulties in any attempt to describe the Church. The first few sentences of the paragraph used the verb 'is' and the last sentence the verb 'ought'. All Christians are compelled to recognize that the Church is not what it ought to be. However much, theologically speaking, one may want to say that the Church 'is' certain things, one also has to recognize that these are also ideals. However much the Church may be the redeemed alternative to natural humanity, its members remain imperfect human beings and itself an imperfect community. I shall want to return to this difference between the ideal Church and the actual Church in a later chapter. The point I want to make here is that there is a parallel between the position of the Church and the Christian in that for each of them there is an ideal. And in each case the ideal is Christ. It is his faithfulness, integrity, self-sacrifice and love which are the marks of the Church. When we talk about the Church in ideal terms we are in a sense talking about Christ himself.

The Pauline image of the Body of Christ is, perhaps, the most familiar of the New Testament ways of describing the Church and the one most frequently used in attempts to devise a theology of the Church which will express the relationship of the actual Christian organisation to that ideal Church which is in some sense Christ himself. And, like every other aspect of Christian theology, the doctrine of the Church has been a matter of considerable debate and disagreement. What is often lost sight of is the fact that when Paul himself uses the image he is not talking about the Church as in some way providing Christ with a physical, concrete medium for action in the world (which is how it is sometimes used by Christians) but as a way of expressing the corporate, interlocking, organic character of the Christian community. The emphasis is upon the *corporate* nature of the Church rather than upon its ability to *act* on Christ's behalf.

However much there may be disagreement about the doctrine of the Church, perhaps the concept of the Church's holiness is less controversial. The Hebrew word for holiness carries the connotation of 'set apart'. Originally it may have had more to do with taboos and the dangers inherent in coming too close to the naked power of the divine, as in the story of Uzzah in II Samuel 6, but the contrast between God's holiness and the 'uncleanness' of the people in the vision in Isaiah 6 shows the beginnings of a moral understanding of holiness. It is clearly difficult, in any case, once one regards moral purity as one of the essential ingredients of holiness, to treat it as a less than absolute quality. To be set apart with and for God must imply a demand for moral perfection.

To demand an absolute moral perfection from a community is to ask the impossible in an even more obvious way than to demand absolute moral perfection from an individual. Not only is there the simple fact that the larger the community becomes the greater are the chances that it will include those who only pay lip-service to its ideals. There is the additional problem that being perfectly communal is itself extraordinarily difficult. Most Christians actually experience the community of the Church in terms of some specific group of people, perhaps a local congregation, in which they know fellowship and from which they draw the strength to live the kind of life to which they are committed. The smaller the group, the more intense its sense of solidarity is likely to be and the more likely it is to provide a springboard for action.

On the other hand the Church cannot be conceived of purely in terms of small and local groups. To do so would be to deny its universality, its unity and its inclusiveness. Something has to hold the groups together. The organisation and the structures which result from that need are very different from the small groupings in which Christian community is most easily demonstrated. F. D. Maurice's vision of a Church as closely knit as a family yet wide enough to embrace the whole human race is a moving one. It is also one which all our experience and sociological expertise label as impossible. Structures and organisations operate politically, in the broad sense of the term. There are conflicts of interests, schools of thought, disagreements as to policy, competition to control, ambitions for power. To contrast the Church with society is to miss the fact that the actual Church which we experience is not simply a Church of close-knit communities but a Church of structures which operate like any other structures.

There is, moreover, a sense in which it is good that it is so. Structures are currently unpopular and tend to be treated as potentially demonic as, no doubt, they are. But it is not only the large-scale which can be demonic. So can small groups. The very intensity of their unity can make them, not only narrowly exclusive, but too easily convinced that their own understanding of what is the proper way to turn Christian faith into practice is the only way. A group tends to be composed of people who share certain attitudes, anyway. Left to themselves they may develop a monochrome unanimity which is unable to examine and test the morality of what they are doing. One imperative too easily dominates their concerns. The existence of a wider Church, which has to be taken into account, is the one thing which may prevent small and local groups of like-minded Christians from developing the unpleasant and obsessive characteristics of sects – a Ku Klux Klan type of togetherness. For this very reason it is important that the wider Church should be concerned to assert *all* the ideals of Christian morality. A small group, like an individual, striving to apply the demands of Christianity to a particular situation may very easily lose sight of one ideal in its anxiety to live by another – may lose sight of charity in its desire to stamp out adultery. The wider Church, just because it embraces so many different people in a wide variety of situations, has a better chance of stating the truth.

Nor should we minimize the importance of actually *saying* what are the moral truths. It is easy to dismiss attempts to assert moral ideals absolutely on the grounds that it is hypocritical to proclaim them unless we actually live by them. But if the Church does not assert the ideal, it may be lost sight of in the press of events.

If one conceives the Church thus – as a community which is committed to proclaiming an absolute ideal of integrity and love and living in conditions where those ideals are impossible to realise and sometimes seem to conflict – one is reminded again that being a Christian has to be described in language which is as much moral as it is doctrinal. Christianity is a matter of striving to *live out* a belief. The moral dimension is inescapable. No one really believes that faith is *primarily* an intellectual understanding, important though theology is. Faith is something *lived*, not merely thought or talked about, and *how* one lives – morality – is, therefore, the primary affirmation of faith. To strive to be a particular kind of person within a particular kind of community, is to proclaim one's faith. When one perceives this truth, one may begin to understand that, so far from there being an incompatibility between Christian morality and political engagement, being a Christian may actually *require* one to be involved in the attempt to create a certain kind of human society.

It will, however, also involve understanding the 'absolute' quality of Christian morality in a particular way, implicit in the assertion that one ought to be a certain kind of person because God is a certain kind of person. For the term 'absolute morality' is, in fact, used with a variety of different meanings. Some people may chiefly mean, as I have already suggested, a set of inflexible prescriptive regulations like the ten commandments. In such a case it may be feared that the translation of these rules into laws for society might impose Christian morality upon those who do not share its beliefs, as in laws against the sale of contraceptives in Ireland. When the Islamic clergy gained *de facto* power in Iran in 1979 they began to apply in the law courts the prescriptions of the Koran in this way. Even Mrs Whitehouse's campaign to clean up television programmes is thought of as another example of it. But a Christian who has understood that morality is primarily a response *of* love *to* love, will not seek to impose morality by force upon those who can make no such response. What his duty actually is, I shall go into in a later chapter.

'Absolute morality' may also refer not to precise prescriptive rules like 'Thou shalt not steal' but to general principles like 'One ought always to tell the truth' or 'Treat others as you would like them to treat you'. What is feared from this kind of 'absolute morality' is both the self-righteous ruthlessness that Burke feared from the egalitarians and, paradoxically, the weak, good-natured naivety about which President Truman said, 'If you can't stand the heat, get out of the kitchen'.

I have attempted to suggest that even this is not the kind of absolute morality that the Christian will desire. There is another sense in which 'absolute morality' could be used: to refer primarily not to regulative prescriptions or even general principles but to a kind of person – a wholly good man. If I am right in arguing that Christian morality is fundamentally a response of faith and if our faith centres upon a kind of person – Christ – then principles are derivative, descriptive alike of the person Christ is and of the kind of person who responds to him. Morality is primarily about the kind of person one *is* or becomes: the function of general 'principles' is to define that kind of person. They are, in that sense, descriptive rather than prescriptive.

This view of morality does not seem to me to pose a threat of the kinds we have been considering though it may threaten politics in other ways. In the previous chapter I quoted Sir Stuart Hampshire on the subject of the 'threshold' between public and private morality. He has also asserted, as a fundamental starting point for moral philosophy, that 'a human being has the power to reflect on what kind of person he wants to be, and to try to act accordingly'.[5] This seems to me a very significant statement and, though it makes the process sound too easy, closely akin to the view of morality which a Christian will desire to uphold upon the basis which I have tried to expound here. The pattern for the kind of person he will want to be is Christ. Morality is the way we affirm our faith in God's ability to make us like Christ and set out on the path towards the goal of being that sort of person.

Harry Williams, writing about prayer and the path to holiness, has said

> . . . to arrive at my truest self where God dwells, it is necessary for me to pass through some pretty rough and decidedly ugly country. To find God within me I have on the way to encounter aspects of myself from which I tend to run away and hide. . . . I have not only to encounter all those ugly aspects of what I am. Indeed I have to learn to love them as I would love a naughty and wayward child. And that can't be done without considerable turmoil and perhaps agony. I shall find God within me all right. I shall find the love, joy and peace which is my truest self. But

the discovery will for a long time be mixed up with the pain and the discomfort of the journey.'[6]

This is why forgiveness, which is central to Christian faith is also central to Christian morality, because we know that life will be largely a matter of striving rather than succeeding. Integrity, love and community are part of the faith and are to be affirmed in living. But they are also beyond our grasp except partially and in our grandest moments. And that would seem to imply that our affirmation of faith is a very shaky thing. No doubt, even at best, it is. What redeems it from total hypocrisy is that part of what we are affirming is our own fallen nature, our need for redemption, our dependence on grace and the centrality of forgiveness. The self-sacrificing love for which the cross is the focal point says something – if Christ is the key to our understanding of God – of the nature of God himself. It is an understanding of God as one who loves at whatever cost, who forgives in spite of betrayal, infidelity, cowardice, lack of integrity, hatred, cruelty, political intrigue, time-serving and mockery. And because all *that* is at the centre of the proclamation of the faith, it is also at the centre of the living affirmation of it. Morality is partly a matter of picking oneself up out of the dust of each day's failure and doggedly, penitently, asking for the grace to make another attempt.

The centrality of forgiveness is also, of course, the only thing that makes it possible for Christianity to assert an 'absolute' morality of any kind. No Christian is, or can hope to be, sinless. The very fact that perfection is an absolute makes it unattainable. But everyone can hope to be forgiven. Forgiveness, therefore, enables us to accept the reality of imperfect human nature without lowering our standards of what human beings and human life ought to be. Without a concept of forgiveness one has a choice between lowering one's standards to a level which is attainable and is, therefore, a great deal less than 'absolute'; or giving up the whole idea of moral standards, since the only ones worth having are impracticable anyway.

This is not to say that forgiveness is an easy option, as anyone who lives by it knows very well. It is, perhaps, the most difficult way of life of all, for no one easily accepts the fact that he is a failure. One can live with oneself if one is succeeding in attaining whatever goal one has set oneself, even if perhaps it is not very grand. One can live with oneself if one has not set oneself a goal at all. But to live with a goal which one believes to be right, and yet humanly unattainable, involves a continual recognition of one's own inadequacy. But that recognition, with repentance and forgiveness, is what Christian morality is all about.

There is a very delicate point to be captured here – perhaps the most difficult in the whole field of theology – and one has to try and do it with great precision. On the one hand, to recognize that a belief in the atonement necessitates a willingness to live as a sinner in need of forgiveness does *not* mean that one can condone evil or accept any sort of shoddy compromise in the ideals by which one lives. To be a Christian *does* require one to live by absolute standards. I ought not to do anything which I believe God has forbidden me to do. There can be no doubt about that. I must respond to God's love with every ounce of energy I possess. I am called to stand by integrity, selflessness, love and truth. Those should be the marks of my daily life in whatever area I am moving. On the other hand I have to accept that I am going to fail. And I *may*, because of human sinfulness in general, encounter situations in which there appears to be no wholly right course of action, where there genuinely is a choice between two evils rather than between good and evil. But if those situations are usual rather than exceptional; if sin becomes the staple of life rather than the inevitable but tragic error; if the ideal ceases to be sought; then life is no longer an expression of faith and I have to do something radical about it.

The question then is whether there is anything about the political which makes it impossible to live by that concept of what morality is. If being a Christian is a matter of *becoming*, a journey towards God through, as Harry Williams put it, countryside which reveals the worst features of myself, in order to find the love, joy and peace which is my truest self because they are God within me, can the journey be made in political and social terms as well as private ones? And one has to remember that the question has to be asked not just of the professional, the politician and the civil servant, but of every citizen. For, as I have already argued, there is no escape from what is political so long as a man or woman remains part of society. The only alternative is the hermit's cave.

At least it is clear that one false idea has to be discarded. We do not start in some pure and sinless state which might be spoiled and dirtied by politics. Even in private life we are not in that condition. We start out on life as sinners and the business of life, for the Christian, is to come to self-knowledge and to God *through* the battle to live by ideals and through the agony of one's failure to do so.

If it were clear that any kind of involvement in politics *necessarily* involved one in embracing evil then it would be quite unacceptable. It would be comparable with a willing degradation of oneself by embracing the life of a drunkard or seeking employment as a professional assassin. There would be an abandonment of the ideal, the struggle, the search, the journey. One would be saying, 'I affirm evil instead of good'. But this would be true of every citizen as well as of the professional. If one really believed that political life in general were like that, the hermit's cave would be no longer a mere alternative but a necessary condition for living the Christian life.

In setting out what I believe to be the true Christian concept of morality I have admitted that there may be occasions in which it *appears*, at least, that there is only a choice between evils. I have argued that we ought not to accept that this really is the case except after rigorous examination. Even then, in theory, there might conceivably exist some wholly good course of action which simply has not been perceived. But, at any rate, part of common experience in everyday life, even for Christians of the highest moral integrity, is to be in a situation in which *any* course of action seems certain to cause harm. We are all familiar with such situations. They are the stuff of moral theology text books. Discussion of issues such as abortion, euthanasia and divorce raises them at every turn; and these are all issues which are regarded as belonging to private rather than public morality. Sometimes they arise from quite specific acts which can be categorized as sinful. Sometimes they are consequences of material rather than moral evil – disease, accident or some other aspect of the general nature of existence. They are all part of what theologians call the fallenness of man, the imperfection of this world and our life in it. It would be wholly consistent to assume that from time to time political life will also produce situations in which, in a similar way and for similar reasons, there seems to be no wholly right course of action but only a choice between evils. If that were the only problem then it would be possible to say that the political aspect of life was no different from any other.

The problem we have been examining, thus far is the disconsonance between Christianity, concerned with perfection and what is ideal and eternal, and politics which is the art of the *possible*. The assumption has been that what is possible will seldom be perfect because what is possible is defined in terms of what can be managed in an imperfect society of imperfectible human beings. The necessary practicalities of politics crop up naturally, as it were, and because they crop up in society they are bound to reflect human imperfection just because it is in humanity in the aggregate that imperfection is most noticeable. A single man or woman, alone, may be devoted to living by the highest ideals. Put us together in the mass and the sinfulness of each of us will frustrate the attempts of others to be good. In other words, to oppose what is possible, practical or expedient to what is eternal, ideal and perfect, is to talk

– in theological language – about original sin. From that point of view there is no need to assume that politics is necessarily more evil than any other part of the human situation. Our private lives have to be lived within the realities of human imperfection. If our public lives, whether as citizens or as professionals, have to be lived within the same realities this need not condemn us to anything that faith would compel us to avoid. And, in a sense, the concept of Christian life and morality set out in this chapter eases the problem. It is possible to say that, in principle at least, the disconsonance between perfection and possibility need be no worse in politics than in private life.

Politics is not, however, simply about what is *possible*: it is also about power. It is about power in that it is about achieving and maintaining one's own power against others. (And we have to remind ourselves, again, that this does not simply apply to the professionals, though it is more obvious for them. The ordinary citizen often casts his vote because he wishes to acquire or retain power for his class, his race or language group and his section of society.) Politics is about power, also, in the sense of the ability to compel obedience: to the party or people in office, to the public servants who administer government, to the generality of citizens who desire to protect by law their persons or property. Politics is also about power in the sense of being able to secure the interests of one's own country against others. None of those things seem necessarily wrong in themselves. The objectives of the exercise of power, in other words, can be morally acceptable. Nor do I wish to press Acton's law about the corrupting effects of power. For one thing, as will already be apparent, I would be unhappy about any view of human nature which assumed that it starts good and may or may not end up bad. From the point of view of Christian morality, moreover, that corrupting effect – if it does exist – is not a statement about power so much as a statement about those who use it. It is as if one said, 'All alcohol makes one drunk'. In the last resort, however, power involves compulsion, coercion and force; and the use of force, in turn, implies violence. And *even where we recognize that violence is necessary*, even when it can be described as 'deserved', there is something dehumanising about it. It has an obscene quality, as of a kind of rape, a violation of human dignity. It dehumanizes those who use it as well as those who suffer it.

A friend whom I revered as a good and wise Christian once wrote (though he softened his argument later in the article from which I quote):

> . . . to triumph rightly in a conflict which is 'according to nature' is a most honourable achievement. Even those of us who dislike

killing can appreciate the motives of a man who wants to experience victory in a conflict of endurance and alertness with his quarry. . . Nowadays it is absurd to glorify war, but in the traditional songs which do this it is always the danger, exhaustion and courage in the conflict which is extolled . . . [and] in situations of conflict, our human ability to form cohesive groups within which ideas are readily shared intensifies the emotion-arousing power of the situation and brings into play that suppression of individual independence which we call loyalty.[7]

I find it almost impossible to accept this attempt to justify conflict and violence as an aspect of human greatness, if that is what it is intended to be. I can understand conflict as one of the prime evolutionary motors, like suffering.[8] I can glory in the fact that even suffering, conflict and violence can evoke from human beings a noble and heroic response. I can perceive the splendour of loyalty. But conflict and violence themselves I cannot regard as other than of the fallenness of humanity. And loyalty, when it means that 'any individual who resists [the urge to fight] excludes himself from the group and is regarded as "disloyal" ',[9] is a denial of the true sense of community discussed earlier in this chapter.

This is an emotive subject and one in which, as in many other aspects of politics discussed in this book, prejudice is very difficult to avoid. Those who glorify the heroism displayed in war may be sickened by the sight of children in Belfast or Toxteth hurling petrol bombs at human beings 'who are only trying to do their duty as soldiers or policemen'. It is when we are sickened in this way that we ought to pause and ask ourselves whether violence can ever be justified, except possibly as a last desperate resort, regardless of the nobility which human beings are capable of displaying under pressure. Part of what Aldous Huxley seemed to be saying in *Brave New World* was that violence, tragedy and suffering have to be accepted as integral to the human condition because tranquil humanity produces no grandeur, no poetry, no love. But to argue that it is good in itself seems to be a perversion, except at the very simplest level as when one says that the undoubted violence used by a dentist in extracting a tooth is a kind of creative violence.

An article in *The Spectator* in the autumn of 1979, when Gary Gilmore was executed after the revival of the death penalty in the United States, said that there was no tasteful way of killing a human being. This seems much nearer the truth than any argument which relies on the grandeurs produced by human conflict. There was a time, no doubt, when crowds were attracted by the brutalities of a public execution. But even public executions tended to be ritualised to disguise the degradation of the pleasures they offered. A man was expected to 'die well' and display a kind of nobility *in extremis*, reminiscent of the way a public schoolboy used to be taught to say 'Thank you, sir' to the master who had just beaten him. Two young men standing toe-to-toe and hacking away at each other's faces with open razor blades in a Brixton street are recognizable as hooligans. Virtually the same activity, performed for the same reasons, to prove one's virility and one's acceptability in the group, but ritualized and romanticized by the traditional German student fraternities, with their jargon of loyalty, brotherhood and self-discipline, can be made to seem glamorous and heroic. When the heroism is stripped away, when a man refuses to 'die well' and the indignity of violence is displayed, the violation of humanity becomes unbearable for those who inflict as well as those who suffer it. An account of the execution of Ruth Ellis, the last woman to be hanged in England, makes unbearable reading. She was virtually carried to the scaffold. She was terrified and had to be rendered paralytically drunk on brandy. And one gets the impression that this was as much for the sake of her warders as for herself.

In so far, then, as power involves implicit force and violence, even when it can be said to be necessary or justified, it is a deviation from the best that humanity is capable of. Looked at dispassionately imprisonment, execution and war are dehumanising. A sergeant in charge of a group of young soldiers fighting guerrilla forces in a bush war has to teach them, 'If it moves, shoot first, ask questions afterwards'. And he is right to do so; their lives depend on it. How much damage that teaching has done to those young men, even if only to some of them, is something that cannot easily be estimated. Yet it is clear that society could not survive without restraining criminals, punishing the guilty, defending itself against aggression and eliminating the disloyal. Violence seems to be a necessary function of government, even if it is only used to prevent other and worse violence.

Now, of course, the violent use of force is something which only hovers in the background, so to speak, in a civilized society. We no longer indulge in public executions. Many societies have abolished capital punishment altogether. The grosser kinds of physical torture are less blatantly used. The possibilities of war have become so terrible that we hardly dare contemplate using them and we permit only small, local, guerrilla wars with what we call 'conventional' weapons. We have come a very long way in making punishment and imprisonment humane if still undignified. Power has come to depend less on force and violence and it is terribly important that that progress should continue and that we should not allow society to become more violent again. Violence can only be contemplated when it is a genuine exception, a 'lesser of two evils' in the sense that I have defined this consequence of the human condition. So soon as force and violence become more than that, become a way of life, the disconsonance will threaten to become that other kind in which a genuine incompatibility of politics and Christian morality will force us to choose whether to affirm good or evil.

It would be absurd, of course, to suppose that conflict could be entirely eliminated from human life. There will be conflict, in the sense of conflict of interests, of differing views about the proper policies to be pursued in particular circumstances and rivalry over the power to control what is to be done. This seems to be implicit in politics, in any structured society. Most political structures, in fact, seem to develop in order to provide a framework within which such conflicts can be resolved by negotiation, discussion and the balancing of powers in such a way as to avoid a resort to violence. And a good many of the political skills are skills which enable one to obtain the demands of the interest one represents *without* the use of force. Even industrial action is, in one sense, recognized as undesirable by those who decide to take it. Since they also lose by any damage which may be done to the corporation against which the action is taken, the breakdown of negotiation is a real symptom of failure to obtain what they want. The threat of it may be a useful negotiating weapon: the reality is seldom so.

And it would be equally absurd to suppose that the role of the Church or the Christian must always be one which tries to overcome conflict at any price. This is what is wrong with the argument of those who echo Burke's sentiment that 'No sound ought to be heard in the Church but the healing voice of Christian charity'. If the atonement is the proper Christian model for a reconciling role, then reconciliation is not compromise. Christ's reconciling death does not symbolize some mid-point between opposing forces. It symbolizes the uncompromising assertion of what is right, on the one hand, and the self-sacrificing forgiveness of what is wrong, on the other. It is sometimes argued that the violent use of force is good because the destruction of a corrupt system is for the good of the oppressor as well of the oppressed. That is obviously true in the sense that an oppressor or exploiter is being damaged by what he does. But it is only true in an abstract, generalized and hollow sense, for it is difficult to see how any individual oppressor benefits by being killed. It is not a very convincing way to expound the ideal that one ought to love one's enemies. At best it seems, once again, a desperate attempt to justify, as a last resort, the use of force and violence to destroy something which is itself destructive.

If that last resort is not to be resorted to, then power must rest upon persuasion. And here, too, there is a difficulty, for persuasion so easily becomes manipulation. Power in government is won by the party which persuades the electorate to vote for it. It is almost impossible for a politician to avoid the manipulation implicit in slogans, propaganda, clever debating points and the selective use of facts. It is even more difficult for the government of one nation to avoid deception, lies and intrigue if it is to protect itself against the at least equal array of untruth and propaganda employed by its rivals. Hatred and fear of the inhumanity of the state apparatus in Communist Russia, and its apparent determination to draw more and more countries into its orbit, compels us to maintain a security system, a world of official secrets and, therefore, a world of official lies. Indeed it seems that the only way to avoid the violence of war is by resorting to the deception and concealment of an elaborate security operation. Obviously, if this goes beyond a certain point, it becomes self-defeating because there is always the danger that, in a desire to protect the country from a totalitarian enemy, one may create precisely the same kind of totalitarian apparatus in which people are sacrificed to the needs of the state. In South Africa the electorate is always being told that the undemocratic processes of the regime are made necessary by the threat of Communist subversion. Before the general election of 1981, the South African prime minister said, 'We don't have security measures for decent-minded, reasonable people but for underminers of our stability'.[10] And that, of course, is what every government says. We have heard official spokesmen in Communist countries say much the same thing about dissidents there. In itself it means nothing. There is no way of quantifying the 'importance' of the conditions that will justify lies, secrecy and deception. They can only be justifiable as exceptional, tragic failures to find another and better way. Once they become accepted and championed as necessary to our way of life it is no longer possible to argue that they are simply forced upon us by those inevitable choices between evils that arise from time to time out of the imperfectibility of human society. A society that embraces them as desirable in themselves has accepted the fact that politics is irreconcilable with Christian morality. Power that is not based upon persuasion but relies on manipulation and deception is also, in its way, a violation of human dignity.

I have to confess – because I recognize that it may mean that I have judged the nature of power more harshly than most people might – that I have never understood the appeal that power seems to possess. I can understand the attractions of lust, pleasure, importance, comfort and security. I cannot understand the passion of the pure miser, who desires money for its own sake and not for what it can buy. I can understand the person who lusts for power, as for money, for what accompanies it. But there clearly are those who desire power for its own sake, else there would be no grey eminences content to exercise power without even the glory and status that normally go with it. And there have always been those who are prepapred to take the most fearful risks to attain and keep power. I feel about them as a blind man might feel about those who enthuse over the beauty of a picture. I may, therefore, be exaggerating the element of violence and deception in the exercise of power.

Even if this is true and politics does not *necessarily* contain such an element, it is difficult to avoid the impression that the acquisition and exercise of power requires a toughness that is difficult to reconcile with those Christian moral principles inherent in the concepts of love and community. That seems the clear implication of the quotation from James Margach with which this book opened. Part of the disconsonance of politics and Christian morality arises from the fact that Christ's victory is the victory of a man who will die rather than surrender his integrity: the successful politician is the one who wins at whatever cost. Clearly the two styles of victory, each requiring its own kind of courage, are not necessarily bound to conflict *all the time*. A fortunate politician might succeed without ever surrendering integrity. In any case, Christian faith and morality takes account of personal sin and human sinfulness, the unpleasant characteristics of particular politicians or the occasions when there seems no wholly right course of action. What it cannot accommodate is a concept of power which *depends* on and *welcomes* the use of either violence or lies, and infringes the proper dignity of human beings to such an extent (even when it claims to be for their own good) that it amounts to a positive affirmation of what is, in Christian terms, evil.

That is unacceptable because a recognition of the autonomy and dignity of men and women is one of the hallmarks of the Christ of the gospels. Whether one believes those gospels to be a literally accurate account of what actually happened or not,[11] they clearly present him in this way. His characteristic teaching method is the use of parables in which his hearers are left to unravel the point of what he is saying and to apply it to themselves if they have ears to hear. Again and again he presents people with a choice and – as in the case of the rich young man – they are left free to reject him. He consistently refuses to perform miracles in order to compel acceptance of his claims. And there is a clear distinction between miracles performed on people and on things. Christ simply commands inanimate objects. He does not treat people like that. They have to want to be healed. So one is left with the picture of a man of undoubted authority who will never use that authority to violate the dignity of another human being, whether by force or by manipulation. On the basis of the view of morality set out in this chapter, therefore, to affirm belief in Christ involves living a life which upholds the dignity and autonomy of other human beings. Though one may recognize that there will be occasions when one's own sin or the general sinfulness of humanity causes one to fall short of that ideal, there can be no question of committing oneself to a political way of life if it involves an outright *denial* of the ideal. Whether the necessities of politics involve such a denial or whether they can be accommodated within the Christian scheme of faith and morals with its recognition of human sinfulness is, of course, the crucial question. The best way to start the process of finding an answer is, perhaps, to consider the Christian's moral duty as a citizen.

Notes

1. For the most part, the style of this chapter is closer to that of the actual lectures than is the case in most chapters. It is much more of a personal statement than an academic argument, which would have had to cover the whole field of theology. As a result the first person singular intrudes more often than is really desirable and footnotes are rather sparse.
2. For a fuller account of how I understand Christian believing see P. Hinchliff and D. Young, *The Human Potential*, Darton Longman & Todd 1981.
3. This account of the nature of Christian morality was not originally one of the Bampton lectures but was contained in a paper read to the annual consultation of the Community of the Cross of Nails in Coventry in 1979 and published by the Community in E. E. Lester (ed.), *In Search of a Living Faith*, pp. 32ff.
4. David Clark, *Basic Communities*, S.P.C.K. 1977, for instance, repeatedly suggests that true community ought to involve a sexual openness that would override the narrower bonds of marriage. The logical implication of this would be that a real community could only exist when there was a sexual relationship between each member and every other member, regardless of gender or age.
5. S. Hampshire, 'Morality and Pessimism' in S. Hampshire (ed.), *Public and Private Morality*, Cambridge University Press 1978, p. 6.
6. H. A. Williams, *Becoming What I Am*, Darton Longman & Todd 1977, pp. 86f.
7. D. W. Bandey, 'A Positive Evaluation of Conflict', *Journal of Theology for Southern Africa*, 31, pp. 18f.
8. See P. Hinchliff and D. Young, *op.cit.*, p. 56.
9. D. W. Bandey, *op.cit.*, p. 19.
10. *The Times*, 11 April 1981.
11. For a discussion of the reliability of the New Testament account of the kind of person Jesus was see P. Hinchliff ad D. Young, *op.cit.*, pp. 62ff. and n.b. p. 76 for its bearing on the particular point under discussion here.

4

A SINGLE MORAL STANDARD

The New Testament is not silent on the subject of the Christian's proper attitude to the state. In Romans (13:1–3) St Paul says

> Let every person be subject to the governing authorities. For there is no authority except from God, and those that exist have been instituted by God. Therefore he who resists authority resists what God has appointed, and those who resist will incur judgement. For rulers are not a terror to good conduct but to bad.

This seems quite clear. God has appointed those who govern and Christians have an entirely passive role – obedience. They are to pay their taxes, honour their rulers and obey them.

This does not seem to offer any solution to the problem of the disconsonance of politics with Christian morality. Indeed it actually creates a new dimension to the problem. If St Paul means that the state must always be obeyed in every conceivable situation and without question; if he means that God has authorised every regime and every policy of every regime; he may have solved our practical problem for us. We need no longer ask questions about what we *ought* to do: we simply do what the state tells us. But the moral problem would have been eased by simply evacuating morality of all meaning.

One has only to remember Tertullian's interpretation of Christ's saying about rendering to Caesar what is Caesar's, to become aware that Christians have never been prepared to accept that St Paul was enunciating a divinely inspired command requiring unconditional obedience to the state. Tertullian was arguing that Christians must die rather than obey the state if it commanded apostasy. And if one is not to obey *such* a law, why should one obey *any* law that conflicts with conscience? It is true that some early Christian writers seem almost to think that the state is to be obeyed in all things with the single exception – when it prevents the worship of the true God. St Augustine, for instance, says that Christians will not wish to disobey customs, laws and institutions so long as they do not hinder religion and the worship of God.[1] But Augustine is, by implication, talking of a good and peaceful, even if not necessarily Christian, society and probably of 'religion' in a wider sense than merely formal acts of worship. At all events it would be highly illogical to argue that the state was to be obeyed except only when it commanded apostasy or forbad the worship of God. For if one is not to obey laws of that kind why should one obey laws which command genocide or adultery or even the wearing of safety helmets, if one believes that God has forbidden them. Whatever St Paul may have meant in Romans 13, it is clear that Christian tradition did not interpret the passage as compelling an absolute and unqualified obedience.

The same Christian tradition also modified the starkness of what Paul appears to be saying in another way, too. Paul's emphasis is all upon subjection. But Christians seem to have thought that this did not prevent their playing a more active role of service under the state provided that they were not involved in some blatantly un-Christian action, like swearing by pagan gods. In other words they were prepared to be active participants in government, not merely obedient subjects to it. No doubt the fact that the Old Testament represents the ruler as the Lord's anointed made it easy for Christians to participate actively in government when the ruler was himself sympathetic to Christianity. This Old Testament theme would also make it easier for a Christian to accept political responsibilities as being, in a sense, to do God's work. To command as well as to obey could be a role open to the Christian.

The New Testament itself plainly does not present a single, monolithic teaching on the subject of obedience to government. The first epistle of Peter (2:13) says,

> Be subject, for the Lord's sake to every human institution, whether it be to the emperor as supreme, or to governors as sent by him to punish those who do wrong and to praise those who do right. For it is God's will that by doing right you should put to silence the ignorance of foolish men.

Though at first sight this, also, sounds like a simple injunction to obedience, it is less clearly so. For what if the governors punish those who do right rather than those who do wrong? Does the writer mean that subjects, like the slaves he was to mention a few verses later, are to suffer wrongfully and take it patiently? Or is he saying that if one leads a good life by Christian standards, then the critics of Christianity will be silenced? Or is he urging Christians to concentrate on living their private lives by those standards so that, even if they were to suffer at the hands of rulers, their own consciences would be clear? The case is far less clear cut than in Romans.

If Babylon, the great harlot seated upon seven mountains and drunk with the blood of the martyrs of Jesus, is indeed intended in the Revelation of St John the Divine (17:5ff) to represent Rome, then perhaps there is here yet another stage in New Testament thought. With the tempo of persecution increasing, or rather with the state playing a larger direct part in it, it was less possible to think of the powers that be as ordained of God (other than in the most general terms). It was easier and more natural to think of the state as the enemy and as the instrument of evil.

Nevertheless, we are forced to take seriously the undoubted *fact* that the New Testament asserts that the state does have a claim upon our obedience. It says, quite categorically, though not perhaps consistently, that the proper attitude of Christians towards political authority is obedience. And we ought to treat this the more seriously because it is, perhaps, surprising. The history of Judaism would not, at least on the surface, seem a propitious soil for the growth of a tradition which said that one ought to obey, almost at all costs, even those rulers who were outside the people of God. What one might have expected was a transposition of Old Testament ideas so that non-Christian rulers could be identified with the foreign tyrants and oppressors of Israel's history just as Christian or sympathetic rulers could be identified with the Davids and Cyruses of that history.

In fact that did not happen. We know that Constantine's 'conversion' (though he was not baptised till he was dying and Christianity did not finally become the sole official religion of the empire till several generations later) was hailed by Christians with some extravagant language.[2] We know that it was a standard ploy of early Christian apologetic to argue that those emperors who were the most savage persecutors were also those whom even the Romans themselves regarded as heartless tyrants.[3] But, in spite of the temptations, Christians seem to have held that even pagan rulers, even bad rulers, possessed a legitimate authority, as long as they did not abuse it.

Now of course it may be the case that this attitude was adopted as a sort of propaganda tactic. If Christians consistently advocated obedience then the authorities might become convinced that there was nothing subversive about the new religion and might be less likely to persecute its adherents. 'Have Christians been condemned as felonious followers of an executed felon? [The author of Luke and Acts] will show that Christ and his disciples have justly been pronounced innocent by representatives of Roman law'.[4] 'Luke consciously creates the impression that Christianity can spread without trouble. That this image does not correspond to reality can be seen from the persecution logia in the Third Gospel as well as from his efforts to prove Christianity to be politically loyal.'[5] These are moderate judgements, not inconsistent with the view that the New Testament writers are genuinely and sincerely advocating an attitude to the state which they believe to be properly Christian. There have been harsher judgements. Some scholars suggest that the later documents within the New Testament attempt to put the blame for the death of Jesus almost entirely upon the Jews in order to curry favour with the Roman government. So Luke is said to emphasise certain features of the passion narrative because he 'is clearly anxious to present the Romans in as favourable a light as possible'. And New Testament literature written after AD 70 can be described as designed 'to confute rather than convince' Judaism, as for example in the way the fourth gospel condemns ' "the Jews" as a whole for actions which the synoptists had more specifically ascribed to the Pharisees or to some other party'.[6] Modern complaints that the Oberammergau passion play is antisemitic may be justified but some of the passages which condemn the Jews and exonerate the Roman authorities are in the gospels themselves not in the additional portions of the script.

There is a complex and difficult problem here. It is possible to argue that controversy between Jews and Christians and between Jewish Christians and Gentile Christians, allied with growing political tensions between Jews and the Roman state in the latter part of the first century, meant that Christians tended to dissociate themselves from the supposedly subversive attitudes of Jewish nationalists. At the same time an almost concurrently increasing persecution of Christians (in which Jews sometimes played a part) might have led to the development of a tradition which set strict limits upon the obedience that Christians were, in practice, willing to render to the state. There is no easy answer to this historical problem but it must be remembered that the passage from Romans 13, which is the most unqualified demand for obedience in the New Testament, is probably earlier than anything in the gospels. Coming from so Jewish a writer as Paul, written in the full knowledge that Christ had been executed by the state, such an uncompromising statement of the duty to obey is very significant. One may regard it as naive and oversimplified. One may say that common sense requires that it should sometimes be qualified or modified. One may recognize that the later Christian tradition, represented by Tertullian, also needs to be taken account of. Nevertheless, if one is to take the New Testament at all seriously, one has to say that there is a *prima facie* obligation laid upon Christians to be dutiful subjects to their political rulers.

Sometimes, no doubt, the tradition of obedience has been grossly exploited by government to make rebellion appear something cursed by God as well as by the king. Nor is this exploitation something that belongs only to the remote and distant past. The history of English missionary activity in the nineteenth century is littered with examples to show that conversion to Christianity was thought of as including a change of political loyalty too; becoming a Christian was, or at least ought to have been, a matter also of becoming a loyal subject of the missionaries' king. Indeed missionaries themselves sometimes sought support from the state on the ground that the extension of Christ's kingdom would be virtually the same thing as the extension of England's kingdom. Thus Joshua Watson, in his capacity as one of those responsible for the finances of the Society for the Propagation of the Gospel, wrote to Archbishop Manners Sutton in 1817, pointing out that it might encourage Lord Liverpool to persuade the Prince Regent to authorise a collection for missions in every parish in England, if he stressed the political advantages of missionary expansion in Ceylon.

> . . . the bringing of a population of 1¼ million of souls . . . to speak the English language, under the mild sway of English laws, and to profess under its purest form the Christian Religion, within the pale of that Church which has ever given the best security for ye loyalty of its members, is confessedly a matter of commanding interest – and if, from the present outgoings of the settlement, its full attainment be considered as beyond the immediate reach of H. M.'s Government, I submit that it might still be effected by the exertions of the Society for the Propagation of the Gospel.[7]

Joshua Watson was, of course, a high churchman and perhaps it was only to be expected that the traditional throne-and-altar attitude of high churchmen should produce thinking of this kind. But it is also to be found in people from a very different tradition. John Philip became the London Missionary Society superintendent in the Cape Colony in 1820. A convinced independent in religion and a disciple of Adam Smith in politics and economics, he was also the champion of the indigenous people of the colony against the white settlers. One of Philip's converts was Jan Tzatzoe or Tshatshu, the son of an independent chief whose land lay beyond the borders of the colony. In 1847 Tzatzoe took part in an attack upon the colony. This 'defection and apostasy' is said to have broken Philip's heart.[8] Such a reaction to the behaviour of the son of an independent ruler can really only be explained by a general assumption that religious conversion ought to have brought with it an automatic loyalty to the British crown even where the crown had no political claim upon that loyalty, not even by right of conquest. If the son of one European ruler had attacked the territories of another, in the same period, there might have been outrage at his aggression. No one would have suggested that it was apostasy or disloyalty.

It is possible for us to recognize that those who saw Christian missions and political interest as so closely intertwined were exaggerating or perverting the tradition of loyalty and obedience which begins with the New Testament. Those nineteenth-century Christians, no doubt, saw it as a natural aspect of the tradition. It was, in other words, symptomatic of the way in which that tradition had become deeply ingrained in Christian thinking. The Pauline teaching that 'the powers that be are ordained of God' had been given a more than merely instructive character: it had led to attempts to adumbrate a *theology* of government. On its foundation some Christians had asserted a doctrine of the divine right of kings, others had argued that the sanctity of government rests in some natural principle of creation, others that there is a separate and divinely constituted sphere of secular authority in which the Church has no voice, yet others that rulers are themselves in a direct sense the ministers of God. Perhaps the most extreme view of all is that all exercise of authority, even the discipline of the Church itself, ought to be in the hands of secular authorities. The same ingrained tradition seems to lie behind that principle of the medieval concept of the just war, which required it to be waged by a lawful ruler. It is also echoed by the reformation variant which said that rebellion even against an ungodly, unbelieving tyrant ought to be undertaken only when authorized by inferior magistrates. And though, no doubt, the tag '*cuius regio eius religio*' was born from pragmatic necessity, the acceptability of so unprincipled a principle must be owing in part at least to a belief in the providential nature of government.

A classical anarchist desires non-government for its own sake. Almost everyone else would, I suppose, believe that *some* kind of order was better than none. One prefers there to be a law requiring motorists to drive on one specified side of the road than that there should be no law on the matter at all. It is easy to believe that government, in general, is in accordance with the will of a God whose creative activity is described by Genesis as the bringing of order out of chaos. In that sense most Christians would have no hesitation in saying that government was providential. But any attempt to develop an actual theology of the state, on the basis of Romans, or 1 Peter or other New Testament passages, runs into the difficulty that it is obliged to grant the state a kind of authority which, even if it is not *strictly* autonomous, is virtually so in practice. If government, simply by virtue of *existing* (the powers that *be*), is clothed with an authority derived from God then it is almost impossible to set limits upon the claims which government may properly make upon the loyalty of Christians. Even the most convinced literalist would hesitate to say that Romans 13:1 is an unqualified divine command enjoining obedience to every whim of a malevolent state. Common sense dictates that the Pauline statement be treated as a sort of general rule to guide behaviour, all others things being equal, and not as an expression of the will of God which must be applied in every conceivable case or as the revealed truth upon which a theological system is to be constructed.

Granted, then, that Christian subjects have a *prima facie* duty to obey – though not without question – there remains the problem of why the New Testament should stress the Christian's duty as *subject*. And perhaps the answer is a very simple and practical one – that *that* was what Christians were, subjects not rulers. There is nothing very revolutionary about this suggestion. People often think of the early Church as a community consisting entirely of the poor, the halt, the blind, the outcast and so on. No serious history puts it quite like that but B. J. Kidd's three-volume classic conveys the hint of it. The new converts were drawn from the masses, he thinks, because the ministry was largely peasant and the few rich Christians marred the simplicity of community life.[9] Later on, under Domitian, the execution of Titus Flavius Clemens and the exile of his wife Domitilla can be adduced as evidence that Christianity had made some headway among the upper classes. It is an attractive picture. It combines the romanticism of an appeal to the oppressed with the success story of upper-class conversions. Christian historians have obvious reasons for liking it, therefore,[10] and curiously it gains some support from Marxists. Engels himself described early Christianity as a movement of slaves and emancipated slaves, the rightless poor and dispossessed subject peoples.[11] It was, he thought, a movement of the proletariat.

The truth is that writers like Marx and Engels were transferring the pattern of religious and social groupings from the nineteenth century, when status, wealth and power more or less coincided, to the first and second century, when they did not. One only has to remember how important freedmen ('emancipated slaves') could be in both commerce and politics, and how often the occupants of the imperial throne were of the 'subject peoples', to perceive this fact.

Max Weber's analysis in *Sociology of Religion* is, perhaps, more realistic. He argued that it was especially the lower-middle classes and the artisans who were most open to conversion to Christianity.[12] This is, in one sense, a very different picture from the romantic idea of the Church as a community of the destitute and the outcast. Weber's Church would be largely composed of staunchly independent craftsmen and small businessmen. And this picture is backed up by other information we possess about the early Church. We know that Christianity was essentially an urban religion, found principally in the towns and cities of the empire and spreading along the network of Roman roads, and therefore not really what is usually meant by 'peasant' at all. We know, also, that it was initially disseminated through the Jewish *diaspora*., which was among other things a trading *diaspora*. There is nothing new about either of these pieces of information but they ought to have predisposed us to expect Christianity to be found amongst the urban tradespeople rather than amongst the peasant poor.

Recent research has tended to confirm this picture. A small but seminal work by E. A. Judge argued that the household was the most important unit in early Christianity and that the household in the empire of this period was not only much larger than the nuclear family of modern Western society but also contained a cross-section of many different social classes.[13] Even quite modestly wealthy men might have in their households slaves, freedmen, retainers and clients, hangers-on of one kind or another, who would represent a rather lower class than the head of the family. John G. Gager, building on the work of A. D. Nock, A. H. M. Jones and E. R. Dodds, has shown that Christianity was most unlikely to have made much headway among the Roman aristocracy or the very wealthy but was likely, in the first two centuries, to have been chiefly a religion of the lower and lower-middle, Greek-speaking, urban classes, and certainly not predominantly a slave-religion.[14] The work done by Ramsay MacMullen on social groupings in the empire at this period presents us with an account of city life into which a Church of tradesmen and artisans would fit very easily, with Christians tending to live together in clusters which would be broadly of the same class yet contain, at the same time, considerable variation in wealth from the poor to the modestly well-off.[15] And, of course, apart from anything else, exhortation to Christians to give to the poor implies that there were some Christians who had money they could give away. A. J. Malherbe, attempting to sum up what he calls an emerging consensus on the subject of the social class of Christians in the period, says that this consensus views the Church as comprising a cross-section of most of Roman society. Where scholars have used 1 Corinthians as crucial evidence, he suggests, they tend to say that the Church included at least an influential minority of well-to-do persons as well as a large number of people from the lower classes. When Acts and other later writings are used, scholars are inclined to say that Christianity grew chiefly in urban circles of well-situated artisans and tradespeople.[16]

This consensus is not actually one of complete unanimity. Scholars vary in their assessment of how far conversions from among the very wealthy, on the one hand, and from among slaves and the very poor, on the other, are to be regarded as exceptional. But the general picture is one of urban communities of Christians, socially as well as geographically mobile, centred on household churches, living perhaps in one small quarter of a town or city, containing a cross-section of lower-middle and lower class tradesmen, craftsmen and artisans, with some wealthier leading figures and a number of slaves and the very poor. This is a very different kind of community from that envisaged by either the romantic or the Marxist historian. There is no *evidence* that Christianity made capital out of, or was made use of by, the disaffections or frustrations of any social class.[17] Nor ought one to think of the Church as overwhelmingly made up of the peasants, the proletariat, the destitute, the outcast and the un-persons. It would be more accurate to say that there were lots of poor Christians, very few very rich ones, and a solid core of the petty bourgeoisie and the skilled artisan. In that, it would be an accurate echo of society as a whole. If the Church was different from the world outside, the difference lay in the fact that at least an *attempt* was made to overcome the distinctions between rich and poor.

But, if it is foolish to harbour romantic notions of a Church composed exclusively of the scourings of society or of a Christian movement with thinly disguised but revolutionary political aims, the fact remains that the kind of Church envisaged by the 'consensus' would still have been a Church of subjects rather than rulers. Merchants, tradesmen and artisans in the Roman empire were not likely to have any part in the administration of government or in the making of policies. Their role in society was to render service, to bear imposts, to pay taxes, to keep the machinery going. And this is precisely what they were bidden to do by men like Paul. In so far as they played a part in the business of government at all, people of that class would be petty officials, not sharing in decision-making even at a low level, but concerned rather with collecting from others what was due to Caesar. Even that sort of function was regarded as itself as impost,[18] almost a levy, which consisted in turn of levying imposts upon others. It seems to me that it may not be accidental that there are only two sorts of people whose *political* role is singled out in the New Testament and upon whom a specific moral duty is enjoined. It is done not by Christ nor by any of the apostles, but by John the Baptist.[19] Tax collectors and soldiers are told by him how their jobs are to be done. I know that there is considerable controversy about whether Christians were allowed to serve in the Roman army.[20] But it seems clear that some did and that if Christians were to be found *anywhere* in the ranks of government servants, these were precisely the two jobs they would be most likely to be doing. There would be no point in the New Testament laying down rules for magistrates, policy-makers or decision-takers. Christians would not occupy such posts. Government *was* as St Paul implies, a *given*. In so far as Christians were involved with it at all they were its subjects or, at most, its agents, and in no sense the architects of its policies. All that was necessary was to tell them to perform these roles in a Christian manner.

I do not believe that the conversion of Constantine made a great deal of immediate difference to the way in which political *morality* was dealt with, however much it may have led to dramatic changes in other aspects of the relationship between religion and politics. Church and state found themselves in an entirely new alliance. Christians began to occupy positions in which they could actually affect the policies and decisions of government. No doubt there was some unevenness and certain exceptions. But by and large the assumptions seem not to have changed. Christians took with them into government the acceptance of authority as a given. But a Christian in government was subject to the same moral code as any Christian private citizen. An act which would have been wrong if done by any individual was wrong if done by the emperor. Whatever one's role was, one was to perform it in a Christian manner.

This comes out very clearly in the behaviour of Ambrose, Bishop of Milan from 374 to 397, that is to say some three generations after the conversion of Constantine. What makes him significant is that he was the son of the praetorian prefect of Gaul, that he had been trained as a lawyer and was, at the time of his election as bishop, governor of Aemilia-Liguria, which had Milan as its capital city. He was, in other words, familiar with the political world from the inside. Moreover the imperial court was often in residence in or near Milan so that Ambrose had first-hand dealings with emperors and was caught up in a succession of political events.

The most dramatic of these were:

(1) In the winter of 383/4, at the request of the emperor's mother, Justina, he went on an ambassage to the usurper Maximus to negotiate terms for the young emperor Valentinian II;

(2) In 384 he persuaded Valentinian not to permit the restoration of the altar of Victory in the Senate;

(3) In 385 and 386 he successfully resisted the attempts of Justina to acquire a church in Milan for the use of Arian heretics, largely by enlisting popular support on his side;
(4) In 388 he refused to proceed with a celebration of the eucharist until the emperor Theodosius withdrew a decision compelling the local bishop to use church funds to pay for the restoration of a synagogue at Callinicum, destroyed by Christian rioters;
(5) In 390 he compelled Theodosius to do penance for massacring several thousand Thessalonians after the assassination of a barbarian general.

It has been argued that Ambrose, while he would in theory have subscribed to a kind of Church and state dualism, was in fact set upon establishing an ascendancy of Church over state. It has also been suggested that this attempt at an ascendancy was, for the most part, not very creditable to Ambrose, particularly as regards the Callinicum episode.[21] It is, of course, very easy to agree that Ambrose paid too little attention to the demands of justice and fairness in the case of the rebuilding of the synagogue but he lived in an era when government was still largely a personal affair. It is true that by the fourth century Roman Law made a clear distinction between the emperor as emperor and the emperor as a private person, particularly as regards ownership of property. But this is different from making clear distinctions between actions performed by the emperor as a human being and those performed by government as an institution. In any case it would not always be possible to tell one from the other. And the pagan world, with its ideal of the philosopher-king, would tend to suppose that an emperor ought to behave *better* than anyone else. It would have been very difficult for Ambrose to adopt the mode of thought which says that there is a 'different' morality applicable to political action. His was also an age when a secular state, neutral in religion, would have been literally inconceivable – even though it was an age of religious pluralism. The state had a duty to maintain religious observance in order to express society's dependence upon divine tutelage. It was possible, of course, to be cynical about such a duty. It was possible to argue that all religions were attempts to give expression to different understandings of one divine reality. It was also possible to say that one could not be certain which were the right gods to worship and that it was better for all men to worship as they saw fit and thus ensure that all gods were propitiated. None of these is quite what we now mean by secular pluralism. From Ambrose's point of view it would have been extremely difficult to make a distinction between a neutral justice in matters of religion, exercised by the emperor as emperor, and his personal commitment to Christianity as a human being. If the state was to maintain a religion, it could hardly have been one which was incompatible with the emperor's own. The emperor would have to use his 'given' authority to support the truths which he claimed to embrace. And there would be no way in which Ambrose could accept an argument that the emperor was somehow to be permitted to behave less morally than any other Christian.

For these reasons it is something of an anachronism to formulate Ambrose's attitude as if it were a theory of relations between Church and state, unless one is trying to explain what his ideas would mean if one were to transpose them into the context of mdern thought. He would neither have conceived of Church and state as a dualism nor would he consciously have been thinking in terms of establishing an ascendancy of Church over state as some of the medieval popes did. Indeed, the only possible hypothesis that makes consistent sense of Ambrose's opinions and actions is that he was, in each and every situation, applying the principle that what would be sin for any other Christian would be sin for the emperor. In fact he specifically argued that case quite openly on several occasions, notably in a letter to Valentinian II in answer to the petition to the emperor for the restoration of the altar of Victory.[22] And it makes sense of each of his actions in turn. A Christian simply could not actively support the erection of a pagan altar. A Christian could not force a bishop to court martyrdom by refusing to use Church funds for the rebuilding of a Jewish synagogue. A Christian could not insist upon the surrender of a church to heretics. A Christian could not massacre 7,000 people, whatever the claims of political expediency. The emperor is simply a Christian layman (Ambrose would not even allow Theodosius a special seat in the sanctuary because that honour was reserved for the ordained clergy) and so he could not possibly do any of these things either. If he were to try to do so he would be a persecutor like any heathen tyrant and there would be open resistance. Hence Ambrose's enlisting of popular resistance to the empress's attempt to take over one of the Milanese churches.

But if Ambrose had really been concerned to establish an ascendancy of Church over State – or even his own personal ascendancy – in terms of political power, his actions in the case of the usurper Maximus were inconsistent and unintelligible. In 383 Maximus seemed to be the rising star. The young Valentinian was almost powerless. The eastern emperor, Theodosius, was in no position to take effective action against the usurper. Maximus was making a great display of his piety and orthodoxy by harrying the supposedly heretical Priscillianists (whom Ambrose had already opposed). Justina, on the other hand, had just begun openly to avow her Arian opinions. If Ambrose had wished to assert an authority to depose a possibly heretical ruler and substitute an orthodox alternative, and thus demonstrate the supremacy of the Church, it was the ideal opportunity. Instead, however, he persuaded Maximus to divide the western empire with Valentinian and guarantee his safety. Ambrose does not seem to have seen it as his (or the Church's) business to decide who should be the ruler. The powers that were, were. They were still a given. It was Ambrose's business to tell them how they ought to behave if they claimed to be Christians, not to determine who should be the powers that be.

What is even more significant is that Augustine in *The City of God* saw the relations between Ambrose and Theodosius in precisely this way,[23] that is to say as the relations between a Christian bishop and a Christian layman and not as the relations between representatives of Church and State. He repeatedly emphasised the fact that what mattered about Theodosius was whether he was a good Christian layman and not whether he was a successful empire-builder. Theodosius may not have been nearly such a splendid human being as Augustine supposed. He has been described as weak, vacillating and the victim, by turns, of indolence and rage.[24] In a sense this does not matter. What matters is not whether, in fact, Theodosius was a good, moral, Christian but that that was what Ambrose and Augustine thought *important*. That he was also an emperor was almost irrelevant. No concessions were made to political expediency. Rulership was the role Theodosius happened to have to play. For him, as for those Christians who occupied the role of subject, the moral obligation was the same. The role was to be filled in a Christian manner. And the secular importance of the emperor certainly gave him no immunity from either the necessity to behave morally or the consequences of behaving immorally. This comes out very clearly in what Augustine says about Theodosius:

> Could anything have been more remarkable than his humility? On the occasion of the Thessalonian outbreak, at the petitions of the bishops he had promised indulgence, but under the pressure of his officers he had felt obliged to exact vengeance. Then yielding to ecclesiastical discipline he carried out his penance. . . .[25]

There is a hint here to which I shall want to return later but for the present the important thing is to notice that the pattern to which the emperor is expected to conform is that of any Christian layman. It is no doubt an unrealistic and flattering picture, but again and again Theodosius is represented by Christian writers[26] as the type of the Christian layman because he recognised that his imperial office gave him no special moral exemptions and that like any other layman, he was subject to the authority of the Church and bishops in matters of morality.

This raises all sorts of interesting points. Even if one were to accept the theory which I have attributed to Ambrose, there would clearly be all sorts of cases where the apparent effect would be precisely the same as if he were asserting that the Church had a right to determine the *political* policies pursued by the State. By ruling that the emperor, because he was a Christian, could not follow a course of action that was immoral, and by claiming further that as a bishop he possessed the authority to pronounce on the morality or immorality of an action, Ambrose was, *in effect*, exercising a decisive political power. This is a state of affairs which clearly can be pried open at several points. It could be argued that no bishop (or any other agent or organ of the Church) is in principle clothed with the authority to decide with that degree of finality that a specific course of action is immoral. Or it could be argued that, while some of these rulings are sound others can be mistaken – in this particular context, that massacring 7,000 people is manifestly wrong for a Christian but recompensing non-Christians for damage done to their place of worship is not – and that, if a bishop can be mistaken, then, whatever the supposed principle in the matter, his rulings can be of little value in practice. Or it could be argued that the role occupied by a Christian does, in fact, make a difference to the way in which moral rules are applied to him, at least in certain respects. Or it could be argued that government has a representative character (not in a elective sense only but because even an autocrat is in some sense the symbol of the people he rules) and that, therefore, private moral rules can only be applied to him if they are shared by society as a whole. All these are issues which have been raised from time to time in the history of Christian moral theology and political thought. Some of them will be raised again in later chapters but others, for the sake of tidiness, need to be briefly pursued here.

It seems to me clear, because of the repeated emphasis upon Theodosius's humility in the sources, that people like Ambrose and Augustine were less concerned with considering issues of political expediency and the corporate as opposed to the private character of a ruler, than with the question of power and importance. The real principle they are at pains to establish is that secular or political importance does not confer any moral exemption on the holders of high office. This is an obvious point that hardly, perhaps, needs to be argued. It is, at any rate, very clearly a New Testament principle. In spite of the fact that the New Testament is most often concerned to stress the subject's duty to obey, it is equally insistent that earthly power and glory is no excuse for behaving wickedly.

Luke 22:25–6 attributes to Jesus the saying, 'The kings of the Gentiles exercise lordship over them; and those in authority over them are called benefactors. But not so with you: rather let the greatest among you become as the youngest, and the leader as one who serves.' The verb in the first clause could best be translated as 'lord it' if that had not come, in English, to have a purely pejorative meaning. 'Benefactor' was a soubriquet often given to (or perhaps assumed by) Hellenistic rulers. Presumably the sentence can be understood as either straightforward and serious or as a subtle irony. In either case it seems to mean that secular rulers rule by being the master and that the exercise of power *per se* is regarded in the secular world as doing well. Since this is immediately followed by a command prohibiting the disciples from adopting this style of authority and leadership, the point of the saying must be that they are to reject that *pattern* of authority. The pattern which is then exhibited as the right one is that of the servant. The greatest is to be as the youngest, the leader as the servant (diakonos). The proper pattern of Christian leadership is that of service, which was Christ's own pattern, as the passage then proceeds to point out. 'For which is the greater, one who sits at table, or one who serves?. . . But I am among you as one who serves.' The implication clearly is that he is greater than they are and that he is their leader, otherwise the whole rhetorical question loses its point. Nevertheless the authority or leadership which he exercises is not that of the lord who possesses dominion nor of the 'benefactor' with absolute power. It is the authority and leadership of the servant.

It will, of course, be argued that the saying *could* not mean this, since servants do not have any authority. Their status precludes the very possibility of it. But anyone who has known a faithful, conscientious college servant will know that this is simply not true. Even a bad college servant of many years standing can establish a kind of control over what is done and what is not done. Such an authority is not, as has been hinted, necessarily a good one. It can be as unscrupulous and as selfish as the authority of the exercisers of power. The point is that it is an authority of a quite different pattern, the authority of the person who serves.

In origin, therefore, the thrust of this passage seems to me to have been quite different from that of the apparently similar saying which appears in all three synoptic gospels (Matthew 18:1ff; Mark 9:33ff; Luke 9:46ff). In those passages the point that is made, explicitly or implicitly, is that to be great in the kingdom of heaven one has to have the simplicity and humility of a child. The force of the saying is that the great must be humble. The other passage, found in Luke alone, is much more subtle. There the point is the difference between a Christian and a secular *pattern* of authority.

Once the imperial throne was occupied by a Christian the force of the saying about the pattern of Christian leadership and authority, taken with other sayings about humility in the great, must have been redoubled. It must have seemed specially applicable to Christian rulers, urging them to seek not only humility but a spirit of service. And, even if the saying was originally meant to apply to the ecclesiastical rather than the political leadership, it cannot be said to be wrong to give it the wider application. High office does not, in itself, entitle a Christian to be well thought of. The exercise of authority is not in itself a benefaction. Authority is a benefaction when it is an unwearying, unremitting, self-giving *service*. Therefore, so far from there being a kind of moral immunity conferred on rulers by their high office, there is actually an additional demand made upon them, that they exercise their authority in conformity with a particular pattern, a pattern derived from Christ. It is this pattern which, in fact, unifies the role of the ruler and the role of the subject. Both service and obedience are expressions of the humility of Christ.

It is obvious that one of the ways in which our situation is very different from that of Christians in the time when the New Testament was written is that there is no longer quite so sharp and simple a division between ruler and subject. Whatever vestiges of personal sovereignty and prerogative power may have been preserved in the language and even the law of the United Kingdom, the truth is that the citizen is no longer simply subject: he or she has at least some degree of political power and may actually acquire a great deal of it. The theoretical sovereign wields very little real power as a ruler: the *de facto* rulers do not cease to be citizens and subjects. Most of us possess a mixed character, part subject, part ruler, and even if one part of that mixed character seems minimal it is nevertheless real and, as I shall try to argue in the next chapter, places us in what is, morally, a peculiarly difficult position. The main significance of Ambrose's treatment of Theodosius is, however, strengthened rather than weakened by the fact that the division between ruler and subject has been replaced by a sliding scale. An absolute ruler, if he is a Christian, cannot claim that his secular importance frees him from the demands of morality. But even if he could, at what point on a sliding scale can one be said to cease to be a subject and become a ruler?

If the New Testament, then, enunciates as a first principle that subjects are to be obedient to the state, provided it does not command what is evil, it sets alongside it a second principle – which the Church stressed more firmly as government also became a role which Christians could occupy – that political and secular importance confers no immunity upon the ruler. There may be other ways in which the holding of public office modifies the *manner* in which one responds to the demands of morality: the moral principles and values by which one attempts to live cannot be different. This might seem so obvious as to be hardly worthy saying if it were not for the fact that actual experience seems to suggest otherwise. Thomas Nagel,[27] writing about the way in which public crimes do not seem to be fully attributable to the individuals responsible for them, says that public roles and offices undoubtedly 'have a profound effect on the behaviour of those who fill them, partly restrictive but significantly liberating.'

The liberating effect he describes as follows:

> Sometimes they confer great power, but even where they do not, as in the case of the infantryman or the police interrogator, they can produce a feeling of moral insulation that has strong attractions. The combination of special requirements and release from some of the usual restrictions, the ability to say that one is only following orders or doing one's job or meeting one's responsibilities, the sense that one is the agent of vast impersonal forces or the servant of institutions larger than any individual – all these ideas form a heady and sometimes corrupting brew.

Over against this there is the sense in which public office is restricting:

> Public figures are not supposed to use their powers openly to enrich themselves or their families, or to obtain sexual favors . . . personal detachment in the exercise of official functions is thought to guarantee their good moral standing. The exchange seems fairly straightforward. The exercise of publc power is to be liberated from certain constraints by the imposition of others, which are primarily personal. Because the office is supposedly shielded from the personal interests of the one who fills it, what he does in his official capacity seems also to be depersonalized. This nourishes the illusion that personal morality does not apply to it with any force, and that it cannot be strictly assigned to his moral account. The office he occupies gets between him and his depersonalized acts.

There is some evidence to support the correctness of Nagel's analysis and the existence of the state of mind which he is attacking. Of a substantial number of Canadian public servants employed by central government agencies who were asked to say where they believed their responsibility to lie in the performance of their work, only 9.8 per cent mentioned their own conscience and less than 40 per cent mentioned anything other than their superiors (whether ministerial or official) or the structure of the agency itself.[28] Admittedly the question was so put that the respondents might have assumed that matters of morality and conscience were not what was really at issue, since they were asked to suggest where they felt their own accountability to lie rather than being asked to choose from a selection of possible answers provided by the questionnaire. It is, nevertheless, alarming that so very few thought of moral accountability as even entering into the picture.

It is quite clear that a Christian *ought* to feel morally accountable in whatever role he occupies and *ought* to agree with Nagel that there is something distorted about a view of public office which regards it as conferring freedom or immunity from moral constraints. No matter where he believed himself to fall on the subject/ruler sliding scale he would have to hold to the same moral values. Logic and commonsense, other passages from the New Testament and the Christian tradition, all make it obvious that Romans 13 does not clothe government with an absolute authority which makes its morality irrelevant. This, in itself, implies that Christians in positions of authority are not free from the constraints of morality, besides suggesting that Christians subject to authority have an obligation to ask whether that authority is behaving morally or not. When one adds to that the consideration that the Christian ruler is not primarily a ruler in order to exercise power or to be a successful builder of power-structures but to serve, it is plain that the mere importance of the office cannot be allowed to confer moral immunity. In Christian terms Ambrose was plainly right in arguing that what would be sin in a private person is sin in an emperor. The distortion of which Nagel complains is not something compatible with Christian morality.

I have carefully avoided formulating this in terms like 'What it would be wrong for a private individual to *do*, it would be wrong for a public official to *do*'. Partly this is because it would be to lay myself open to the retort that there are some things which have traditionally been regarded as proper when done by the representative of the state but not when done by the private citizen – imprisoning someone, for instance. I am not, actually, entirely certain that there is a real moral, as opposed to a legal, distinction here. One may recognize that there are all sorts of reasons why society may need to do things which it would be undesirable for a private citizen to do. But *the mere fact* that certain actions are desired and authorized by society does not give them a status that lifts them above criticism on moral grounds. Societies have done, and do, acts against individuals which are plainly immoral, and their immorality does not lie in the nature of the act performed but in the nature of the society which authorizes it. A Christian might argue from the principle of obedience, from God's character as a God of order and from man's natural need to live in society, to the conclusion that it was perfectly proper for society to imprison the subversive and the antisocial. This seems a perfectly acceptable view. But there are societies which define 'subversive' and 'antisocial' (and do so with the overwhelming support of most members of that society) in such a way as to make their actions quite immoral.

And that indicates the second reason why I have not said 'What it would be wrong for a private individual to do, it would be wrong for a public official to do.' In the account of Christian morality given in the previous chapter it is clear that sin is not to be defined simply in terms of the action performed. The concern is with the kind of person one is, and the kind of person one becomes, rather than with prescriptive rules or even general principles. Even if my understanding of Christian morality were thought to be defective, it is uncontroversial that the New Testament presents Jesus as being concerned with much more than the action performed. He is insistent upon the importance of interior motives, thoughts and state of mind. It is not enough to avoid acts of murder or adultery. Hatred and lust, as states of mind, are as bad. The *intention* of the woman who poured spikenard on Jesus matters more than the waste of valuable oil which might have been sold for charity. The publican who sees himself as a sinner is better than the pharisee who has performed all the right actions.

This is not to say, of course, that the action does not matter. That a man who has looked upon a woman to lust after her has committed adultery in his heart already, does not mean that the actual act of adultery is neither here nor there. Conversely, it is meaningless to talk of interior states of mind as though they could exist independently. A loving person who did not ever do loving things would be a contradiction in terms. What Jesus does is not to make the action performed irrelevant but to penetrate behind the action to the kind of person involved in it. Moral judgement is made in the interplay between action and state of mind. There are no precise quantitative measures that can be applied in assessing one against the other, but neither can be ignored. Moral judgement must take account of the factual context out of which action develops and the factual situation which action produces, as well as the state of mind and the motives of the agent, the kind of person he is and the kind of person he may become as a result of the action.

It cannot be denied that the Jesus of the gospels is represented as being concerned to interiorize morality. Inevitably this interiorizing also has the effect of individualizing morality. In spite of the fact that the New Testament, in many other aspects of its teaching, emphasizes the corporate over against the individual, and it would be wrong to minimize that emphasis, yet clearly the Christian concept of *morality* is bound to stress the individual. It simply is not possible to interiorize the corporate. Language about collective conscience is bound to be in some degree metaphorical. Society does not and cannot act with a uniform corporate motivation and conscience. In that sense a private morality which depends upon the interplay of the interior state of mind with the external circumstances cannot simply be transferred to the public morality of a whole society and its corporate activities.

That takes us back to another aspect of the passage I have quoted from Nagel, the impersonality of modern government and the way this sometimes appears to insulate its servants from the constraints of morality. No doubt, when government was clearly exercised personally by a single ruler and his servants, as in the case of Theodosius, it was relatively easy to apply the standards and values of an interiorized Christian morality to the actions of the human being in his public capacity. One could still ask questions about his motives, his state of mind, what kind of person he was. In a modern society, where government is both more complex and more impersonal and where the whole of society is, in a sense, involved in what happens, it is much more difficult to ask those questions. One can still, of course, ask questions about what kind of society requires these actions to be done on its behalf and what kind of society will result from such actions. That kind of questioning is, indeed, essential. One can also ask 'interior' questions about individual agents of government and their participation in the decisions and actions. But it is not just that 'the sense that one is the agent of vast impersonal forces or the servant of institutions larger than any individual' seems to nourish 'the illusion that personal morality does not apply to it with any force'. For the Christian, at least, there is the genuine difficulty that the interiorisation of morality which is such a marked feature of Christ's teaching is impossible to transfer from the personal to the corporate sphere. It is not surprising, then, that as government has become more complex and more impersonal, it should prove more difficult to apply Christian moral values to its workings. It will be the purpose of the next chapter to consider briefly the effects of that process.

Notes

1. *Civitas Dei*, XIX. 17.
2. See e.g. the conclusion to Eusebius, *Ecclesiastical History*, X.9.6ff.
3. See e.g. Tertullian, *Apologeticum*, V.
4. G. B. Caird, *The Gospel of Luke*, Penguin Books 1963, p. 14.
5. H. Conzelmann, 'Luke's Place in the Development of Early Christianity' in L. E. Keck and J. L. Martyn (eds.), *Studies in Luke–Acts*, S.P.C.K. 1968, p. 301.
6. James Parkes, *The Conflict of the Church and the Synagogue*, Meridian Books (reprint) 1961, pp. 47 and ix.
7. U.S.P.G. Archives: C/IND/Gen. 4: Watson to Manners Sutton, Dec. 1817.
8. J. du Plessis, *History of Christian Missions in South Africa*, Longmans 1911, pp. 152, 248.
9. B. J. Kidd, *History of the Church to A.D. 461*, O.U.P. 1922, vol. I, pp. 24f.
10. Cf. e.g. M. Green, *Evangelism in the Early Church*, Hodder and Stoughton 1970, pp. 118f.
11. F. Engels, 'On the History of Early Christianity' in K. Marx and F. Engels, *On Religion*, Foreign Languages Publishing House Moscow 1957, p. 313.
12. M. Weber, *The Sociology of Religion* (tr. E. Fishoff), Methuen paperback reprint 1971, pp. 95ff.
13. E. A. Judge, *The Social Pattern of Christian Groups in the First Century*, Tyndale Press 1960, pp. 30ff.
14. John G. Gager, 'Religion and Social Class in the Early Roman Empire' in S. Benko and J. J. O'Rourke (eds.), *The Catacombs and the Colosseum*, Judson Press 1971, pp. 99ff.
15. See R. MacMullen, *Roman Social Relations*, Yale University Press 1974, particularly chapter 3 for a consideration of urban society and what Jewish and Christian participation in it might have been and chapter 4 for the question of what 'middle class' might mean in the context of the empire of the second and third centuries.
16. A. J. Malherbe, *Social Aspects of Early Christianity*, Louisiana State University Press 1977, pp. 87, 29 and 30.
17. C. L. Lee, 'Social Unrest and Primitive Christianity' in Benko and O'Rourke (eds.), *op.cit.*, pp. 133ff.
18. R. MacMullen, *Roman Government's Response to Crisis*, Yale University Press 1976, pp. 129ff. and 153ff., shows how this became increasingly obvious in the third century.
19. Luke 3:12–14.
20. For a balanced survey of the evidence see J. Helgeland, 'Christians and the Roman Army, A.D. 173–337', *Church History*, vol. 43, pp. 149ff.
21. S. L. Greenslade, *Church and State from Constantine to Theodosius*, S. C. M. 1954, p. 71; and H. Chadwick, *The Early Church*, Penguin Books 1967, p. 167.
22. Ambrose, *Ep.* xviii. 9 and 18.
23. *Civitas Dei*, V. 26.
24. B. J. Kidd, *op. cit.*, vol. II, pp. 360 and 362.
25. J. W. C. Wand (ed.), *St Augustine's City of God*, O.U.P. 1963, p. 117.
26. Cf. the story told about Theodosius's admiration for Ambrose in Sozomen, *Historia Ecclesiae*, VII, xxv. 9 and Theodoret, *Historia Ecclesiae*, V, xviii, 20ff.
27. T. Nagel, 'Ruthlessness in Public Life', in S. Hampshire (ed.), *Public and Private Morality*, Cambridge University Press 1978, pp. 76f.
28. C. Campbell and G. J. Szablowski, *The Superbureaucrats*, Gage Publishing 1979, p. 194.

5

A GOOD POLITICAL ANIMAL

In an ideal world I ought now to do two things. I ought to trace the development of the institutions of government from the relatively simple situation of personal rule to the complex and corporate organisation of a modern state and show how political philosophers have explained the relation of citizen to society at each stage of that development. I ought also to give an account of what Christian theologians have said about the application of morality to the same process of changing governmental structures. But it would be absurd even to attempt that in the time and space available. One could take a score of people, from the early Middle Ages on, whose ideas about political morality or the relationship between personal and social roles were of seminal importance, and write a whole book about any one of them.[1] In this chapter I shall glance briefly at the views of four or five people. I do not pretend that this provides even a sketchy account of the history of relevant ideas. It is simply that to look at a few examples, different yet related, may cast some light on the central problem I am discussing.

In the last chapter I mentioned Augustine's opinion of Theodosius as the type of the good Christian layman who also happened to be the emperor but was still to be judged, and was willing to be judged, by the standards of Christian morality even in his political actions. And there was, of course, every reason for a Christian bishop and theologian to approve such virtue. Whether it is politically desirable is a more difficult question to answer. The emperor Constantine, Augustine points out, received political rewards for his Christian devotion, died in his bed at a ripe old age and left sons to rule after him. But Augustine was not so naive as to believe that good *men* are always successful *kings* or that they always get their political deserts in this life. There is, I think, a quality of naivety in *The City of God* in that Augustine often seems to be discussing an earthly polity which has very little to do with the Roman Empire of the fourth century, but he is certainly aware of the difficulty of reconciling the hard facts of political necessity with the personal morality of the politician. Having talked about Constantine's reward, Augustine adds: 'But to prevent any emperor from becoming a Christian merely in order to share the good fortune of Constantine . . . God carried off Christian Jovian more rapidly than pagan Julian and allowed Gratian to be slain by a rival's sword.'[2]

Augustine became involved in this rather tedious argument about providence and history since one of the aims of *The City of God* was to answer the charge that the empire was collapsing because the ancient gods had been abandoned in favour of Christianity. But an even more important theme of the book is the theme of that verse of Hebrews (13:14) which runs, 'For here we have no lasting city, but we seek the city which is to come'. The argument that, by and large, God rewards the good, Christian ruler and punishes the wicked, pagan one was not so much a simplistic generalisation about history. It was really an assertion that the values of the eternal city are reflected even in the temporal, earthly city. For Augustine believed that all men, even if only for selfish reasons, desire peace and therefore will tend to seek order and justice and will be concerned to take thought for others. Even that 'earthly city, which does not live by faith, seeks an earthly peace, and therein contrives a civic harmony of command and obedience, so that there is among the citizens a sort of coherence of human wills in matters belonging to this mortal life'.[3] Here is a natural-law approach of an uncomplicated kind. It seems a curiously optimistic view for one who is sometimes described as the man who invented original sin. But the truth is that there is an underlying deeper pessimism in Augustine which regards all government as a concession to human sinfulness. He does not really believe that the earthly city is very often satisfactory and, in any case, it is hardly important. Even though there may be 'virtuous' citizens of the earthly city, the end of the earthly city is damnation.[4] Only the heavenly city matters. Men are not really intended to rule each other. They ought to need no government but God's. That is the true community of the heavenly city.[5]

This view allows Augustine to deal very simply and easily with the question of whether Christians will wish to have a political role. Since all human laws, customs and institutions, however much they may differ from place to place, will be aimed at achieving temporal peace, Christians could have no interest in breaking or rescinding them – provided they do not hinder the worship of the true God.[6]

Augustine's view, like Plato's, has a simplicity and wholeness in which good is good – whether one is ruler or subject, Christian or pagan. 'The peace of the universe is the serenity of order.'[7] To be a good man *is* to be a good king, a good *paterfamilias*, a good citizen. This is not an unsophisticated view. It is, in fact, a very profound one. Its simplicity depends upon the belief that it is the *eternal* city which matters. Augustine can afford to assert a single, unchanging standard of what is good.

It is sometimes said to be puzzling that Augustine has come to be regarded as the father both of a unitary conception of society and of the belief that the Church ought to be the dominant partner in relations between Church and State.[8] But such views need not be even formally contradictory and, in any case, there is the same kind of misunderstanding here as in the case of Ambrose discussed in the previous chapter.[9] Both Ambrose and Augustine saw matters in an essentially simple way. What is morally right is the right thing to do. Such a view could be better expressed in terms such as, 'The emperor is one of my parishioners' rather than in terms of such abstractions as 'Church' and 'State'. Augustine, like Plato, is talking of a single society where there is only one standard of what is good, just and right.

Of Plato Walter Ullmann has remarked that it is hardly possible to draw a satisfactory distinction in his writings between ethics and politics. 'The *Republic* could be equally entitled "The Ten Books about Ethics" or "The Ten Books about Politics": politics and ethics were interchangeable with him.'[10] In the history of Christian thought it is usually Aquinas who is given the credit, if credit it is, for making the clear distinction between the two; though even for Aquinas politics was a branch of ethics. No doubt, in fact, it came about gradually and unevenly but, to paraphrase Ullman again, it was Aquinas who, by his flexible adjustment of Aristotelian concepts, made it possible to treat man in society as existing in his own right not merely as an extension of Christian man. 'The idea of a double ordering constituted a major advance in doctrine because . . . full value could now be ascribed to the natural and the supranatural.'[11]

But it would be a great mistake to attribute too sharp a distinction to Aquinas. He often quoted that best-known (and much abused) dictum of Aristotle's – that man is a political animal. Aristotle did not mean, of course, that man is an incorrigible politico, an animal who thinks that the most exciting thing in the world is, for example, moving a complicated amendment at a student body meeting. And, as if to drive that point home, Aquinas usually says that man is a *social* and political animal (*animal sociale et politicum*).[12] Man, we might say, is a collegiate or an associative animal.

Men live together because, in isolation, each man is unable to procure what he needs for life. Living together, human beings need government and, in relation to government, must behave as good citizens. And Aquinas said quite specifically in his commentary on Aristotle's *Politics* that the quality (*virtus*) of a good man is not necessarily the same as the quality of a good citizen.[13] It is difficult to discover precisely what Aquinas thought the quality proper to the good citizen is. He says a great deal, directly and by metaphor, about everyone having his proper role to play. But, apart from the fact that prudence is the primary virtue upon which the others depend and that the good citizen is one who devotes himself to the preservation of society, Aquinas is not specific about how exactly a good citizen is distinct from a good man. Perhaps it is worth noting that repeatedly, on each of the several occasions on which he makes the distinction, Aquinas says that the strength or quality of the good citizen is not simply (*simpliciter*) that of the good man. So it is probably a mistake to be looking for some definition of political virtue which would be *wholly* different from private virtue. A good citizen may be a particular version of what it is to be a good human being.

Aquinas differs from Augustine in that he regards political life as something good in itself. Just as he advanced the view that there was a natural theology which was both possible and appropriate to man apart from revelation, so he believed that there was a natural law upon which all political relations were properly to be grounded, from which human justice derived and to which rational and moral values were related. Just as revealed theology did not deny or obliterate natural theology but perfected and transformed it, so the essentially human standard of justice was neither vitiated by sin nor contradictory to the divine. What was proper to man by nature was always perfected, not abolished, by the grace of God. So the basic human virtues of justice, temperance, prudence and fortitude, the political virtues, were no less real than the theological virtues – the god-centred virtues – faith, hope and love. But this does not mean that the two kinds of virtue are divorced from each other or that political excellence is to be measured by some independent yardstick of success or political skill. The end of politics is the common good and therefore implies a moral responsibility. For if grace does not abolish nature, then nature is not strictly autonomous or different from the sphere of grace. What is evil when measured by the standards of grace cannot suddenly become good when measured by the standards of nature. The best in nature may be imperfect but it is only recognized as 'best' by the same standards for which perfection itself stands.

When Aquinas wrote about heretics, Jews and pagans he was by no means indifferent or even-handed. Toleration of non-Christian rites is permitted – like the toleration of prostitution – lest worse should follow.[14] Nevertheless it is possible to feel that, if we had the theoretical framework of his thinking about natural and political virtues to guide us, we might have been able to deal rather more satisfactorily with problems of government than say Augustine or Ambrose were. In the case of the synagogue at Callinicum[15] we might argue with Ambrose that no Christian could, consistently with his commitment to the truth of the gospel, use Church funds to build non-Christian places of worship. Yet with Aquinas's distinction between natural virtue and theological virtue we might have been able to perceive that both justice and prudence – in the sense of political wisdom – required a ruler to insist on reparation being made to the Jewish community for the damage done by Christian hooligans.

Neither Aquinas nor Augustine is much concerned with what one might call political casuistry – using 'casuistry' in its proper sense, of course, the application of principles to cases. They discuss the general nature of political associations and the motives of those engaged in them. It is not always clear when they are discussing what actually is the case and when they are discussing what ought to be the case. But on those occasions when Aquinas is more specific – his consideration of the just war, for instance – it is clear that he is no more concerned to maintain a double standard of morality than Augustine. The discussion of the just war, defined with some precision and sophistication, makes it plain that Aquinas would actually regard most wars as evil for he would say that the motives behind nearly every war deprives it of the right to be called 'just'. He quotes Augustine: 'The desire to hurt, the cruelty of vendetta, the stern and implacable spirit, arrogance in victory, the thirst for power, and all that is similar, all these are justly condemned in war.'[16]

For all that we may feel that Aquinas has somehow come to terms with the realities of politics more satisfactorily than Augustine did, there is, therefore, no question of his having discovered a different moral *standard* for political behaviour. Good is still good. Whatever it is that distinguishes a good citizen from a good man, it is not another and more flexible morality. Aquinas is *not* saying that political success is the yardstick by which political behaviour is to be measured. Aquinas was not a proto-Machiavelli.

Over fifty years ago F. J. C. Hearnshaw remarked of Machiavelli's *Prince*, 'Those who read it should realize that they were not meant to do so'.[17] It is a marvellous remark because, at one stroke, we find ourselves in the manipulative, shifting, looking-glass world of political judgement upon political behaviour. Scholars detect certain contradictions between what Machiavelli wrote in the *Discourses* and in *The Prince*. They may well ask themselves whether this is because he hoped to manipulate whatever real prince it was on whom he had set his hopes, by pandering to his selfish interests, and so persuading him into the course of action which Machiavelli believed to be for the public good. Once one accepts that manipulation is justified, everything one says becomes open to question as being designed to achieve an end other than that which is being publicly asserted. Motives, means and ends may all be other than they seem to be. There is no certain patch of truth upon which one may stand to measure and assess the realities of what appears to be happening.

What Machiavelli desired was the stability of Italy. This, he believed, could only be secured by the expansion of certain states under the government of politically adept rulers. One of the recurring themes of *The Prince* is that the strong get stronger and the weak get weaker. Another is that success is not determined simply by fate, chance or fortune but by men whose temperaments coincide with the needs of moment.[18] Are we to understand these as the author's general observations on the way he thought that things actually were – of the same order, that is, as Augustine's maxim that everyone (even he who makes war) desires peace? If that were the case we might argue that either writer was wrong, naive or mistaken, without actually calling in question his sincerity. But Machiavelli believed that the successful political operator has to learn to manipulate others by pretending to be motivated otherwise than he actually is.[19] He may be saying these things merely in order to plant in his prince's mind the beliefs which would lead him to pursue policies which would achieve what Machiavelli actually desired. It is fascinating to see, for instance, how his observations on the interplay of fortune and temperament lead to an account of the disastrous condition of contemporary Italy and then, just when one might expect the hard-headed, pragmatic realist to advocate prudence and caution lest things deteriorate further, there is the assertion that now is the moment for the bold adventurer to take action.[20] Is the prince being manipulated into seizing the opportunity? Maybe. But if I were the prince in receipt of this advice from such an author I should be asking whether I was someone whom Machiavelli wished to remove from the scene.

I need not go on about this. It does not greatly matter whether Machiavelli was enunciating a coherent and consistent system of thought or whether he was himself merely operating on the basis of the pragmatic advice he offered to others. In the context with which we are concerned – the relationship of morality to political action

– Machiavelli is quite clear that they have little to do with one another. And that is precisely his importance. Not only did he separate ethics from politics firmly and clearly, but he subscribed to no concept like Aquinas's natural law.[21] This is not to say, however, that he believed that the politically necessary and successful acts he advocated were *good*. What makes some of his statement so shocking is not that they show a totally amoral disregard for goodness. They are not simply cynical. What shocks us is that they recognize that there are such things as good and evil, but that political situations demand evil actions. 'And you have to understand this,' he says to his prince, that you 'cannot observe all those things for which men are esteemed, being often forced, in order to maintain the state, to act contrary to fidelity, friendship, humanity and religion.'[22]

Bernard Crick, following Isaiah Berlin, has indeed argued that Machiavelli perceived two quite separate moralities[23] – a Christian morality and a sort of 'old Roman' pagan morality – and does not attempt to synthesize them. Even R. H. Tawney, anxious though he was to maintain a Christian morality applicable to the social and economic issues of the modern world, thought that the medieval ethic collapsed because it really had nothing to offer in terms of the new social situation and because it made no distinction between personal and social morality.[24] Machiavelli, Tawney believed, helped to emancipate social theory from the stiff ecclesiastical framework of the Middle Ages.[25] But Tawney's judgement has to be seen in its context. He was not asking for a 'different' social and economic morality. He perceived the significance of the medieval understanding of the nature of society (enshrined in the concept of natural law) and the undesirable consequences of severing economics from morality.[26] What he lamented was really the lost opportunity when what was still a Christian society failed to find a way of applying morality to its new patterns and structures.

And it may be that, in the political rather than the economic field, Machiavelli was not so much taking sides against morality as asserting that there simply was no way of applying it. To cite Crick again, Machiavelli may perceive two separate moralities but there are times when he does not follow either of them. The advice he gives would be immoral by *any* standard. 'There are times when it is necessary to do admittedly evil things for the preservation and welfare of the political community – and if one is not so willing, one is simply skipping outside politics and, incidentally, abandoning it to those who have no scruples. But if one is willing, then, he seems to say, for God and man's sake, recognize that what for the moment you are doing is evil, and do not fall into calling it good.'[27]

It is this that makes it important to look at Machiavelli as well as Augustine and Aquinas. For I have not set these three up as archetypes merely in order to reiterate more elaborately the irreconcilability of morality and politics. The real interest lies in the relationship between being a good man and being a good citizen or perhaps – since Machiavelli was much more interested in the ruler than the citizen – the relationship between being a good man and being 'a good political animal'.

Augustine would probably say that the strength or quality of a good man and a good political animal were the same thing. Aquinas, as we have seen, is prepared to admit that they are not so, *simpliciter.* Machiavelli maintains that they cannot be – at least, not all the time.

It is partly a matter of how long a perspective one takes. Augustine is really looking at it *in the long run.* It is the eternal city with which he is concerned and, though we may believe him to be right about the necessity of maintaining moral absolutes we may also feel that an 'eternal run' is just a bit too long to be of much practical use. Machiavelli offers us the advantage of a practical and down-to-earth view. He does not ask us to deny goodness, merely to admit that it isn't very practical. But like most consequentialists he is bound to concern himself with a very short run. His technique is anecdotal. This is what so-and-so did from this or that motive. It failed and therefore this is not a very wise policy to adopt. It is only the *immediate* consequences he can take into account because that is the only point at which he can assess the probabilities with any certainty. By contrast Aquinas seems the most attractive of the three – a sort of 'medium run' – because he appears to offer a way of maintaining moral standards while recognising practicalities. The snag is that the theory is more attractive in appearance than convenient in operation. As in the case of the just war, by the time one has defined the precise points at which moral and practical demands meet (supposing that one can, in fact, weigh off such very different kinds of thing against each other) one has defined the well-nigh impossible.

These are not remote, theoretical questions applicable only to prime ministers and presidents. In a social democracy such as ours, we occupy a mixed status. We are not simply subjects. Though most of us would not think of ourselves as rulers, nevertheless even as citizens we have a quite definite political responsibility. We do determine who the government shall be and we do, by and large, get the government we deserve. It is, in fact, a peculiarly difficult responsibility to shoulder, for it is only very 'by and large' that we can determine how power shall be exercised. Not only is our choice very limited, it is also exercised infrequently. Large areas of government are out of our reach because we are simply not consulted about them. Moreover to quote Stanley Benn:

> . . . in matters to be decided by a majority of a mass electorate, where the difference between total success and total failure depends on whether a critical threshold (for instance, 50% of valid votes cast) is crossed, to vote is almost always a waste of time, energy and resources. Anyone would have a better chance of making positive gains in utility by pursuing some private end, where his action would make a difference. Consequently, for anyone to participate in mass political action will generally be irrational.[28]

At the same time we also recognize (as Benn himself does) that there is more to be said on the matter than this, for, if we *all* decided that it was irrational to vote, the whole democratic system would break down. And we know that even apathy has its political consequences. How often do we not hear conservative undergraduates complain that student politics are managed by a small and unrepresentative group of left-wing militants? Apathy may be, as someone once remarked, the acceptable face of conservatism but it is no use complaining afterwards that the silent majority has not said anything.

More seriously, we know that apathy can permit democracy to be replaced by totalitarianism and once one has lived in a country which has allowed tyranny to gain control by default no kind of logic will persuade one of the inutility of exercising one's generalized and limited political responsibilities. One *has* a responsibility, and therefore a guilt, if disaster follows one's failure to vote. One has a responsibility, and therefore a guilt, if one votes for a party which subsequently governs badly. Yet one has little positive ability to control events. The frustrations are part of the price we pay for democracy and they are inevitable. To quote Stanley Benn again it is not the rational utility of our actions which determines our sense of responsibility towards society but our concern for the *telos*, the end to which it is tending.[29]

Morally speaking this is, perhaps, the most difficult situation anyone could possibly be in. To have an inescapable responsibility and yet have very little power to affect what is done is far more testing than simply to be the subject of a 'given' government for which one has no responsibility at all. There is, however, no point in a nostalgic hankering after the conditions that obtained when the New Testament was written. A constant agonising no less than a constant vigilance seems to be the price of democracy. There is no need for me to go over again the arguments of the first chapter to explain why withdrawal cannot be the Christian answer. Even silence is not enough. We have to ask, at the very least, the questions that I began to touch upon in the previous chapter in relation to the interiorising of morality effected by the teaching of the New Testament: 'What kind of society takes this kind of action?' and 'What kind of society will result from this kind of action?' Should the answer be inconsistent with the values of Christian morality, we have no option but to dissent and make our dissent quite clear. This is not merely a matter of salving our own consciences by a refusal to condone what we believe to be wrong but is a matter of exercising our own responsibility towards government. All modern governments, in some sense, claim to govern in the name (or at least with the consent of) the governed. To leave dissent unexpressed is to allow silence to seem like consent and may, even, allow a government to assume quite sincerely that it has the support of citizens generally when it does not. In the case of a totalitarian regime it can actually make it seem to possess a democratic legitimacy.

Moreover, as I have already argued, there is something peculiarly immoral in permitting someone else to do, on our behalf, something that we believe it would be wrong to do ourselves. One hears people say, 'That is a dirty (i.e. morally distasteful) job but it has to be done. I am glad not to have to do it myself.' This is a perfectly natural reaction but one which conflicts with any ideal of integrity. To will the end is to will the agent and his action just as much as to will the means. To will them and to deny them in the same breath is disintegrative. It is, also, disintegrative in the sense that willing something which implies that other people should will the opposite is disintegrative. I can set a selfish aim as my ultimate goal in life. To attain that goal really requires that most other people should be *un*selfish. I am then willing myself to be one kind of person and everyone else to be the opposite kind of person – an ambivalence of values which is hardly conducive to integrity. It will not do, therefore, to vote Labour while hoping for a Conservative victory in which I shall individually be more prosperous. Nor is it a mark of integrity to hold one ideal for society while, at least tacitly, encouraging those who shape the actual nature of society to move in another direction.

No one appreciated the difficult moral questions facing a Christian citizen of a modern state more acutely, perhaps, than Dietrich Bonhoeffer. His theology, whether in general or in relation to political morality, is notoriously difficult to interpret,[30] probably because it was occasional, and sometimes fragmentary, rather than systematic. His most widely known phrases – 'religionless Christianity' and 'man come of age' – have sometimes been taken to mean that he looked for a new kind of attitude which, while it would hold to Christian values, would break free from the liturgical, doctrinal and devotional forms of Christianity and express itself in terms which would be wholly secular and without any conscious reliance on what was overtly religious. Though it is clear that Bonhoeffer's ideas changed and developed in the course of his life, this seems to me to be a complete misunderstanding of what he really taught. It is very difficult to believe that he ever hoped for a world that would have cut itself free from an awareness of God through Christ. Indeed, if this had been what he hoped for it would have been better described as 'Christianityless religion' rather than as 'religionless Christianity'. His own spirituality remained traditional, almost conventional, to the end. He was anxious to break free from empty forms and to see the real and much more challenging truths which lay beneath them. He clearly believed that the secularisation of western Europe and great technological advances had created a new situation for the Church. Things which had previously seemed inexplicable were now understood by man and were under man's control and that meant that man must accept moral responsibility for his own actions and their consequences.[31] It was no longer sufficient to say that all *that* was in the hands of providence. What made the situation more difficult for a Christian was that the Church no longer exercised the kind of authority that could impose moral values on European civilisation. The world in which man had acquired so much control, and therefore responsibility, was a secular world. But to try and retreat from that responsibility would be pointless as well as unchristian.

His political actions seem to me to be entirely in line with this understanding of his theology.[32] If, in some such way as I have already argued, to be a citizen *now* means that one has some degree of responsibility for the existence of a law or a regime, then mere *obedience* to that law or that regime does not exhaust one's moral obligations in the political field. Government has ceased to be, as it was for the New Testament Church, simply a 'given'. It is what it is, not because of an 'act of God' but because of an act of society in which (even if only by one's apathy) one has played one's part. If it is evil, one has some responsibility for it. It is no good merely praying, as it were, for an act of God to undo it. One has a responsibility for seeing to that, also.

Bonhoeffer himself probably arrived at his conclusions through a rethinking of traditional Lutheran theology about the orders or structures of creation,[33] rather than through classical moral theology based on Aquinas. Yet it is probably easiest to perceive the different conditions which he believed that modern society had created by looking at the medieval natural-law discussion about tyrannicide and its applicability to Bonhoeffer's situation.

Aquinas argued[34] that if tyranny is not too oppressive it is better to put up with it than risk the collapse of ordered society. But if tyranny becomes insupportable then lawful opposition is the right course to take rather than individual violence. If the ruler has been elected by the people he may justly be deposed for abuse of power. If he holds power by delegation from a higher authority, it is the duty of that authority to remove him. If no other remedy can be found then it is proper to pray to God to remove the tyrant or change his heart, remembering always that God may have permitted the tyrant to rule in order to punish his subjects for their sinfulness.

To this argument Bonhoeffer might have replied:

(1) that Hitler's tyranny had become insupportable;

(2) that his authority derived from the people, not from a higher authority, and that Hitler was always claiming that he not only represented but symbolized the people;

(3) that the people had no practical constitutional means of deposing him;

(4) that to use prayer as a reason for inaction was to abdicate the moral responsibility modern man had acquired;

(5) and that, while a Christian might accept suffering as a consequence of his own sinfulness, to use that argument when the principal suffering was falling on the Jews would merely reinforce the appalling racial philosophy of the Nazi regime.

Some such reasoning as this, as I take it, led him to associate himself with the plots against Hitler.

I used to be puzzled by an apparent illogicality of Bonhoeffer's attitude. He seemed to say both that he had taken this action because he felt morally compelled to it *and yet* that the action was wrong. Curiously enough it was through reading Machiavelli that I came to understand what Bonhoeffer meant – which is why Machiavelli has taken a place alongside Augustine and Aquinas in this chapter. Forget for a moment Machiavelli's reputation for cynicism and brutal expediency and think of him, as Crick represents him, as a man who accepted political necessity yet would never fall into calling evil good. Then listen to Bonhoeffer writing about what he called 'civil courage' and 'free responsibility'. This responsibility he says, 'depends on a God who demands responsible action in a bold venture of faith, and who promises forgiveness and consolation to the man who becomes a sinner in that venture'. And he added:

> In the last resort success makes history; and the Ruler of History repeatedly brings good out of evil over the heads of the history-makers. Simply to ignore the ethical significance of success is a short circuit created by dogmatists who think unhistorically and irresponsibly; and it is good for us sometimes to be compelled to grapple seriously with the ethical problem of success. As long as goodness is successful we can afford the luxury of regarding it [i.e. success] as having no ethical significance; it is when success is achieved by evil means that the problem arises. . . . In short, it is much easier to see a thing through from the point of view of abstract principle than from that of concrete responsibility.[35]

It seems clear to me that in these passages Bonhoeffer is closer to Machiavelli than he is to either Augustine or Aquinas. It is a shocking thing to suggest, of course, that the man whom the twentieth century has regarded as a saint and martyr should be bracketed with the man whose name has come to be used as a synonym for cynical political pragmatism. And I do not wish to suggest that Bonhoeffer was, in *that* sense, Machiavellian. There was nothing of the manipulative or the devious in him. But he plainly differed from Augustine and agreed with Machiavelli in believing that the good political animal could not always behave like a good man – that there were times when there simply was not available to one a course of political action which was free from sin. He would also have argued that it was not possible to devise *rules* for determining what is an acceptable course of action for a political animal finding himself in such a situation. He would have said that one has to live with the fact that one has been unable to find a wholly good solution to a problem for which one bears some responsibility.

There are, of course, those who say that there are no irresoluble conflicts of obligation and that to admit that they exist is simply to reveal that one is thinking about morality at an intuitive level and has not pursued the matter sufficiently rigorously and critically.[36] This seems to involve making a distinction between 'ought' and 'must' and suggests that when one has decided what one 'must' do, the rival 'ought' has no further claim upon one. The Christian view of sin, as any deviation from what is ideal, is not compatible with such a case. Moral theology has always said that Christian duty remains one's duty even if one *cannot* do it. That is part of what the doctrine of the fall means. One may recognize good and even desire it but be incapable of it. In that sense sin is precisely when 'oughts' fail to become 'musts'.

Moreover it can be simply demonstrated that one has obligations, if not duties, which conflict. If I owe a sum of £100 each to X and

Y which are both repayable on 1st July and when that date arrives I possess only £100, there is no way in which I can discharge my obligations. X or Y, or both, are going to suffer wrong, whatever I decide to do. To say that I cannot repay them both does not imply that my thinking has been incomplete: it means that £100 is not £200. The facts are intractable however far I take my thinking. The crucial thing is that I shall have wronged one or both. And the 'wrong' is not merely a guilt in my mind but something they suffer. There does not seem to be any reason to suppose that the case is different if one is considering less material kinds of obligation.

Nevertheless, an insistence that one ought not to take one's moral decisions at a purely intuitive level may be a healthy reminder that an acceptance of the lesser of two evils is all too often an easy way out.[37] That acceptance ought to come, not as an immediate gut-reaction (if that is what intuition is thought to be), but only after serious, critical and rigorously rational examination. But in the end one has to act; in order to act one has to decide which course to follow; in order to decide one has to resolve the conflict. In that sense only there are no irresoluble conflicts.

Just how difficult this whole area of discussion is may be illustrated from the fact that Karl Barth, who seemed to regard a pause for reflection as essentially contrary to the whole nature of ethics as action, also believed that there could be only one possible right action in a given context. 'But, amongst all the possibilities,' he wrote, 'God's command always purposes and wills one thing only, this or that specific thing. Our obedience has to consist in an exact and concrete doing of this or that, as a human correspondence to the specific divine precept.'[38] It seems probable, however, that Barth intended this in a sense wholly different from that in which we have been discussing what is good and right political action in this chapter. He did not mean that God commands, for example, 'Thou shalt not kill' and that this constitutes an imperative which may or may not conflict, in certain circumstances, with other divine imperatives like 'Thou shalt not suffer a witch (or, conceivably, a tyrant) to live'.

Barth, indeed, rejected the whole idea that Christian ethics was a matter of statements of principle which could be treated as norms or graded in a hierarchy. Christian ethical action is always a preparing to participate in the action of God. 'Strictly speaking, there is only *one* action which is ethical, and that is an action moving the world in its totality from death to life, from judgement to forgiveness.'[39] That means that God's commands cannot simply be conceived of as prescriptive regulations drawn from the text of scripture. One has to understand how God is acting in a given situation and to prepare to participate in that action. The context, however, is not to be found simply in the factual circumstances surrounding one but is also 'the context provided by God's eternal decision and action in electing man to covenant, which was accomplished in Jesus Christ' and 'the context of response provided by the emergence and continuity of the covenant community, Israel and the Church'.[40] Since, moreover, man is really incapable of full participation in the one and only ethical action, man is always in need of forgiveness, whatever he does. 'The only possibility open to man is that of realising a total inability to provide an answer.'[41]

The trouble is that though I am always stirred and moved by the splendour of Barth's ideas, I do not really understand what they would mean in practice and am, therefore, uncertain how one would actually go about behaving in the manner described. Clearly, such a concept of Christian ethical action fits precisely with Barth's theology of the primacy of God and the total depravity of man. Equally clearly, Barth could not have written about the ethical problems of *success* in the way in which Bonhoeffer wrote. Perhaps that explains the practical differences between the ways in which the two men reacted to Nazism and Barth's later attitude to socialism, for Barth would never allow that any human political or social programme could possess an independent status – independent, that is, of the kingdom of God. Neither the existing order nor social protest is in itself good. God's kingdom 'is the revolution which is before all revolutions, as it is before the whole prevailing order of things'.[42] To have committed himself to political action like Bonhoeffer's might have seemed like conferring an absolute and independent status upon a social programme.

Nevertheless, I find myself asking whether, if one held Barth's beliefs about the necessary sinfulness of man's actions and the over-arching context of divine activity in Christ, one would not in practice be in a situation very like the one which Bonhoeffer described – where one could see no wholly right action and where one knew oneself to be a sinner in need of forgiveness. So much seems to depend upon the theological basis for the ethical terminology one uses. If one rejects with Barth the idea that ethical norms are to be found in *principles*, one may be able to assert that there is only one right action in any given situation. But that need not necessarily be different from saying that one is a sinner in acting as one does act. Perhaps one can say of Bonhoeffer at least, that as he understood the nature of sin, it is possible to find oneself in a situation where every course open to one seems sinful.

In South Africa in the early 1960s that seemed a very obvious truth. It was the aftermath of Sharpeville. The horrors of the political situation were inescapable. One was burdened with a terrible sense of responsibility and guilt for a society of which one could not wash one's hands nor do very much to improve. It was also just the period when Bonhoeffer's reputation and influence was at its height. It was hardly possible not to look at one's own dilemma (even if only at an intuitive level) through his eyes.

A close friend and colleague of mine, D. C. S. Oosthuizen, a professional philosopher, a deeply committed Christian and member of the Dutch Reformed Church, wrote three papers in that period in which he developed ideas very like Bonhoeffer's. They were published, after his early death in 1969, in a volume entitled *The Ethics of Illegal Action*.[43] The philosopher was systematically (rigorously and critically) seeking a solution to the problem that would avoid Bonhoeffer's apparent illogicality. The Christian failed to find one. Significantly, the first essay considered the views of Helmuth von Moltke and the second the views of von Stauffenberg, both conspirators against Hitler's life. Oosthuizen came to reject the whole notion that there could be an *ethic* which would justify such action, for the obligation to perform it cannot be universalized. One cannot say, 'Everyone must assassinate an evil ruler.' A Christian has a responsibility to interpret the situation in which he is, as well as the moral precepts which guide his response to it. 'Sin' and 'moral guilt', he concluded, are two quite different things, and there are overtones of Barth here as well as Bonhoeffer:

> One can escape moral guilt by doing what one ought to do, and where one *cannot* do what in general ought to be done, one cannot be *blamed*. . . . [But] one does not escape being *sinful* merely by doing what one ought to do, and of course quite often one *cannot* do what *ought* to be done, yet one cannot divorce oneself from responsibility [in a religious sense] *for* that situation.[44]

But what should a Christian *do* in a situation like that, one cries, when the good seems to be impossible and responsibility seems inescapable?

I remember being involved, with Oosthuizen and others, in a serious discussion about whether we ought to form a 'confessing Church', as a kind of ultimate Christian political action, setting 'the Church' in stark opposition to government, going underground and virtually courting persecution. The inspiration behind this suggestion was, again, Bonhoeffer and the events in which he was involved in Germany in the thirties. There were certain apparent similarities between that situation and the situation which seemed to obtain in South Africa.

The position of the German churches and their attitude to the rise to power of the Nazis in 1933 has been described as follows:

> Largely conservative . . . many churches had welcomed the advent of the new regime which initially had emphasised the Christian-national character of their revolution . . . [and] the party programme hailed 'positive Christianity' as a factor in the fight against Marxist atheism.[45]

Many of us would have felt that this almost exactly described the position in South Africa after the Nationalist government came to power in 1948 and in the decades following. Many members of the churches, if not the ecclesiastical institutions themselves, were politically conservative. Political power for black people did not seem to them a necessary implication of Christian principles. The regime claimed that white South Africa was a bastion of Christian civilisation in the face of Communist attack. 'Christian National' was even the label applied to the education policy of the ruling party. There was the same tendency to demand total obedience and loyalty to the state, the nationalist ideology and the policies which put it into effect. It seemed to us that there was a very similar kind of discrimination, as in Germany, against a part of the population identified by race alone. And it often appeared to have cruel effects even if it was not so deliberately vicious as Nazi anti-semitism. There was also the same suspension of the rule of law.

But the situation was also very different in certain important respects.[46] The Nazi regime had attempted to apply its programme of co-ordination or streamlining (*Gleichschaltung*) directly to the Church, centralising it under a *Reichsbischof*, abolishing its synodical structures and bringing it under state control. This, fortuitously, made it easier for members of the confessing movement to give their action organisational form. The protest against the state quite naturally became a structured dissent, a quasi-denominational separation, involving eventually several thousand protestant clergymen with an organisation, synodical meetings and a formal leadership of its own. It was, in fact, something not totally unlike the Great Disruption in Scotland in 1843 when the Free Kirk came into existence. Indeed at first the movement was not so much confessing as confessional, credal, asserting the true theological formulation of the Church's faith. Only a few became directly involved in the confessing phase, the political action, the heroic witnessing against evil. At first the movement was an assertion of the Church's right freely to proclaim, and to determine the true content of, the Christian faith.

This is not to minimize the courage required even for that. The famous Barmen declaration of May 1934, which reasserted the Church's faith, also spelled out what was deemed to be unchristian in the policies of the regime.[47] But by and large the movement was what Ernst Wolf has called 'an involuntary resistance movement',[48] the organisational Church preserving its true self against state pressure.

The situation in South Africa was quite different. Quite apart from the fact that there was a much wider spectrum of fragmented denominations to begin with – and some of the largest supported the regime with apparent unanimity – there was no overt pressure from the state aimed at taking over the organisational structure of the churches. To become a confessing Church would have had to be a directly *political* action with none of the ambiguity of the confessional/confessing movement in Germany. It is always easier to rally the support of Church members as a whole when the offensive is clearly seen to come from the State rather than from the Church. Certainly that has been true in South Africa.[49] Whatever the reasons, whether there is a genuine corporate sense that the Church is not the proper agent for the initiation of political action or whether it is simply a desire not to invite trouble, it is a real fact to be reckoned with.

I shall turn, in a later chapter, to the question of whether it is proper or possible for the Church to take political action:[50] at this point I wish merely to record the reasons why, as it seems to me, no confessing church movement came into existence in South Africa in the sixties. In addition to the sheer impracticability of creating any quasi-denominational body on the German model, in the very different circumstances that obtained in South Africa, many of us felt that there were genuine theological reasons for not attempting that course of action. Since the official structures and doctrines of the churches were not openly being attacked any constitution designed for a new 'Church' would have had to assert that opposition to *apartheid* was one of its fundamental principles and that would have seemed like a proclamation that a political opinion was of the *esse* of the Church. We should also have been further dividing an already disunited Christendom. And there were many who believed, in any case, that the confessing (rather than confessional) aspect of such a movement would still have to be the concern of individuals rather than an institution. 'Confessing', like martyrdom, has to be an act of personal decision.

The very great burden that such a conclusion places upon the individual conscience, intolerable though it often seems, is probably inescapable given three things. First, the fact that a secular and pluralist society can have no common Christian moral consensus which would enable the individual to appeal to a wider framework than his own beliefs and conscience. Secondly, the fact that the actual structure of modern society places the citizen in the curiously difficult moral position, described in this chapter, of possessing some responsibility without effective power to control the state of society. Thirdly, the fact that the very great difficulty of applying an interiorised morality to society as a corporate entity must inevitably throw questions of motive, state of mind and intention back on to the individual.

Granted that this is the position, the Christian citizen may sometimes find himself in Bonhoeffer's dilemma. Simple gut-reaction is not enough for the resolution of the problem and a careful and rigorous consideration of every aspect of it is required of him. The relationship between the factual context and the demands of morality have to be faced. It is not inevitable, of course, that the action he may feel obliged to undertake will be as drastic as Bonhoeffer's. In Germany there were particular reasons why killing Hitler might have changed the situation dramatically for the better. Not only was he very much the personal embodiment of the regime but he actually claimed that loyalty to himself, personally, was an overriding obligation. Pressure was being brought to bear upon Christians to make them recognize that claim and so legitimize the policies of the regime.[51] A consideration of the actual facts, moreover, might be held to suggest that there was a feasible course of action open to the conspirators. Their own position or role in society was a factor. Unlike most people, they were in a position where the killing of Hitler was an actual possibility. In other words there was a concatenation of circumstances in which this particular course of action was suggested by the context.

That does not, in itself, make it the morally desirable course of action. One has a duty to ask questions about society. What sort of society is it that does the things Nazi Germany was doing? What sort of society will it become if it continues to do them? How can one stop it doing them and thus make it a different and better society? These questions, as I have argued, are a way of trying to apply the principle of interiorizing, as far as one can, to a corporate entity. And under those particular circumstances there was one man who embodied society and whose motives could be examined and taken account of in a way that is not often possible. The conspirators believed that the nature of society could be altered and bettered by the removal of that one man (whose motives were evil) in a way that is seldom the case in a modern state. Consequentialist arguments, therefore, also had to be taken account of.

But the conspirators were subjects and, therefore, if Romans 13:1

was to be taken seriously, they had a Christian duty to obey. In terms of the arguments I have used in this book there are two reasons why that duty cannot be regarded as over-riding. One is that, even if that is how it was intended by Paul, the rest of the New Testament and the weight of Christian tradition has never treated it like that. The other is that the conspirators were not simply subjects: they had a responsibility for what government was doing in their name. And, once one admits that the state has no right to demand immoral behaviour, one is admitting that the state (as such) does not possess a moral immunity which entitles it to behave in a way which would be evil in an individual. (It is a curious fact that those who would regard themselves as the heirs of Machiavelli and would, therefore, argue that political success justifies the performance of immoral actions, are also those most likely to be shocked when the private citizen acts according to the same principle. It is somehow justifiable to authorize, as an act of state, the assassination of a tiresome investigative journalist who may expose the unsavoury secrets of government. The assassination of a president by a political dissident is a different and more reprehensible matter altogether.)

I think that what has happened is that as Christians first began to occupy positions as rulers and then, in modern democracies, to acquire – even as ordinary citizens – some say in the shape of society, they have come to realize that the 'givenness' of government is more complex than it first seemed. It is not simply that we now occupy a different role. We have come to see that the providence which makes governments is one in which we as well as God play a part. The powers that be are ordained, at least partly, by history and while history is, we believe, the field of God's activity it is also the field of our own. Augustine and Ambrose were right to insist that affairs of state do not possess an *importance* which over-rides everything else. They were right to insist that good is good, whoever one is. But it took a very long time for Christians to see that to say, 'The powers that be are ordained of God' can no longer mean that the existence of government is a simple 'given' when they (Christians themselves) are part of the powers that be.

This is the point of Bonhoeffer's remarks about the ethics of success. He does not sanctify success. He continues to assert that what is evil is evil. But he does think that success is relevant, not for itself, but because it makes history. This is the consequentialism that asks questions about what kind of society will result. My own view, it will be clear, is that the answers to questions about history are likely to be uncertain. But there may be times when they are clearer than at others and questions about their clarity or unclarity, their justifiability or otherwise, apply whether one is considering the state or the citizen.

There is, however, another sense in which facts and morality are related in this argument. Bonhoeffer says that it is when success is achieved by *evil* means that one can no longer avoid the problem. He is implying that the action is evil, even when the motive may be good. This is a matter I have already touched on and have argued that one cannot entirely free the act and the intention from each other. One cannot conceive of a truthful person except in terms of a person who tells the truth. One cannot be concerned to get beyond the act of adultery to the adulterous state of mind without taking the act as one's starting point. One cannot say that an act is justified by an intention without implying that the act requires justification and is therefore an act which is judged to be wrong. In other words, an act has a moral quality in itself. One may be able to look behind it but that does not evacuate it of its immoral quality – because of its effect upon the person who does it or the person who suffers it. Therefore we are not entitled to dismiss it lightly, as though it is merely at first sight that an action has a moral character. To say that killing someone is wrong is a statement to be taken seriously and, even if one were subsequently to come to the conclusion that not killing a tyrant was even more wrong – because of the suffering one was permitting to continue – one would still have to face the fact that the action was wrong. The lesser evil would still be an evil. One would still be a sinner committing a sin. And, quite apart from any other consideration, to maintain one's own conscientious integrity it is better to accept *that* than to claim that one had been good in performing such an action lest one should begin to kill other people too easily and willingly. If the burden is to be borne by the conscience, the conscience had better be super-sensitive. It is also important to note that this means that a factual context and a consequentialist argument do not in themselves over-ride the moral considerations. One is not saying that the *facts* are such that one cannot afford to be bound by what is moral. The facts are important in determining what courses of action are open to one. The final decision is not fact versus morality but one set of facts and their moral implications weighed against another.

In an earlier chapter I gave reasons for thinking that Christian morality was better understood as attempting to be, or to become, a kind of person rather than in terms of general moral principles or of prescriptive moral rules. The distinctions are, perhaps, rather finer than they appear and the relationship between the three attitudes to morality needs to be set out rather more clearly.

If it is accepted that commitment to God as revealed in Christ provides the reason for behaving morally and for wanting to be a particular person, that is to say the kind of person Christ is, then morality is primarily about an ideal. The Christian says, in effect, that he is defining his ideal by pointing at Christ. 'Good' is therefore to be measured in terms of the kind of human being specified by Christ. But *imitatio Christi* cannot simply be a matter of imitating the *behaviour* of Christ, partly because he was himself so concerned to insist that behaviour by itself was too superficial a yardstick for measuring morality and partly because our context is different from his. Simple imitation would be inadequate even if it were possible.

This means that one has to fill out one's understanding of the good, the ideal by which one lives, by trying to describe more precisely and completely what kind of person the ideal is. The only way to do this is in terms which are, in fact, enunciations of general principles. 'That kind of person is unselfish' or 'That kind of person is truthful', descriptive of one's ideal of what is a good person, are almost indistinguishable from saying 'I ought to be unselfish and truthful' – at least in practice. The real difference is that the general principles are grounded in the personal being of Christ, in this case, rather than being simply general principles. One's reasons for holding to them are not merely that one believes that there is some intrinsic worth in the principles themselves. And that, in turn, implies that they could be over-ridden if one believed that, in doing so, one came closer to being the kind of person who is the ideal.

In the same sort of way there is, perhaps, not a great deal of difference, in practice, between general principles and prescriptive rules. Since one believes that Christ is the proper ideal for all humanity, the principles are universal as well as general. One could as easily say 'Everyone ought to be truthful' as 'I ought to be truthful'. But, once again, what really matters is that one's decisions about how to behave are not simply governed by rules which are their own authority. One is striving to become a kind of person. If obedience to rules or principles is an end in itself one has either to face irresoluble moral conflict or specify, qualify and elaborate the rules till they become unworkable as guides for action. Because Christian morality is grounded, rather, in a concept of a kind of person there is a criterion for deciding how to deal with the claims of different absolutes which is rather different from resolving moral conflict. One can recognize that one ought *always* to be truthful and yet that there are exceptional circumstances in which that obligation cannot, as a matter of fact, be met.

At the same time it remains true that one ought to be a truthful kind of person. The fact that one has not been truthful does not mean that a lie is as good as the truth. And one ought to acknowledge that fact by admitting that one's action has not been wholly right, wholly ideal. One is still a sinner in need of forgiveness because the untruth, if willingly embraced, might make one a kind of person wholly other than the ideal to which one is committed. It is only because one acknowledges that the lie is an exception, which itself is accepted on moral rather than merely expedient grounds, that one is able to maintain the ideal of what is good. One is, so to speak, at one and the same time, asserting with Augustine the eternal truth that good is good, recognising with Aquinas that eternal goodness cannot simply be incompatible with temporal goodness, and admitting that when one cannot find a way of reconciling the two completely one has to do the best one can without pretending that it is wholly good.

That which is wrong in principle is being forced upon one, in this view, as a last resort instead of being regarded as a possible course of action which one has treated from the start as something which it might be right to do. For this reason I dislike describing it as 'justified', which implies that it is only at first sight that it appears wrong but that later argument or evidence might persuade one that it was right. Intrinsically the untruth remains wrong. One is excusing rather than justifying it. It is the *only* thing to do, rather than a right thing to do. It has a provisional quality, as the best one could manage under the circumstances.

This is admittedly agonising as well as untidy. It is also inherent in the Christian concept of morality as an ideal which it is impossible to live up to completely. The Christian recognition that no human society can be perfect makes it a particularly acute problem in the political sphere. Christians as citizens do have a responsibility for the shape of society. They have to attempt to influence it in the right direction. But society will not become perfect. Therefore all social and political action is an admission that one is a sinner, part of fallen humanity. And that involves recognising that evil is not good. To take action which is less than wholly good, even if it seems the only thing to do, involves accepting responsibility for the ill that may follow from it, though one may not be able to foresee precisely what that will be. The very fact that the enterprise is human means that sin will be involved. My share in that has to be faced, kept to a resolute minimum, and repented of – not shrugged off nor 'justified'.

To live like that requires tremendous courage. It is the spiritual equivalent of the loneliness of the long-distance runner. But it is not essentially different from what one experiences in one's personal or private life, in the family or job. It is an essential part of being a Christian. There is always the possibility of a crisis in which, in the last resort, no one else can take the decision for us and where the decision cannot be taken in terms of neatly prescribed rules. It is seldom that one has to face a crisis like Bonhoeffer's, but in any moral crisis what is essential is the preservation of integrity and that is not to be done by pretending that evil is good.

In Matthew 12:24–31 Christ is reported as saying that blasphemy against the Holy Spirit is the unforgivable sin. He was casting out an evil spirit and the Pharisees, because he threatened their safely pious world, said that he was doing it by the power of Beelzebub the prince of the devils. They saw him doing something good, in other words, and categorized it as evil. It was this which provoked the saying. The unforgivable sin is to recognize what is good and to call it evil. It is unforgivable because once one has done that, no standards or values mean anything at all. Integrity has gone. Conscience is meaningless. One is unable to see what kind of person one is, let alone how one compares with the kind of person one is committed to being. No moral judgement is possible. Therefore one must remain absolutely clear-eyed about what is good and what is evil and one must never pretend that one is the other. So far from being hypocritical, to assert the ideal even when one cannot do it, is to preserve one's integrity at a deeper level. One is asserting the ideal of the kind of person one desires to be, even when one admits that one is a sinner. By doggedly facing the fact that one has fallen short of the ideal one may also have the best chance of becoming the kind of person who is able to judge when what is less than good is the only thing to be done.

One is bound to ask whether there is not an arrogance in having to decide that one must do what one regards as wrong. There is, indeed, that danger. But the Christian is never free to treat morality as though it were a private possession. He has to face his own sinfulness in the context of his membership of the Church.

Notes

1. A very valuable survey is Q. Skinner, *The Foundations of Modern Political Thought*, Cambridge University Press 1978. The work is in two volumes, the first dealing with the Renaissance and the second with the Reformation.

2. J. W. C. Wand (ed.), *St Augustine's City of God*, O.U.P. 1963, p. 115.
3. *Civitas Dei*, XIX.17.
4. *Ibid.*, V.19; XIV.1. XVI.
5. *Ibid.*, XIX.27.
6. *Ibid.*, XIX.17.

7. *Ibid.*
8. J. W. C. Wand, *op.cit.*, p. xvii.
9. See pp. 78ff.
10. W. Ullmann, *The Individual and Society in the Middle Ages*, Methuen 1967, p. 119.
11. *Ibid.* p. 122f.
12. *Summa Theologica* III–III. qu.61, art. 5 and cf *De Regimine Principum*, 1.4.
13. Commentary on Aristotle's *Politics*, Lib. III, Lect.iii
14. *Summa Theologica*, I–II. qu.40 art.1.
17. F. J. C. Hearnshaw, *Social and Political Ideas of the Renaissance and Reformation*, O.U.P. 1925, p. 108.
18. *Il Principe*, XXV; and cf. *I Discorsi*, II.1.
19. *Il Principe*, XVI and XVII.
20. *Ibid.*, XXV and XXVI.
21. J. W. Allen, *A History of Political Though in the Sixteenth Century*, Methuen (University paperback edn) 1960, p. 472.
22. *Machiavelli: The Prince* (tr. W. K. Marriott), J. M. Dent (Everyman reprint) 1974, p. 99.
23. B. Crick (ed.) *Machiavelli: The Discourses*, Penguin Books (reprint) 1979, pp. 63ff.
24. R. H. Tawney, *Religion and the Rise of Capitalism*, John Murray (2nd edn reprint) 1943, pp. 36ff.; and cf. R. H. Preston, *Religion and the Persistence of Capitalism*, S.C.M. 1979, p. 6. Preston's account of Tawney's view is, in my opinion, exaggerated perhaps because it is so compressed and therefore oversimplified.
25. R. H. Tawney, op. cit., p. 80.
26. *Ibid.*, pp. 60 and 62.
27. B. Crick, *op.cit.*, pp. 66f.
28. S. I. Benn, 'The Problematic Rationality of Political Participation', in P. Laslett and J. Fishkin (eds.), *Philosophy, Politics and Society* (5th series), Blackwell 1979, p. 292.
29. *Ibid.*, p. 312.
30. The standard work is E. Bethge, *Dietrich Bonhoeffer: A Biography*, Collins 1970.
31. See e.g. D. Bonhoeffer, *Letters and Papers from Prison*, S. C. M. (reprint) 1973, pp. 326ff.
32. I am encouraged to find this opinion supported by the judgement of a Bonhoeffer specialist; see R. W. Lovin, 'The Christian and the Authority of the State', in *Journal of Theology for Southern Africa*, 34, pp. 32ff.
33. *Ibid.*, p. 34.
34. *De Regimine Principum*, I.vi.
35. D. Bonhoeffer, 'After Ten Years' in *Letters and Papers from Prison*, S.C.M. (reprint) 1973, pp. 6f.
36. R. M. Hare, *Moral Thinking*, O.U.P. 1981, pp. 23ff and 148ff.
37. Cf. p. 50.
38. K. Barth (ed. G. W. Bromiley and T. F. Torrance), *Church Dogmatics* II.2, T. and T. Clark 1957, pp. 744f.
39. R. E. Willis, *The Ethics of Karl Barth*, E. J. Brill 1971, p. 29. I am greatly indebted to this work for my understanding of Barth.
40. *Ibid.*, p. 181.
41. *Ibid.*, p. 28.
42. K. Barth, *The Word of God and the Word of Man*, quoted in R. E. Willis, *op.cit.*, p. 17.
43. D. C. S. Oosthuizen, *The Ethics of Illegal Action*, Ravan Press 1973. The relevant essays are called 'The Ethics of Illegal Action,' 'Moral Scruples about Illegal Action and Violence' and 'Moral Guilt and Sin'.
44. *Ibid.*, p. 65. The italics are mine.

45. K. D. Bracher, *The German Dictatorship* (tr. J. Steinberg), Penguin Books 1973, p. 471.
46. For a discussion of this point see J. W. de Gruchy, *The Church Struggle in South Africa*, S.P.C.K. 1979, p. 107.
47. See O. G. Rees, 'The Barmen Declaration', in D. Baker (ed.), *Church, Society and Politics*, Studies in Church History 12, Blackwell 1975, pp. 405ff.
48. Quoted in K. D. Bracher, *op.cit.*, p. 474.
49. See J. W. de Gruchy, *op.cit.*, pp. 92ff. for an analysis of the reasons.
50. See pp. 122ff.
51. R. W. Lovin, *op.cit.*, pp. 39ff.

6

THE HOLINESS OF THE CHURCH

I have been arguing so far that Christian morality is a matter of becoming a certain kind of person. The ideal which provides the model for that kind of person is Christ. Because that kind of person is described in terms which are absolutes, Christian morality *is* concerned with absolutes. But these moral absolutes are neither arbitrary nor autonomous, they are derived from and subservient to the ideal. Christian morality also has to take account of the imperfectibility of human beings. It has to recognize that there may be occasions in which no perfect or ideal course of action seems available. There may be situations in which it is impossible to serve every 'absolute' at once. Coping with that situation is not a matter of devising rules to determine when the bad becomes good, as if the 'absolute' could contain provision for over-riding itself, nor of resolving a conflict of obligations, as if one could order the 'absolutes' in a hierarchy of importance and so come to a purely rational conclusion about what one ought to do. But it is not a matter of mere intuition, either. And it is certainly not a matter of deciding that expediency or some supposedly hard facts outweigh the moral considerations. One is asking oneself, rather, which of the possible courses of action will best serve the ideal to which one is striving. One does not pretend that the lesser of two evils has somehow become good: one asks which course of action is closer to the behaviour of the kind of person one desires to be. And that involves the recognition that what one is doing remains less than good. There is, therefore, a tentativeness or provisional character about it. It is 'the best I can manage' or 'the only thing to be done under the circumstances' rather than something which can be described, with absolute confidence or authority, as right. And there does not seem to be an essential difference between the way in which one takes decisions in one's private life and in the political field, at least in this respect, particularly in a pluralist society such as ours where there is no common public morality to serve as an agreed framework. The final judgement about how one ought to behave is left to the individual.

When one turns to consider the Church in terms of morality one very quickly discovers, as I have already suggested in chapter 3, that there is the same tension between the ideal and both the actual and the possible. I can best make the point by returning to the commonly expressed sentiment, which I alluded to in the first chapter, that the Church, being holy, ought not to soil her hands with politics which is a 'dirty game'. Christians do undoubtedly believe that there is a sense in which the Church is holy. We assert that as an article of faith every time we recite the creeds. But it has been recognized ever since the time of the Donatist schism in the fourth and fifth centuries that there are massive theological difficulties (and an obvious foolishness in practice) in supposing that the holiness of the Church either derives from or is dependent upon, the moral purity of her members.

It is an interesting fact that the Donatist schism itself originated in a conflict between Christianity and the state.[1] The schism lasted more than a century and throughout its history constantly raised problems connected with one aspect or another of the relationship between religion and politics. In the great persecution of Christianity under Diocletian, at the beginning of the fourth century, pressure was brought to bear upon the clergy to make surrender (*traditio*) of the scriptures. After the persecution those who had surrendered (*traditores*) were somewhat naturally regarded as having compromised themselves and their ministry. In North Africa two things exacerbated the situation. On the one hand, there was that African tradition of rigorism, to which Tertullian belonged, in which apostasy had been consistently treated as an almost, if not entirely, unforgivable sin. Martyrdom had been glorified in Africa even more than in the rest of Christendom. On the other hand, the African theology of the ministry was such that a sinful bishop could be thought of as spreading the taint of his sinfulness, through his sacramental acts, so that those who continued to receive his ministry might themselves be defiled. The great African hero of half a century earlier, the martyr bishop St Cyprian, had subscribed to, if he did not actually create, this teaching.[2] And this, in spite of the fact that he had himself had trouble with the rigorists and had refused fully to support their views.[3]

The schism which follows Diocletian's persecution divided the African Church on the question whether bishops who were *traditores* could continue their ministry, whether other bishops ordained by them were valid bishops, and whether those who remained in communion with them were part of the true Church. It is a matter of dispute how far this was really a division between the Romanized, cosmopolitan Christians of the coastal cities and the poorer Christians of the interior who maintained indigenous traditions.[4] At all events it seems to have been Donatism which received the support of most North African Christians and it is difficult to believe that there were no social and political overtones to some aspects of the schism.[5] Nor were the persecution in which it originated and the violence which sometimes accompanied it, the only ways in which issues of politics and religion were raised by Donatism. After the accession of Constantine, Donatists as well as 'catholics' appealed to the imperial court for recognition and support. As Christianity became the official religion of the empire attempts were made to use the power of the state to coerce the Donatists into abandoning their separate church.

These political aspects of the schism are not, however, my chief concern. By Augustine's day the schism was primarily about the nature of the Church and its holiness or purity. It is probable that Donatism did not actually claim, as Augustine accused it of claiming, that its members were individually holy and pure. It stood for purity in a more formal, perhaps narrower sense. 'It had kept itself pure', as Peter Brown remarks, 'from a single, unspeakable crime, from *traditio*, the sacrificing of the Christian "Law".'[6] Donatists felt themselves to be preserving a law like the Law of Israel, just as they believed themselves (like Cyprian) to be preserving a priesthood on the pattern of the Temple priesthood. The priesthood by its ritual purity maintained the people's relationship with God. The Law constituted the people of God in terms of moral purity. They 'thought of themselves as a group which existed to preserve and protect an alternative to the society around them. They felt their identity to be constantly threatened: first by persecution, later by compromise. Innocence, ritual purity, meritorious suffering, predominate in their image of themselves.'[7]

In a sense it does not matter whether Augustine either misunderstood the Donatist claims or deliberately caricatured them in order to make his polemical task easier. The debate became a debate (whatever the truth of the actual case) about whether the holiness of the Church depended upon the holiness of its members. And Augustine, harking back to Cyprian to strengthen his claim, for propaganda purposes, to represent the tradition of Africa, cited Cyprian's epistle to the Carthaginian confessors.[8] No man may separate himself from the Church, Cyprian had said, because he believes that there are tares amongst the wheat.[9] The reference is, of course, to the parable in Matthew 13. Augustine, like Cyprian, used it to prove that the Church cannot pretend to be the body of the sinless.

It is true that Matthew's own allegorizing of the parable does not say, 'the field is the *Church*'. It says 'the field is the *world*'. On the other hand, it does say, 'As therefore the tares are gathered and burned in the fire; so shall it be in the end of this world. The Son of man shall send forth his angels, and they shall gather *out of his kingdom* all things that offend, and them which do inquity; and shall cast them into a furnace of fire.'[10] It is just possible, if one takes the words 'his kingdom' to mean 'the Church', to argue that the parable teaches that the Church contains good and bad alike. And this is what Augustine did, though not without reservations.[11]

At all events, no one can seriously maintain that the Church is to consist only of the pure, unless one defines purity in some narrow, formal and ritual sense. Otherwise no one would qualify. Nor can the holiness of the Church be the collective holiness of its members. For it would then be a shabby, greyish kind of holiness. We *believe* in a holy Church yet we cannot believe that it is *our* holiness that makes it holy.

If the holiness of the Church does not derive from its members, there is only one other possible source. It must, in some sense, be from God in Christ that the holiness comes. Augustine clearly believed that the Church was holy because it was Christ's bride 'without spot or wrinkle', the 'garden enclosed' of the Song of Solomon. The Church is the Lord's. Its members derive their holiness from the Holy Spirit in the sacraments, which are Christ's sacraments.[12] But that is not quite the whole story. Augustine was not quite prepared to say that all those who are baptized and therefore part of the actual historic Church are holy. There are those members of that Church whose lives are far from pure. Truthfulness will not allow him to pretend that they are other than they are. But they do not detract from the holiness of the Church nor do they contaminate the good members of the Church. They may be won to repentance and so to holiness. If they are not, God eliminates them from the Church at the last. But those who participate in Christ[13] are the Church and therefore share in his work. It is that *purpose*, too, which makes the Church holy.

There is, perhaps, some ambivalence in what Augustine says. He wishes to assert, on the one hand, that God chooses his saints, that God makes the Church holy through his sacraments, that the sinfulness of some members of the Church does not contaminate others, and that it is as Christ's bride that the Church is spotless. But he also insists that sinners are sinners, that if they persist in their sin there is no salvation for them, and that the Church in love and patience must strive to redeem them and also to convert the world. It is this ambivalence that prevents Augustine from simply equating 'kingdom' and 'Church'. It is also responsible for the fact that he sees the holiness of the Church as being derived from its purpose (the conversion of sinners) as well as from its character as the bride of Christ. In either case, however, holiness comes from Christ whether as source or as goal. In the one sense Christ is its source since it is from him, through the sacraments, that it comes. But even if the Church is to be called holy because its purposes are holy, that still means that holiness derives from Christ because the Church's purpose is Christ's purpose and its members participate in Christ and his work. It is because the Church is Christ's body, his bride, his creation, maintained by his sacraments, guided and vitalised by his Spirit, sharing in his redemption of the world, that it is holy at all.

It is possible to argue that Augustine lands up in what I have called his 'ambivalence' because he is not willing to distinguish clearly between the ideal, invisible Church known only to God and the actual historical Church on earth. He does not do so because he needs to appeal to the authority and traditions of the actual Church while refusing to blind himself to the real sinfulness of some of its members. He argued, for instance, that if sinfulness was capable of destroying the Church, the Church would have ceased to exist very early on and there would have been no Cyprian for his opponents to appeal to. That was to invoke the fact of the historical institution. But, equally plainly, to look at the historical institution is to be compelled to recognize that there are some appallingly bad Christians. One cannot be very happy about asserting that they are part of an ideal and holy Church, ultimate and eternal. So Augustine found himself with a real paradox, which was not just a simple contradiction, because each wing of the paradox seemed logically to require the existence of the other even though it also appeared to contradict it.

We may try to escape from Augustine's ambivalence, for the moment, by trying to define more precisely the different senses of the word 'Church'. The most difficult distinction to make – partly because it is the subject of so much theological disagreement – is between what I shall call 'the ideal Church' and 'the actual Church'. Both those terms are open to criticism but I propose to use them without too much apology and with an attempt to be clear about what I mean when I do use them. By the actual Church I shall mean the Church as it is actually found in this temporal world. Even that can mean a variety of things. Different theologians and different denominational traditions define it in different ways. They may mean those Christians who are in communion with the see of Canterbury, or accept the authority of the Pope, or who love the Lord Jesus, or who are the elect of God and known only to him, and so on. But they all agree that there is some sense in which the Church is present in the world as the Church militant, actual people within the space–time continuum.

By the ideal Church I shall mean the Body of Christ. As I have already suggested in chapter 3, the term appears to be used by St Paul to do two things. First it implies an identity between Christ and the Church. The ideal Church is is some sense (perhaps a mystical sense, perhaps a metaphorical sense) one with Christ himself. Yet it is also, in some sense, the community of Christian people. Secondly, the language of Body of Christ is always used precisely when it is the corporate, organic character of the Church which is in mind. It seems to me, therefore, that what this language reaches for is an attempt to represent Christ as if under a corporate or communal character. The ideal Church is Christ but not Christ as a single individual human person (as was Jesus of Nazareth) but Christ as defining the human race as it ought to be. One might say that if one conceived of or imagined the Jesus Christ of the gospels translated into a community, that is what the ideal Church, the Body of Christ, stood for. It is Christ in his corporate and representational aspect.

Now I am perfectly well aware that this is, in itself, a controversial matter. Christians will disagree about whether this ideal, corporate 'Christ' has a merely notional quality or a real existence (and this is why I have preferred to call the other sense of the Church 'actual' rather than 'real'); and, if real, how its reality is to be understood – as mystical or metaphysical or in some other way. They will also disagree about the relationship between the ideal and the actual Church and how closely the two are to be identified. Yet it seems to me that, if we remember that we are concerned with questions of morality, it is possible to propound a view which will be generally acceptable without having to wait for the theological disagreements to be resolved.

Anyone who wishes to proclaim a belief in a *holy* Church will agree that he or she is not talking about the actual Church, without qualification. It is the ideal Church one is concerned with, even if the only difference one intends is a difference between those members of the Church who are perfect and those who are not. Such a person will also agree that the ideal Church and its holiness are in some sense to be defined in terms of Christ, whether they are thinking in terms of a mystical union, or of the perfected for whom Christ died and whose perfection is therefore Christ's, or of qualities of perfection which are eternal, in the sense of being unchanging values, and yet real, in the sense of having been instantiated historically in Christ himself. He or she would also agree that, though the actual and the ideal Church are not exactly the same thing, there is some connection between them and that the actual Church ought, so far as possible, to conform to the ideal Church.

All that seems to me to add up to an assertion, which may not be very controversial after all, that there is much the same relationship in morality between the actual Church and the ideal Church, at the corporate level, as between the individual Christian and Christ himself, at the personal level. The concept of the ideal Church is Christ somehow conceived of as corporate. He stands, in this corporate character, to the Church militant here on earth as he stands, personally, to the Christian. In each case morality consists of a striving to become the ideal though attainment of the ideal may be impossible.

If this distinction between what I am calling the ideal and the actual Church is accepted, it seems to me that one can usefully proceed to look at the four principal senses in which the word 'Church' is used in our own day:

(1) as the theological concept, the ideal Church, the Body of Christ, the perfect and spotless bride of Christ;

(2) as the congregation of Christian people, either 'throughout the world' or in its local manifestation;

(3) as the denomination, with its institutional structure and organization;

(4) as the clergy or the ecclesiastical leadership, as in the sentence 'John is going into the Church', which means 'John hopes to be ordained' not 'John hopes to be baptized'.[14]

It has to be noted that in some cases these are not just shades of meaning but are actually different things. The last two senses of the word, and particularly the fourth, are improper uses of it. Nevertheless the word is used with all these meanings and there clearly is some sort of link between them. It is, I think, only when we are absolutely clear as to the sense in which the word is used on any given occasion that it is possible to talk sensibly about the Church in relation to politics.

William Temple used to say, with wry humour, that when people said, 'Why doesn't the Church do something?' they really meant, 'Why doesn't the Archbishop of Canterbury do something?'[15] And he made this joke in the context of an issue of national importance – which is to say, in a political context. He was really saying that, in the question, 'Why doesn't the Church do something?' 'Church' is being used in sense (4), to mean 'the ecclesiastical leadership'.

And it is in this sense that 'Church' is usually used in a political context. In Temple's joke it is being used in a positive sense – the ecclesiastical leadership *ought* to be doing something. Much more frequently it is used in the negative sense, meaning that it ought *not*. 'The Church shouldn't interfere in politics' is usually said when a bishop or clergyman has made a political statement and, again, 'Church' means the ecclesiastical leadership.

But consider the sentence which I cited early in this chapter and which is often used to explain why 'the Church' ought not to interfere in politics: 'The Church, being holy, ought not to soil its hands by meddling in politics, which is a dirty game.' There is a massive but hidden confusion in that statement. With Augustine we should wish to recognize how dangerous it is to claim that the Church, in the second or fourth sense is holy. The congregation of Christian people is not pure and holy for it is a body of fallen human beings, a body of sinners. There are tares as well as wheat among them. For the same reason, the leadership is not pure either: one of the points at issue in the debate with the Donatists was whether the unworthiness of the minister prevented the sacraments from being efficacious. As to sense (3), the denominational organization, it hardly needs to be said that an institution is unlikely to be holy! Augustine would have said that the only holiness it possessed came from the fact that its purposes might be holy.

It is only in sense 1 that the Church can truly be said to be holy. The Church is holy, because it is Christ's body. Its holiness derives from him and not from its members. The sentence, 'The Church is holy and therefore ought not to soil its hands with politics which is a dirty game,' ought really to read, 'The body of Christ is holy and therefore. . . .' But can the ideal Church interfere in politics and get its hands dirty? A child, hearing that the Prime Minister was calling a general election and 'was going to the country', might ask, 'What is she doing in London, then?' The legal style of my college is 'The masters and scholars of Balliol College, Oxford,' but the notice on the gate, 'The college is closed to visitors,' does not mean that the masters and scholars are closed to visitors. With one proviso, a statement that the holy Church ought not to soil itself with politics, is making a confusion of a similar kind.

The one proviso is that one could make the statement if one held a doctrine of the Church which identified the temporal 'denominational' institution, simply, absolutely and without remainder, with the body of Christ in a sense which also located the ability to *be* the Church in an organ of the institution capable of political action. One would have to believe, for instance, that the Pope *was* the Church of Rome and that the Church of Rome was the one and only true Church on earth and that that visible and institutional Church *was* absolutely identified with the body of Christ. Then one could say that the Pope ought not to vote in a general election lest he should soil the body of Christ by identifying it with a less than perfect political party. But not even the most old-fashioned supporter of ultra-Montane papalism believed *that.* The decree on infallibility defines very precisely the moments when the Pope is the embodiment of the Church, when he declares the truth in matters of faith or morals – when he *speaks,* in fact, on certain subjects. But the cry, 'Why doesn't the Church *do* something?' almost always intends 'do' in sharp contrast to 'speak'. 'Why doesn't the Church do something?' means 'Stop talking and take action'. But it is, in fact, very difficult to see how 'the Church', in any of the four senses, can *do* anything political.

We have already seen that it is extremely difficult to imagine the ideal Church taking political action. There is the same kind of problem connected with the Church in the second sense, the fellowship of faithful Christian people. It is possible to maintain that there is a close connection between that fellowship and the ideal Church as Christ's body, as Augustine did. Just precisely how one perceives the connection will depend upon how one defines 'faithful' and what one regards as constituting real rather than nominal membership of the visible Church. But, however one tackles those problems, it is still difficult to imagine the whole body of true Christian people throughout the world taking political action. What takes action will be less than the whole Church.

If one is thinking of the fellowship of the faithful at a local level, one may still hold that there is a close connection between it and the body of Christ. A congregational theology of the Church asserts that the local, 'gathered' body of Christians is, and possesses the authority of, the Church. In a strong form, where it is claimed that each congregation has a full and independent right to determine doctrine, ministry and moral standards, such a theology could be very similar in its effect to the doctrine of papal infallibility, at least in the particular context of this present consideration. It could amount to an assertion that there is a visible and identifiable organ, capable of action in the world, which really *is* the Church in a theological sense. But, again, even in that form the claim is that it acts *for* rather than exclusively *as* the Church.

Theology apart, moreover, there would obviously be practical difficulties in a local congregation taking political action. The local Church, like the denominational institution, is a sociological entity as well as a theological one. People become members of the Church, in that sense, for such a wide variety of motives (partial and mixed even when good) that concerted action is impracticable. Moreover, even at a local level, decisions are usually taken by the leadership or the institutional organs of the Church rather than by the whole body of the faithful. The real question, therefore, is how far, even in an admittedly improper sense, one ought to regard synods, committees, officers, clergyman and other agents of that kind as speaking for the Church.

In this connection, whether at a local or at a denominational level, two problems arise. One is that our reasons for calling our own part of the fragmented Christian Church on earth 'the Church' are often unsatisfactory ones. There is an implicit claim, perhaps, that other Christians are not really part of the Church. Or we may dislike being thought of as a 'denomination' because we wish to be regarded as *the* national Church. At all events most of us will recognize that the actual Church in sense (3), to which we belong, is not the ideal Church. Certainly its institutional organization is not the most important part of its claim even to approximate to the Church as the body of Christ. In fact, in these days, the institutional aspect of the denomination often appears the least Christian part of it. To say that one belongs to this or that *Church* is to be claiming for the institution no more than a *connection* with the ideal Church. We would not wish to assert that a decision taken by a committee of the local congregation, or by a synod or assembly or conference, or by any department or council or secretariat of the national organization, was without doubt an expression of 'the mind of the one true Church of Christ'.

The other problem is that even if we were certain that the institutional organs *really represented* the ideal Church, it is not easy to see how they could take political action. The function of these bodies is to legislate for or administer the denomination, or to speak to or on behalf of the organization as a whole. It is worth noting that the word 'speak' has come back into the discussion and it is important to remember that it is the job of ecclesiastical assemblies to *speak*. The pressure to stop talking and *do* something, when applied to bodies of this sort, is in fact misconceived. It derives, I think from the false assumption that an ecclesiastical assembly or synod or council is a kind of parliament. The analogy is responsible for much that is wrong with the synodical structure of the Church of England, as anyone will realize who has watched the General Synod trying to cope with its rules of procedure. It is true that, as a result of historical accident, some decisions of the Synod have the force of law but it is nevertheless a serious mistake to think of it as a body like parliament. Parliament's job is to legislate and its legislation *will result in action.* There are coercive powers to be used if the action does not follow.

In the case of ecclesiastical bodies it doesn't work quite like that. Legislation, with the one exception already noted in the case of the Church of England, can only affect internal matters, the organization, officers, finances and activities of the denomination itself. Any attempt to say, 'Every Christian shall do X or Y,' can only be an exhortation, difficult if not impossible to enforce, and the only possible sanction is expulsion. In other words ecclesiastical legislation does not produce universal activity in the way parliamentary legislation does. And such activity as it does produce is internal. Resolutions about politics and society, or even about the duty of Christians towards politics and society, cannot be legislative decisions resulting in assured *action.* They can only be exhortations, *statements* (sayings) about what the institutional organs believe to be the moral duty of Christian people. They are, or can be, of great value. They are part of the proper function of the organ and they ought not to be criticized for being words and not actions. It is not the function of a synod, as such, to *do* politics. It *is* part of its proper function to say what it believes to be the moral truth about politics.

It is, moreover, almost impossible to conceive of any way in which the actual Church, expressed in terms of organizational structures, *could* take direct political action (as I suggested earlier when I was discussing the reasons why it was difficult to launch a confessing Church in South Africa).[16]

The denominational institution only *approximates* to the ideal Church. And the same is true of the clergy and leadership. They can only be said even to be the actual Church in the sense that they are members of it. They certainly are not the ideal Church.

Temple's joke drew attention to the confusion implicit in an assumption that even an archbishop could *be* the Church. yet it was a confusion he was not above making himself. In *Christianity and the Social Order* he drew a careful distinction between the political function of the Church and that of Christian citizens. 'The Church must announce Christian principles,' he said, and Christian citizens must undertake 'the task of reshaping the existing order in closer conformity to the principles.' He then ruined the careful distinction by reintroducing precisely the same old muddle which talks about Christian leaders as though they were the Church. Arguing that one of the reasons why 'the Church' ought not to attempt to devise specific political programmes was that it lacked the technical knowledge, Temple drew an analogy with the construction of a bridge. 'If a bridge is to be built, the Church may remind the engineer that it is his obligation to provide a really safe bridge; but it is not entitled to tell him whether, in fact, his design meets this requirement: a particular theologian may also be a competent engineer and, if he is, his judgement on this point is entitled to attention; but this is altogether because he is a competent engineer and his theological equipment has nothing whatever to do with it.[17] The plain implication of this enormous sentence is that the theologian here stands for the Church, and clearly for the Church as denomination. But the theologian, whether a competent engineer or not, simply is *not* the Church. He may be a member of a denomination, part of its leadership, or a thinker within it. Clearly he can take political action. But he is not the Church except in the wholly improper fourth sense.

Temple was absolutely right to distinguish between the role of the Church and the role of the Christian citizen in relation to politics and society. It is a great pity that he allowed the muddle to creep in and also that he did not provide any clear reasons for making his distinction. The only reason he gave, other than lack of expertise, was that no human society and no political programme could be perfect. Because of original sin, man's dealings with man would always fall short of perfection. Therefore any social order could rightly be critized on moral grounds by the Church, as denomination. But, any alternative human policy must equally be imperfect and the Church ought not to endorse it as though it were morally beyond criticism.[18]

Here, too, Temple was clearly right as far as he went. A very important conclusion follows. When the Church as denomination exercises its claim to approximate to the Church as the body and bride of Christ or to speak for the whole congregation of faithful people, it will have to content itself largely with making negative statements. To use Temple's words again, 'The Church must announce Christian principles and point out where the existing social order at any time is in conflict with them.' There will be enormous pressure for it to go beyond that and propose practical alternatives. It ought to resist that pressure, in spite of the fact that it will lay itself open to the criticism that it has no positive solutions to offer to practical problems.

This will seem to many (as it would have seemed to me when I began to prepare these lectures) to be an unsatisfactory position to adopt. If one believes that Christianity has an importance for this life then it is natural to assume that 'the Church' ought to be able to do something politically. But, in fact, the more one tries to work out how 'the Church' could take political action, the more impossible it seems. The ideal Church cannot take political action any more than Jesus Christ himself can personally take direct political action now. It is very difficult to envisage any way in which the *actual* Church could take political action, either. When one can envisage some form of action – as opposed to speaking – which it might do, one discovers that it is only part of the actual Church, or certain members of it, or something which only represents or approximates to it, that one is dealing with.

It is significant that there is a sense in which it is proper for the actual Church to *speak* even when it is impossible for it to take political action. For, curiously, it is when the actual Church *speaks* enunciating moral principles and saying what it believes to be the moral truth about politics – that the actual Church may approximate most clearly to the ideal Church. That is to say that, though it may not be possible for it to *be* holy, it can say what is believes holiness to be. By asserting the absolute value it may come closest to the ideal of Christ himself. This reinforces the suggestion that there is a parallel between the moral position of the actual Church and the Christian. Both strive towards an ideal. Both ought to assert the ideal, even when they cannot live up to it. Part, therefore, of the actual Church's claim even to approximate to the ideal Church will be that it will insist that evil is not good and that a political programme, which will necessarily be imperfect, may be the best one can do but is still less than good.

This is not to say, however, that there is no obligation upon members and leaders and parts of the actual Church to take such political action as they can. The point at which the Church, in any sense of the word, comes closest to *doing* anything, is when it is the second sense which is intended – the body of Christian people. Admittedly it is a practical impossibility for the whole universal body to take concerted action, so it will necessarily be individuals and groups who do so. And this will apply in political action also. Moreover it is most likely to happen, as I argued in chapter 3, in small groups. This has been the practical experience of those who engage in liberation theology where basic communities, groups of Christians working out the political implications of their faith in specific contexts, are an essential part of the theological system. But it is not only liberation theologians who discover this. Any kind of Christian action tends to flow from such groups. But, as we have already seen, such groups do not correspond in practice even to the whole of the local Church or congregation. There is always the problem of preventing them from becoming virtually sectarian in character. So it is clear that, once again, they cannot actually claim to *be* the Church. They speak and act for themselves.

This is not to say that they are wrong to act. In fact neither Christian groups nor Christian individuals can escape doing political things. They do not have to 'go into politics'. By virtue of being citizens they are in politics already and even if they decided, for instance, not to vote in a general election, their abstention would have political consequences and would, therefore, be a political action. But it does mean that they cannot claim the same kind of authority or certainty for their political action as might be claimed for assertions of moral ideals by 'the Church'. There is a tentativeness, a provisional character, about what they do or the action they commend. They are saying that this seems to them to be the best that can be done.

There is, therefore, a very close parallel between the position of the actual Church and the individual Christian. Both ought to assert the ideal, even when they cannot live by it. Both may have to do what is possible without claiming an absolute certainty for it. There is this difference, however, that it is very difficult in practice to envisage action taken even by the actual Church as such. Action taken will be taken by members or groups or organs or leaders of the actual Church. There is an obligation upon them not to claim any greater weight for their decisions than the fact that they are *their* decisions.

Temple was clearly right in saying that it is the Christian citizen rather than 'the Church' which has the primary duty actively to reshape the existing order, even though he failed to give clear reasons for his opinion and fell back into the muddle of calling bishops and theologians 'the Church'. Christians, whether they are laymen, bishops, theologians or anything else are citizens and will do political things. The shape society has will be partly a consequence of their actions.

There is a rather unexpected consequence of this view, which Temple does not draw attention to. If there is acceptance of the argument of my first chapter – that there are not two separate and autonomous spheres, one belonging to God and the other to the state – then there can be no question of the Christian citizen acting now as Christian and now as citizen. He does not have two separate functions. When he acts as citizen, he acts as Christian. If he votes Labour, it is the Christian who is voting Labour not some person who is sometimes a Christian but is for the moment a Labourite rather than a Christian. He is also, by definition, a member of the Church in both the second and third (and in some cases also in the fourth) senses. And because he is a Christian he has no business to act, even when he acts politically, from motives of self-interest. Nor is he ever free to forget about moral values. His vote has to be an expression of his Christian determination to do the best he can.

This means that individual Christians or groups of Christians, however much one has to insist that they are not in any theologically justifiable sense actually the one holy, catholic Church when they take political action, are members of it and represent it, however indirectly. In every Christian's activity there is an earthing process by which the bride and body of Christ is involved in what is done. So the ideal concept of the Church is not totally unrelated to what is done by Christians as members of the actual Church. In this respect laymen are not different from clergymen. The only justifiable difference is that clergymen will, because of the office they hold, be marked in the public eye as spokesmen for the actual Church and there will be an automatic assumption that they are somehow committing not only the actual Church but the ideal Church by what they say or do. In other words a claim to be representing the ideal Church will be forced upon them unless they specifically disclaim it. This may be unfair and undesirable but it seems an inescapable facet of what is actually the case in practice.

Of course the actual Church has other functions besides that of taking decisions and making statements about moral issues. It has a pastoral role, which may lead it to say that it can understand why, in particular circumstances, people may feel compelled to take action in a way which is less than wholly good. This sort of statement, which is a kind of counselling rather than a pronouncement upon moral truth, is concerned with specific people and circumstances and it is usually exercised through specific people, the pastors of the actual Church, or by one Christian advising another. When they offer that sort of advice they do not claim for themselves the certainty of being right: they are trying to guide each other towards what seems to be the best that can be done in circumstances where no wholly right course of action seems possible. Their advice is tentative and provisional.

The actual Church has yet other functions. It has legislative functions, though we have seen that that is a limited and internal function. The actual Church has no way of legislating for the world and no business to be doing so. It also has the function of being a community, providing a bond and a forum for its members as they strive to apply the moral ideals in what are sometimes complex and potentially tragic situations. In so far as the denominations, or other institutional structures of the actual Church, attempt to do this they will inevitably become 'political' themselves, not in the sense of becoming mixed up in secular politics but in the sense in which any institution or organization has a politics of its own. Decisions are arrived at through conflict of interests, disagreements about policies and decisions, negotiation and compromise.

Just how complex and difficult the role of the actual Church is can be very well illustrated by the notorious decision of the World Council of Churches' Programme to Combat Racism to make grants to organizations involved in guerrilla warfare in Africa. This is such an emotive issue that cool, rational discussion of it is almost impossible. To keep it in perspective one has to remember that the entire annual budget of the Programme would not be enough to purchase a single first division footballer.[19] I have written elsewhere on the subject[20] and I imagine that my sympathies have been apparent in what I have written. I believe that the Christians in those guerrilla organizations have as much justice on their side as in any war in history. I believe that a very good case can be made for the existence of a fund to help their cause. The publicity for the grants was, however, badly handled and both sides in the controversy have permitted or actually encouraged so many misconceptions about the significance of what was being done that it became distorted.

The actual situation confronting the organization of the World Council was one where a war already existed. More than one moral absolute applied. War is undoubtedly (as I shall argue in chapter 8) an evil. But so are injustice, exploitation and oppression. It is not possible to say that one of those evils is clearly and obviously more immoral than another. But both the advocates and the opponents of the Programme have allowed themselves to talk as though they were dealing with a situation in which there was only one immorality and that they alone support the moral position. Both sides have therefore become entangled in blatant inconsistencies.

Much of the pressure which led to the establishment of the fund depended on the argument that 'the Church' would lose credibility if it did not take action. A favourite slogan was that the Church, which had so often condemned racialism, ought to put its money where its mouth was. This was a wholly illogical argument. The W.C.C. is not even the actual Church. Moreover, in so far as it claimed any sort of right to represent the ideal Church, its job was to assert the truth of the ideal – no war, no injustice, no oppression, no exploitation. Even if it had been the actual Church there would have been no *necessary* obligation upon it to stop talking and start acting, for there are, as we have seen, many bodies within the ecclesiastical organization whose function is precisely to talk, to discuss and to proclaim, and which are simply not designed to engage in direct action. It is not clear to me, in any case, that the Programme actually means that those who had previously done the talking now engage in direct action. We all know how giving a donation can be a way of avoiding the necessity of direct action.

What the W.C.C. was doing was really, in response to the needs of Christians actually caught up in a desperate situation, to declare its sympathies and to provide a channel whereby donations could be made for non-military purposes. Nevertheless both sides discussed the issue as though it were a case of the world-wide Church actually *doing* something of dramatic significance.

Another slogan of which we heard a great deal when the Programme was first mooted seems worth examining carefully. 'Racism', we were told, 'is moral heresy.' This is Donatist language. It may be possible to distinguish moral from immoral heresy. There might, that is to say, be heresies which are adopted for moral reasons – as Martin Luther seemed to think that his campaign against indulgences was one in which his 'heterodox' belief was required by conscience.[21] But a moral heresy, in the sense of a deviation from orthodox morality, there cannot be. There is only sin, as Bishop Alphaeus Zulu (himself a black South African) pointed out when the Programme was being discussed at the Central Committee of the W.C.C. at Canterbury in 1969. And one does not deal with sin by means of a 'programme'.

Divested of the grandiose claims which were made for it, however, there was much to be said for the Council's decision. If it had been more clearly seen as a decision taken by a gathering of Christians (rather than 'the Church'), faced with a tremendously difficult situation in which no wholly right course of action seemed to be possible, trying to do the best they could and saying where they believed justice lay, it would hardly have been objectionable. Indeed, many of those who did object would have no hesitation in saying that 'the Church' in Britain, say, ought to support any war in which Britain might become involved. Many of the other objections were equally illogical. The Salvation Army has since withdrawn from the W.C.C. because of the Programme. I do not know precisely what reasons it gave for its decision, but the W.C.C. reply suggests that the Salvation Army alleged that the motives behind the Programme were political rather than religious. If this is what the Salvation Army said that, too, is an absurd argument. It is senseless to talk about motive when one is dealing with a corporate body, especially a large one, for each member of it may have a different motive. This is the wrong way to attempt to apply the New Testament principle of interiorization to the corporate.

But that, in turn, reminds us that when one is dealing with any institution its activities will be, in a sense, political. It will arrive at its decisions by a process in which conflict of interests, manoeuvring, compromise and debating points will play their part. Legally and constitutionally the W.C.C. had every right to do what it did.

Legally and constitutionally it specifically disclaims the ambition of being the actual Church. It cannot *be* the ideal Church. But, short of a much more insistent disclaimer and a more vigorous assertion of the moral ideals, its grants were bound to be misunderstood. Even though it specified that the money was not to be used for military purposes it was bound to be misunderstood as saying, 'This war is good,' and thus seeming to condone all those inevitable horrors to which any war gives birth.

No one, of course, can be blamed for being misunderstood provided he has taken the trouble to make his position clear. In terms of morality, the W.C.C. action ought not to be seen as 'the Church' proclaiming absolute and certain moral ideals and translating that pronouncement into direct activity. It has to be understood as the action of a group of Christian men and women, faced with a situation in which there seemed no clear and simple answer, doing the best they could in the circumstances, and arriving at their decision by the kind of internal 'political' transactions inevitable in any organization. And that means, as a necessary corollary, that their decision has only a tentative and provisional character and carries, in moral terms, only the authority of those persons who actually supported it.

Notes

1. The standard work on the subject is W.H.C. Frend, *The Donatist Church*, O.U.P. 1952.
2. See P. Hinchliff, *Cyprian of Carthage and the Unity of the Christian Church*, Geoffrey Chapman 1974, pp. 89 and 103f.
3. *Ibid.*, pp. 53ff.
4. This is Frend's thesis but it has been criticized by R.A. Markus and others.
5. See B. J. Kidd, *A History of the Church to A.D. 461*, O.U.P. 1922, vol. II, p. 111 – written long before it became fashionable to regard Donatism as a movement of social protest.
6. P. Brown, *Augustine of Hippo*, Faber 1967, p. 219.
7. *Ibid.*, p. 214.
8. Augustine, *De Baptismo Contra Donatistas*, V. 23; and *Epistle* XCIII. 41.
9. Cyprian, *Epistle* LIV.
10. Matthew 13:32–42.
11. The tares and wheat parable is a favourite of Augustine's, see e.g. *Epistle* XLIII and *Civitas Dei*, XX.9; but he also uses the net and the fish parable (Matthew 13:47ff.) and in *Epistle* XCIII talks of the net of the Lord in which the Church swims along with the bad fish. So he is not simply equating kingdom and Church.
12. *Epistle* XCIII and *De Baptismo Contra Donatistas*, V.

13. Cf. *Contra Epistulam Parmeniani*, II. iv and xxi.
14. That part of this chapter which deals with these four different senses and their bearing on what it means for the Church to be involved in politics is based on *P. Hinchliff*, 'Can the Church "do" politics?' in *Theology*, LXXXIV, pp. 341ff. and is reproduced here by permission of the editors.
15. F. A. Iremonger, *William Temple, His Life and Letters*, O.U.P. 1948, p. 565.
16. See p. 107.
17. W. Temple, *Christianity and the Social Order*, S.P.C.K. (new edn) 1976, p. 58.
18. *Ibid.*, pp. 56f.
19. A fact pointed out by a speaker at the final meeting of the Anglican Consultative Council at Limuru, Kenya, in 1971.
20. P. Hinchliff, 'Religion and Politics: The Harsh Reality' in H. Willmer (ed.), *Christian Faith and Political Hopes*, Epworth Press 1979, pp. 19ff.
21. See the version of Luther's famous cry at Worms which actually appears in the original record – E. G. Rupp, 'Luther and the German Reformation' in G. R. Elton (ed.), *The New Cambridge Modern History*, vol. II, Cambridge University Press 1958, p. 82.

7

PUBLIC AND PRIVATE MORALITY

I have been trying to show that it is one of the appropriate functions of the Christian – whether as an individual, or as a member of a group, or of the denominational organization and its leadership, or of the local congregation – to 'earth' the Church in politics. It ought not to be supposed that that activity either degrades the Church or makes the Christian himself less holy than he ought to be. The holiness of the Church does not derive from its members and cannot, therefore, be compromised by what they do. The holiness of a Christian is not a pristine possession, which may be degraded, but something to be sought in the processes of life. The social and political aspects of life are as important as any other – job, family, friendship. We need not feel guilty if we are concerned about the condition of the society in which we live nor are we betraying that which is eternal if we care about what is temporal. But this is not intended to suggest that Christian morality is a convenient sanctifier of political duplicity as though it really did not matter how one behaved. That human beings are always sinners and dependent on God's forgiveness does not justify their saying that they will do whatever seems politically expedient knowing that God will forgive them. *Of course* politics devoid of morality is undesirable – and probably self-defeating in the long run. The question is how one is to 'earth' holiness without either anticipating utopia or abandoning ideals. In other words, when we turn from the Christian in relation to the Church to the Christian in relation to society, we are back with the problem defined in the second chapter – the relationship between private and public morality and the role of the Christian as, in some sense, the one possible bridge over the gap between the two.

The starting point for any reconsideration of this problem ought always to be the reminder that the Christian citizen, in so far as he is a subject, is called to the humility of obedience and, in so far as he is ruler, to the humility of service. That is the real significance of his inability to be anything other than a sinner. He is never the master. Since he cannot succeed in mastering himself he had better be reluctant to play the master over others.

Various answers are given from time to time about the relationship between what is demanded of the Christian by the gospel and what he or she is able to achieve in the reform of society. Those who are most acutely aware of the sinfulness of human society, the personal commitment necessary to the Christian life and the radical transformation that commitment brings, tend to suggest that it is only by conversion that social reform can be achieved. A former Archbishop of Cape Town has said:

> The fact is that to attempt to superimpose a particular spirituality, a teaching on Christian ethics, or social action as an expression of the love of God, upon lives that do not know his love for them in Jesus Christ, and who do not experience the power of his Holy Spirit, is an exercise in futility. It leads to frustration, boredom, irritation and unbelief. To renew society with unrenewed Christians is like a non-swimmer trying to rescue a drowning man.[1]

I am sure, from other things said in the same article, that the archbishop does not really intend to make social action sound as impossible as, perhaps, that quotation suggests at first sight. Nevertheless, it is perfectly clear that, if the improvement of an iniquitous society is made to wait upon the conversion and renewal of all its members, it will have to wait a very long time. It is not surprising that Christians who emphasize the priority of personal conversion have tended to withdraw from all attempts at social reform altogether.

I am equally sure that the archbishop does not intend to sound as though he, as a 'renewed' Christian, is being arrogantly sarcastic at the expense of the 'unrenewed'. But he *is* scathing about those who, like himself in his 'unrenewed' days, try to persuade governments to express love in terms of justice, to prove *apartheid* theologically inconsistent with the gospel, to de-racise Christians, or to draw up latter-day Barmen declarations. He suggests, instead, 'that when a man says "yes" to God and is filled with his Spirit, he is set free to respond with love to the Father's love and also to love his neighbour. The Holy Spirit both awakens a social conscience and conveys the means by which it is expressed.'[2] Intentionally or not, this suggests that, while one works towards the permanently unreachable time when all men are converted, one ought to love one's neighbour rather than take social action aimed at dismantling *apartheid*. And this, in turn, though once again possibly unintentionally, suggests that what one ought to do is to behave lovingly at a person-to-person level rather than attempt to change society.

Over against such views as this there are those, and they are not just the radicals of the political theology movement, who argue that a merely personal Christian morality does not go nearly far enough. There are evils in the world that simply are not touched by the gospel if morality remains purely personal.

> The church seems to proclaim and is certainly heard to proclaim, an ethic of personal good behaviour rather than an ethic of social change and discontinuity. . . . The Church will . . . continue to limit the faith she proclaims until we are ready to be the pioneers in helping our society to pay the price the Gospel demands. Our vested interest in the 'liberal egalitarian' society for example, makes it hard for us to hear what the majority of our fellow-Christians are telling us – that our concern for human rights is not easy to hear when it is spoken by those who maintain, and benefit from, the poverty and degradation of two-thirds of the world. It is very hard for our middle-class church to recognize this – for to recognize it is to demand changes which will be unpopular and uncomfortable and perhaps even downright dangerous.[3]

The danger referred to here is not revolution or the armed struggle, I think, but simply the danger of unpopularity. What the writer is implying is that it is not enough for an employer to be personally good, kind and generous to his employees within the structure or system as given. He may have to change the structure. And the same kind of moral demand may be made upon a whole society in relation to other societies in other parts of the world. This is a sense, wholly different from what is normally intended, in which public morality may be 'different' from private morality.

But this view is no freer from snags than the first. If one is not careful, a demand for a change in the structures can become an assertion that one knows what the right structures should be and, therefore, either utopian or arrogant. Moreover, if human society is imperfectible, if a middle-class Church finds one's programme too radical, and if the Church is, in any case, unable to influence society, perpetual failure will create just that disastrous state of mind about which the archbishop wrote – frustration, boredom, irritation and (when God's cause seems to get nowhere) unbelief.

Moreover, an objection very similar to the objection levelled at the archbishop's view can equally be brought against this one. It does not provide us with an answer to the question, 'How do we apply the demands of Christian morality to society *now*?' If to wait for the conversion of every member of society is to put off social reform for a very long time, waiting till society can be persuaded to 'pay the price of the gospel' in social, economic and political terms, may have an equally dilatory effect. Those who choose the first option can at least put all their energies into mission and comfort themselves with the thought that they are doing something. Those who choose the second option may find that society turns a blind eye to all their efforts and may, in the end, find themselves driven to the theology of armed revolution. As I shall attempt to argue later, it is very difficult to maintain that such a course is never justifiable but it is clearly not what anyone would wish to regard as the normal way for Christians to influence society.

It appears that the second approach is really assuming that the proper and normal way for Christians to influence society is by being themselves, as the Church, a community of love. This clearly is an implication, also, of my argument in chapter 3. If the Church is a community, defined in terms of love and integrity, whose existence flows from the self-sacrificing life of Christ, then part of its function in God's scheme of things is that it should provide a paradigm or example of the way all human communities or societies ought to be. But it is also implicit in what I have been saying in chapter 6 that, though the denomination, the local Church and any group of Christians or their leaders, are the ways the ideal Church is 'earthed', the actual Church as a human community cannot expect to be a perfect community. Indeed the author whom I have been quoting says as much.

> We claim to be a community of love but very often the church looks like any other human organization or community with all the same jealousies, all the same hidden agendas, all the same fears. How often is our activity (and even perhaps the good we do) determined less by our love for one another and common life in Christ than by our own needs, fears and ambitions?[4]

But if this is true, then such a view offers no better guide to our immediate need than the archbishop's does. Being realistic necessitates an acceptance of the fact that most people will remain 'unrenewed' and that the ideal Church will not be perfectly realized in the Christian churches. Meanwhile Christians continue to live in society and to bear some responsibility for the shape it has.

It would, of course, be very easy to say that the truth lies somewhere between the two options we have been looking at. Christians need to be renewed. They need to convert other members of society. The Church needs to be a better community and to set a better example to society as a whole. All these things need to be done simultaneously. None is an exclusive panacea by itself.

As a theoretical statement of the truth this is quite unexceptionable. As a practical guide it is not a great deal of help. And it appears that it is always precisely at this practical level of what one ought to do, here and now, in this particular moment in the history of this particular society, that the application of Christian morality to politics breaks down. I referred, in an earlier chapter, to the criticism levelled at the churches in respect of their apparent inability to say anything practical about nuclear armaments. Another example of precisely the same difficulty is discussed in *Crucible*, the journal of the Church of England Board for Social Responsibility, for the last quarter of 1980. This is the case of Mr Patrick Jenkin and the British churches.

Earlier in 1980 the chairmen of the social responsibility departments of 'the six main' churches had written a letter to *The Times* asking that those responsible for framing the country's budget make provision for a substantial increase in child benefit. Mr Jenkin, Secretary of State for Social Services, made a television appearance to reply that he was surprised that the churches should resort to behaving like a political pressure group. It seemed to him that the churches were deserting their real task, helping people to work out their own salvation, and that – if they were going to exercise political pressure – they must also accept the responsibility accompanying such activity. They must say how their request was to be paid for. In other words, they must suggest practical alternatives to the policies they were criticizing. Editorial comment in the journal admitted the justice of the latter comment. It said that the churches needed to take account of practical realities, to try to develop a view on such issues as public sector borrowing and recognize the difficult task faced by politicians in formulating policies. It then went on to suggest that the role of the Church was an 'alternation of withdrawal and engagement, penitence and celebration', sometimes concerned with spiritual and sometimes with social questions, sometimes stressing utter realism and sometimes expressing simple moral outrage. But, having said, 'The cash-value of the Church's political attitudes will be found in its own life', the author concluded with the question, 'How do we fare?'[5]

In the context of the purpose which this editorial was intended to serve, this was no doubt as far as the author needed to go. But many of his readers must have asked themselves just exactly what it meant in practice. Did he think that this was an instance in which moral outrage was the correct response or was it one where realism necessitated a practical answer to the question of what the preferred policy should be? If the latter, where was the money to come from? In what sense could the Church's political attitude on child benefit be given cash value in its own life? Should the Church raise money for poor families rather than seek to influence government policies? In the end one was left, once again, with the feeling that the argument was wholly right – the Church must concern itself with the nature of society – but that there was no overcoming the main objections to the argument. The Church seems to content itself with expressing moral outrage and has no practical alternatives to offer.

I believe, in fact, that the editorial made one very significant contribution to the debate by drawing attention to an important fact which is seldom recognized by either side. It said that Mr Jenkin's argument:

> . . . takes us right to the heart of the problem of the citizen's responsibility in a representative political system. He or she can, and frequently does, express preferences and voice criticisms: it lies with Government to form a complete view, to decide and to carry the can. The mark of a mature democracy is that the people share with Government not simply in its goals, but also in accepting the costs (which include the goals which have been foregone).[6]

In that brief paragraph there are a large number of vital points. One is that the formulation of practical alternatives lies with governments and prospective governments. It is not really possible for anyone else to propose in detail the alternative preferred to the policy being criticized. And pressure groups are not normally expected to do more than indicate what they would regard as an area in which compensating sacrifices would be acceptable. This was certainly the case when, in 1981, Conservative back-bench MPs, representing rural interests, attacked the sharp increase in petrol taxes proposed by the budget. Clearly the Church cannot be expected to do *more* than any other political pressure group. But, since the Church's criticism ought to be an expression of a moral concern and since Christians ought to have a sense of pastoral responsibility towards those in office,[7] it would seem appropriate for the Church to say, at least, where it thinks the cost of what it is asking for should fall; increased taxation or whatever may be the case.

In other words, what is really being revealed here is the complex variety and inter-relation of roles which is disguised by terms like 'Church' and 'politics'. Following the kind of analysis I have attempted in earlier chapters, it is possible to suggest what ought to be done in a case of this sort. First, the chairmen of the departments (as part of the denominational leadership) were perfectly right to express the hope that poorer families would receive the help they needed. That was a wholly proper statement of a moral ideal. It was their duty as spokesmen making an implicit claim to represent the ideal Church and the absolute holiness for which it ought always to stand. But they might, perhaps, have made a virtue out of their apparent weakness and asserted boldly that, in that role, it was not their business to go beyond the implied criticism of society and suggest a detailed and practical alternative. History, as I have argued, is an untidy and unpredictable business. We are never in a position in which there is a real beginning.[8] The existence of a variety of left-over 'ends' limits the range of options and there are only certain possible policies and programmes which are available at any given moment.

The prime responsibility for assessing the options and formulating policies rests squarely upon government. What the leadership of the institutional Church has to accept is a pastoral concern for those who have that responsibility. And that will inevitably affect the way in which its criticisms are formulated – in terms of 'what sort of society is concerned for poorer families?' rather than an attack on politicians as such. It is, after all, part of their other role, as citizens, to accept responsibility for the shape society has. But, given that there is a limited range of possibilities, and that the formulation of policies in response to those possibilities *cannot* be done by anyone other than government, the chairmen also had a role (as Christian citizens) to indicate the areas where they would, themselves, have seen it morally right to accept sacrifices. 'We would be prepared to pay higher taxes to provide an increased child benefit.' As part of the leadership of their denominations, moreover, they also have a duty to teach, to urge and to campaign for, the members of those denominations to accept the necessary sacrifices. They would be saying, in effect, 'This is not a course which is wholly perfect, but it is the best course, morally, in the present situation.'

Finally, because those leaders are also members of local congregations, committees and informal groups of Christians, they would also be doing everything they could in those roles to persuade other Christians to make the necessary sacrifice, to give 'cash-value' to the Church's political attitudes and to care in practical ways for actual poor families on their doorstep.

Even at this level, of course, there are practical difficulties. No single person can embrace every cause or care for every sufferer. One has to do the best one can and this is a very good reason why William Temple's distinction between the role of the Church, as critic of society, and of the individual Christian, as active reformer, is obviously sensible. And that, in turn, draws attention to another practical function of the Church in its local and institutional manifestation. It is a community, not a chance agglomeration of individuals, and part of its job as community is to bring and hold together a variety of people who see the political application of their Christian faith differently just because human beings are limited in what they are able to care about and do. And this is, perhaps, the aspect of the Church's role which is, in practice, least obvious in this country at present. The churches look more like chance agglomerations of individuals than like communities.

There are, no doubt, many reasons for this. 'Going to church' rather than 'being the Church' is the way most people probably articulate the nature of their membership. But there are special problems in the area of political and social concern. In part these seem plainly to be a consequence of what I have called the civil-service pattern of neutrality which has so often been advocated as the correct one for the Church.[9] It is only right and proper that members of all parties should be welcome in the Church. Unfortunately that means that, in practice, political matters are avoided because they might be divisive. Only too often, when one talks about what Christians ought to do about, for instance, poverty in the Third World, one will hear someone say that no concerted action is possible because we hold different political opinions. There are two things to be said about this. The first is very simple: if the Church really were a community which was born out of the love of God revealed in Christ, the bonds which held it together would be strong enough to permit it to discuss *any* issue, however divisive potentially, without its corporate life being destroyed.

The second point is rather more difficult to capture. It seems to me that, if party political differences are strong enough to destroy the religious unity of Christians, that suggests that those political convictions must be stronger than, or at least as strong as, the religious convictions of the Christians concerned. And that would imply an entirely different state of affairs, a different kind of understanding of the Christian life, than the one I have been assuming in this book and which I tried to set out in chapter 3. If being a Christian means that one's commitment to God revealed in Christ is expressed in the life one tries to live, that implies a situation in which *everything* else becomes secondary, including one's politics. One may still be a committed and enthusiastic member of a political party but that will be because one has come to the conclusion that *that* party is the best vehicle for one's concern that society should reflect the proper values. One is not a Christian *and* a Conservative but a Conservative *because* one is a Christian. If one has two separate and autonomous commitments one may find it difficult to be part of a community with someone who shares only one of them. So it will be wholly appropriate to say that it would be better not to talk politics at the Rotary Club or in the senior common room. But if one has a common, over-riding commitment, from which all others derive, and one shares *that* with someone else, political differences will remain but they will be seen as different ways of expressing the same faith. And, in such a context, it ought to be possible to discuss and compare radically different ways of putting the religious commitment into political practice.

Now plainly even this contains a good deal of wishful thinking. We are still up against the problem that Christians and the actual Church, no less than society, are imperfectible. My contention is, however, that when one analyses the various roles which an individual may play, even within one single issue, instead of presenting the problem simply in terms of a sharp opposition between 'the Church' and 'politics', the whole thing begins to look far less intractable. It may be no less difficult to put into practice but it is, at least, not wholly outside the realm of practical action. But merely to state the priority of Christian commitment over political commitment is a reminder that we live in a society where Christianity no longer dominates and in which, for most people, politics is not an expression of Christian faith. How far ought Christians, even if they were able, to seek to move society in what *they* regard as a moral direction? If they can not, what ought their response to their failure to be?

This necessitates some consideration of just what the connection between politics and morality is thought to be in a contemporary secular society. My own understanding of this was illuminated by my being present at a seminar (attended by undergraduates, tutors and businessmen) to discuss factors affecting the taking of decisions in large commercial enterprises. The subject was introduced by representatives of a multi-national corporation who said that decision-taking was best understood as a complex process they described as 'moral arithmetic'. The examples given of the kind of calculation they had in mind were, for instance, where one had to balance immediate profits against the demands of home government, public opinion or the government of the developing country where a new investment was to be made: 'If we build a road from A to B it will cost us a lot but it will help our local image.' There were clearly moral implications to the decisions since they might affect the welfare of workers or benefit the whole society of the developing country. The moral attitudes of government and public at home also had to be considered. But it was perfectly clear that *for the corporation itself* it was a calculation that had very little to do with morality. What they were weighing against immediate profits were longer-term factors such as the necessity of having the support of government or potential investors, without which the commercial venture would soon cease to be viable. This became abundantly clear when there was an attempt to argue that there was an exact parallel between these cases and such calculations as the cost of ambulance services against the need to save the lives of people hurt in accidents. But even this 'cost-effective' approach to ethics was at least concerned with a moral consequence, whereas the former case was simply a tactical calculation as between short- and long-term commercial benefits. When this was pointed out, the speakers took refuge in saying that altruism is always the same thing as long-term enlightened self-interest: being generous and charitable will pay off in 'good will' (a curiously strong echo of nineteenth-century ideas). 'The ordinary man in the street', we were assured, 'would say that *that* was how to decide on the right thing to do even if philosophers and theologians would not.'

If that assessment was in any sense a correct judgement on public ethical standards, then the man in the street decides upon what is right in purely consequentialist and materialist terms. He asks himself what results will flow from various possible courses of action and judges the 'right' one to be that which suits his own selfish interests best. No doubt this is how he sometimes, perhaps often, proceeds. And, equally often, his political judgements are also taken on no more moral a basis than that. But in that case it is difficult to account for another feature of public life – the effect of scandal in political affairs.

There seems to be a widespread assumption, which is less logical than the point made by Nagel and quoted in a previous chapter (see page 85), that if I stick to a firm moral code in my *private* life then my public persona will also be worthy of approbation. Of course, we all realize that this does not actually follow. It is possible for a man to be chaste, unbribable and a teetotaller, and yet be a tyrant. But the belief that there is a simple connection between private respectability and public integrity dies hard, even in these days of almost total permissiveness. One can see that a politician who embezzles ought not to be trusted with public funds and that a politician who shares a mistress with an agent of a foreign power is a security risk. Someone who panics after a road accident and tries to cover it up may not be the best person to take the country through a crisis. But a public figure caught visiting a brothel may also find himself pressured into resignation, even though no issue other than his private morality is called in question. And that is curious for it does not follow that his conduct of public affairs need be corrupt or even that most members of the public regard visiting a brothel as immoral. Why do we make these demands?

If we were asked to say what we required most of all from our rulers, we should probably reply that it was actual competence, an ability to keep the economy expanding, to protect us from outside interference and so on. Many Americans, once the shock of Watergate had worn off, and particularly in the latter part of President Carter's term of office, were prepared to say quite openly that competence was preferable to high-mindedness. Bernard Williams tells the story of a politician 'who used to say "that is not a serious political argument" to mean, more or less, "that is an argument about what to do in politics which mentions a non-political consideration" – in particular, a moral consideration'. And I remember once having a furious discussion with the then president of my college Junior Common Room who rejected any argument which contained the word 'ought' as 'moralistic' not 'political'. As I was arguing that we 'ought' to do certain things on very practical grounds – the necessity to balance the budget, for instance – I found this concept of what makes an argument 'moralistic' somewhat confusing. And it soon became apparent that he was really defining 'political' as 'what the Junior Common Room wanted' – that is in terms of interests. This is 'moral arithmetic' like that of the multinational corporation.

Admittedly 'ought' is sometimes used in a confusing way, however. 'This is what I ought to do' often means simply 'this is the thing to be done in view of the practicalities of the situation.' It is, therefore, what I would call a political argument, about the art of the practical or the necessary expediencies, rather than about morality. When my wife says, 'I ought to cook the pork tonight because it has been out of the freezer longer than the beef,' that is not a judgement arrived at as a result of moral considerations.

In the sixties contextual ethics (not to be confused with situational ethics) gained some popularity in Christian circles and contextual ethics maintains that neither prescriptive regulations nor general moral principles are as important as that one should understand the situation, fully, in detail and with a clear perception of what is really happening. The economist and the sociologist will enable one to understand what action is necessary. One seeks to reduce 'ought' statements to 'is' statements. I take this to mean that contextual ethicists believe that a careful analysis of a situation will reveal that one course of action alone is feasible, or at least so obviously better on practical, political or expedient grounds, that there really is no choice. So you cook the pork tonight, as it were.

Contextual ethics receives its religious justification, in writers like

Paul Lehmann for instance, from the argument that God is at work in the world and in history and that what is required of us is to work with him.[10] There are echoes of Barth here, yet the total affect is very different. To discover what is happening *will* reveal (ought to reveal?) our own proper course of action.

I am, as may be apparent, somewhat sceptical. Specialists seldom come up with a clear-cut, *agreed*, answer about what *is* happening. Moreover, when one has listened to all the specialists one is not often in a position to make a judgement upon what they have told one. And, finally, unless one accepts a determinist view of history, it is seldom the case that one single course of action emerges from the analysis. One would still be faced with weighing op the projections like any consequentialist and asking the question about which was the *right* course to take. And, once it is clear that there is no one *obvious* course, then the 'is' and the 'ought' separate out again and one is looking for the standards which will determine right from wrong, even if they are practical rather than moralistic ones. Religious contextualism, moreover, is dangerous because, having cut itself free from statements of general principle, its proponents are able to claim to discern precisely what God *is* doing in history. It is easy to fall into an arrogant certainty that one is doing what God's action in the events of history require one to do. If natural law concepts of the relationship between politics and morality tend to sanctify the *status quo*, because they inevitably use arguments likely to appeal to the common sense of the majority, contextualist morality tends to sanctify violent change because it assumes that it is in the revolutionary events that God is at work. The humility of Bonhoeffer is to be found precisely in the fact that he did not claim some kind of divine authority for his action.

The boundary between 'is' and 'ought' is, however, always difficult to draw – 'I ought to do this because it is the only way to balance the budget,' which sounds like a practical, an 'is' statement in disguise, may actually mean what it says, 'I have a moral obligation to balance the budget'. It is that difficulty which seems to me to be largely responsible for the implicit contradiction, discussed earlier, in our attitude towards those who govern. On the one hand we would argue that our first requirement is that they *ought* to be competent and successful at a practical level. But we are also, though often hypocritically, inclined to demand that they *ought* to be morally respectable as well.

There is a very good reason why we *should* prefer to be governed by people who are moral as well as competent. This is quite simply that no one wants to be exploited or oppressed or to be manipulated and lied to or to be defrauded or to be unjustly treated. Each of us resents those things for himself and would therefore prefer in theory, at least, and as a matter of sheer self-interest, that the politicians who govern our society should be honest and just, not cruel or arbitrary. This is to look at the question from the 'moral arithmetic' point of view.

Justice is, perhaps, the crux of the thing because justice is about how each of us is treated relative to each other and to society. Anyone who writes about justice tends at some point to talk about the relationship between justice and fairness or justice and equality.[11] And many of the arguments about how to achieve justice consist of attempts to envisage a situation in which each person, in order to achieve what will suit *him* best, will be compelled to press for conditions which will be equally advantageous for anyone else. So one moves from 'moral arithmetic' to a genuinely moral consideration, however pragmatic. It is fascinating to see that John Rawls, who has written what is probably the best known modern book on the theory of justice, adopts a device not unlike that of Plato himself.[12] Each, in effect, says, 'Let's suppose that we were sitting down to create a new society from scratch. How should we achieve justice then?' (Though that is where the agreement ends, for Plato can appeal to eternal values while Rawls cannot.) The attempt to imagine the creation of a new society is the obvious device to adopt, for in those conditions all men are equal partners and each may be able to stand in another man's shoes and see things from his point of view. In fact Rawls tries to build in artificial and not entirely satisfactory conditions, what he calls a 'veil of ignorance', to ensure this.[13]

Rawls needs his 'veil of ignorance' because justice accompanies self-interest only when I am compelled to take account of others' needs lest I should one day find myself in their shoes. Pure self-interest does not say, 'Do as you would be done by' (as in *The Water Babies*); it says, 'Do to me as I would that you should, bearing in mind that I may wish you to do quite differently to various other people.' I do not, in other words, want politicians to lie to *me* but I may actually like them to lie to politicians who represent another party or another nation. Electioneering slogans may turn out to be quite obviously dishonest. But this does not lead those who benefit from them to say that they are despicable; they often continue to be regarded as a very successful P. R. job. Nor do I recall a single protest when, over the 1980 Moscow Olympics, almost all British politicians performed a painless *volte face* on the matter of politics in sport. Political competence is supposed to require that sort of thing and we resent it only when it is practised at our own expense.

Much of this is, no doubt, an example of the way we are blinkered by our own prejudices, but one logical consequence of it needs to be noted. In an earlier chapter I argued that when objections were raised to the application of absolute morality to the practicalities of politics, two different objections to two different senses of 'absolute morality' were often at issue. Absolute morality, if conceived of as prescriptive regulations, is feared because it might lead to the enactment of tyrannical laws. Absolute morality, even if understood as general principles, is also mistrusted because it might imply a lack of ruthlessness. In other words, I fear that the politician might treat everyone else with exactly the same kindness with which I want him to treat me. And, on occasion, that might be disastrous. So I would like him to be a good man (in the sense of possessing qualities like honesty, truthfulness, kindness, generosity and so on) because otherwise he might treat me badly. But I do not wish him to exercise those qualities absolutely and indiscriminately. Part of the competence I expect of him is the ability to know when the practical expediencies of national or international politics require him *not* to exercise them.

Cynical though this may sound, I do not intend it so. If one is considering the question, 'What does the ordinary man in the street think that politicians *ought* to do?', which is the point we are concerned with, I think the true answer is the somewhat muddled one that is beginning to emerge. But the muddle is itself significant. It is a recognition that moral qualities, the kind of person one is, are the most important thing. What is desirable is that a ruler should possess personal moral qualities rather than that either the style or the content of his governing should be a direct reflection of regulative moral prescriptions or general moral principles.

One can maintain the desirability of this for very down-to-earth reasons. Sissela Bok does so, using evidence from American opinion polls in 1975 and 1976. Of those then questioned 69 per cent asserted that they believed that the country's leaders had consistently lied to the nation. This led her to say:

> Voters and candidates alike are the losers when a political system has reached such a low level of trust. Once elected, officials find that their warnings and their calls to common sacrifice meet with disbelief and apathy, even when co-operation is most urgently needed.[14]

Too much lying, in other words, can destroy the practical effectiveness of a government. Because we expect some degree of moral probity, a ruler known to be dishonest will cease to be effective.

This makes it clear, as it seems to me, that the man in the street is operating at a level above that of the 'moral arithmetic' of the representatives of the multinational corporations. However much his attitudes may be based upon a pragmatic, cost-effective consequentialism and self-interest, he is actually concerned that there should be moral values and that politicians should possess them. However much he may recognize that effectiveness sometimes requires the performance of an action which would normally be regarded as immoral, he also fears the triumph of a politics totally without morality. And that, in turn, will tend to create support for moral values for their own sake.

> For what would it mean to care deeply for freedom and justice if one did not express one's concern in any of the standard ways on those occasions when its objects were abused? To remain passive and silent then would seem inconsistent with being the sort of moral agent one claims to be, with the moral concerns one claims to have.[15]

To be concerned for justice lest one be treated unjustly oneself may lead one to protest the cause of justice even when it is not especially in one's own interest, at that moment, to do so.

The 'muddle' of which I spoke earlier is, in fact, a paradox which we all recognize intuitively even if we do not manage to articulate it. It is not something only to be encountered in the upper reaches of moral philosophy. A scientist conducting experiments on living animals in order to discover a cure for human disease may well say, 'I believe I have to do it, but I feel that it is wrong, all the same'.

Bernard Williams says of this paradox, when applied to politics: 'It is a predictable and probable hazard of public life that there will be those situations in which something morally disagreeable is clearly required. To refuse on moral grounds ever to do anything of that sort is more than likely to mean that one cannot pursue even the moral ends of politics.'[16] Williams drives the paradox home by adding that 'the moral disagreeableness of these acts is not merely cancelled by the fact that they are necessary, and this comes out above all in the consideration that the victims can justly complain that they have been wronged'. The conclusion he draws is that politicians ought to 'hold on to the idea, that there are actions which *remain morally disagreeable even when politically justified*'. He hastens to point out that he is not simply saying that it is edifying for politicians to be ruthless but unhappy about it. 'Sackcloth is not suitable dress for politicians, least of all successful ones.'[17] It is partly that, if they are not unhappy, if they do not recognize the paradox, they are likely to be the kind of person who will do the morally disagreeable thing, *even when it is not necessary*. But it is also partly a matter of what he calls a 'sensibility to moral cost' – 'not just an initial hesitation in reaching for the answer, but genuine disquiet when one arrives at it'.

Margaret Boden has produced some fascinating arguments in relation to computers in an attempt to show that subjectivity can arise within a basically mechanistic universe. Her purpose is to counter the view of humanists and theists alike that human beings possess a freedom of intention which makes them entirely different from machines. I do not wish to concern myself with that aspect of her argument but simply to draw attention to the section of her article called 'Moral Responsibility'. She recognizes that, to make her case, a computer (a machine) would have to be made capable of moral choice. A programme able to achieve this has not yet been devised but she believes it to be possible in principle. For it to be done computers would have to be able to choose, not only *for* an ethical consideration *against* the strongest desire, but to deliberate on mutually exclusive goals and 'judiciously change their minds'.

> We have already seen examples of programmes capable of reasoning about their choices so as to avoid what might initially seem the 'obvious' option. . . . So there is no reason to suppose that specifically moral considerations could not also enter into such deliberation, and so decisively affect the generation of action, provided that one could give a programme a moral sense of what it should be worrying about.[18]

That sounds very like saying that computers will become morally responsible when they can be made to 'agonize', a further reason for supposing that what we are talking about is not simply a subjective guilt-feeling to bolster up one's estimate of oneself as a worthy person, but a real and important factor in the decision. It ought to be difficult to choose to do morally disagreeable things.

Most attempts to resolve the dilemma adopt one of two approaches, which both attempt to devise a formula for determining the circumstances when morally disagreeable actions are justified. What they attempt to do, in other words, is not to dissolve the moral absolute nor to circumnavigate the apparent necessity but to find ways of defining or testing justifiable exceptions. It *is* morally disagreeable ruthlessly to sacrifice the interests of worthy persons to those of unworthy persons. Yet it may seem to be a necessity of politics. One of the ways of justifying the necessity relies upon a quantitative principle – the size of the group or body for which the politician or public servant acts. The utilitarian principle of the greatest happiness of the greatest number is probably the best known and most openly invoked variety of this approach. But I quoted an example of another variant in an earlier chapter, an example in which it was argued that there was a 'moral threshold' which is crossed on 'the assumption of a political role, and of the power to change men's lives *on a large scale*'.[19] This quantitative element is reinforced by one of the criteria cited by Sir Stuart Hampshire in that example – accountability to one's followers. The argument seems to be, in fact, that the representative character of a public servant and his responsibility for a large number of other people is what puts him on the other side of the threshold. It is, I suppose, a very similar kind of argument which bases itself upon the claims of state, government or society over against the individual. An official may say, 'Government regulations require me to do this,' in a context in which he is about to act in a manner which would normally be described as 'morally disagreeable'. He does not say it when handing one a tax refund. The safety of the state in wartime is widely recognized as justifying such things as the deception and exploitation of one's own people and one's allies as well as unethical acts against the enemy, such as the killing of 'innocent' civilians in bombing raids.

The other group of arguments relies mainly upon the sheer intractability of political facts themselves and, in that sense, resembles contextual ethics. An examination of the situation reveals that one course of action, however morally disagreeable, is for practical reasons the obvious one to take because any morally acceptable course appears to involve inevitable disaster. 'That being the case', the argument runs, 'I was right to do it.' In this category belong the attempts to defend morally disagreeable actions on the grounds that the end justifies the means, the inevitability of compromise or the choice between two evils.

The trouble is that all the variants in both approaches can only too easily become morally shabby. The end justifying the means is notoriously so. 'Government regulations required me to do it' was, in effect, the standard defence of many of the war criminals at Nuremberg. Even the choice of the lesser of two evils is not actually as safe as it appears. Tutors who act as referees to undergraduates applying to certain branches of the civil service may encounter questions from the security officers who vet the candidates which seem less than wholly ethical. A referee may be asked about the wife of an applicant in a way that implies that the investigator has evidence that she is sexually promiscuous when, in fact, there is no such evidence. It is simply an attempt to fish for possible 'weakness'. If one protests, one is told that it is better that the woman's reputation be damaged than that the safety of the whole nation be in the hands of a security risk. That a very large number of people will be at risk in the second case is used to suggest that it is obviously the greater evil. But there is, in fact, a hole in the argument. The statement 'X is non-existent' is incompatible with the statement 'X is greater than Y', as Anselm pointed out in his ontological argument for the existence of God. If there *was* no evidence that the woman was promiscuous, the danger to the state was hypothetical, the evil non-existent. It could not possibly, therefore, be the greater evil of the two.

The trouble is that there is not always this sort of hole in the argument. Sometimes there is a genuine conflict between two morally desirable goals, and the fact that one can demonstrate that both categories of argument are open to abuse does not alter the fact that on some occasions there is no evading them. Even the notorious end-justifying-the-means argument is one which we all use, and properly, on occasion. The problem really is that there seems to be no way to devise a general principle which will tell us when it is proper to use them – or, rather, it does not seem possible to devise general moral principles which of themselves will also tell us when we may abrogate them legitimately.

What is really being indicated here is the inadequacy of general moral principles. They are generalizations which have to assert apparent absolutes. Otherwise they would have to be formulated as near-contradictions; 'One ought always to tell the truth except when one ought to tell a lie.' And that, apart from being unhelpful, appears to treat truth and lies as of equal moral value.

If we ask what people usually mean when they formulate a general moral principle, it is clear that they are really concerned to assert the preferability of truth over lies, the *prima facie* superiority of one kind of intention and action over another. At that moment they are not concerned with possible exceptions arising from conflicts between two moral principles. Kant's categorical imperative may be more than this but Jesus's 'Judge not that ye be not judged' does not prevent his passing judgement on the Pharisees. The fact is that general moral principles are assertions of personal ideals which are believed to have an intrinsic worth. No doubt they ought to be more precisely formulated. One ought to say, 'Telling the truth is the good thing and cases where one does not do so ought to be very rare indeed.' But that so weakens the force of the injunction that it does not do justice to the ideal one is concerned to assert.

Moreover if one wished to make one's injunction strictly universalizable one would have to spell out every possible exception in very precise detail, with as many clauses as the most complex statute, and then it would require a judicial authority to interpret it. We should in fact find ourselves relying upon case law, or its equivalent in moral theology – casuistry. And what has given casuistry a bad name is precisely that there are always cases where the principle, once it is reduced to a prescriptive regulation, cannot be applied. Nor can there be rules about when it is moral to behave immorally. Quite apart from their inherently hypocritical character, they inevitably seem clever, unagonizing, or even faintly comic. The need to do, in exceptional circumstances, what is usually wrong cannot be expressed as part of the assertion of what is usually right. It is a matter of fine, agonizing and sensitive judgement. The decision has to be the responsibility of a person not a rule.

What I am trying to show is that the experience of having to do what is usually wrong and the belief that what are called moral absolutes are really assertions about personal ideals, is not peculiarly Christian. There may be differences between Christians and non-Christians about what the ideals are or about how one arrives at and defends them. But, accepting that there are principles which enshrine ideals in this way, those who hold to them usually recognize that there will be difficult cases in which it appears impossible to apply them. Where it seems to me that Christians will be in a rather different position is that they ought not to be surprised at the paradox and ought to be clearer and more articulate about what it means and how it is to be dealt with. They ought to be aware of the imperfectibility of man, his inability to choose the good, his need for forgiveness and the cost of his sinfulness. All this seems implicit in the view of morality set out in earlier chapters. Christians ought also to realize very clearly the importance of being the kind of person who can judge these situations.

I can best illustrate what I mean by taking a hypothetical case devised by Bernard Williams.[20] It was invented by Williams as part of an argument against utilitarianism. In brief it is this: a man called Jim visits a South American town to find that a firing squad is about to execute twenty Indians. Pedro, the captain in charge of the squad, offers to free nineteen of the Indians if Jim will shoot the other one. In strict utilitarianism, assuming that death does not contribute to happiness, Jim should clearly agree to shoot one in order to free nineteen. But, says Williams, '. . . even one who came to think that perhaps that *was* the answer, might well wonder whether it was *obviously* the answer'. One's intuition might tell one differently.

Jonathan Glover has attempted to answer Williams and argue for strict consequentialism by maintaining that the only thing which would really prevent anyone from shooting the Indian was a concern for his own virtue.[21] It would be a kind of higher selfishness, as it were. One's own personal regard for one's own virtue would be destroyed if one shot the Indian. What really matters is not, however, the moral qualities of the person but whether the action has good or bad consequences.

R. F. Holland, in an article significantly entitled 'Absolute Ethics, Mathematics and the Impossibility of Politics',[22] on the other hand, has argued that the hypothetical case is fanciful and therefore likely to divert attention from what really matters in genuine cases of that kind, the sense of outrage and agony. I am sure this is important and I am equally sure that there is another aspect of the fancifulness of hypothetical examples which is related to the first and almost as important. They are unreal because they lack the detail necessary to give them credibility. After all Frederick Forsyth's best seller, *The Devil's Alternative*, needed nearly five hundred pages to convey the complexity of the interplay of factors of all kinds, including personalities, which normally enter into a real moral dilemma. Forsyth's story is about a fictional American president faced with a choice between permitting an ecological disaster or the outbreak of World War III. Both these courses are politically (and morally) unacceptable, so he is compelled to accept the immoral decision to murder two men whose freedom has been guaranteed. Detail such as Forsyth provides – which is obviously out of the question for a philosopher wanting a brief illustration of a theoretical point – is important not just because it conveys something of the agonizing involved but because, sometimes, it is in the very detail that the grounds for taking the proper decision are to be found.

Holland also introduced into Williams's story the possibility that Jim might be a saint and do surprising things – like arranging to be shot himself in place of the twenty Indians. This is really another way of arguing that we need the detail and the personalities in order to make a judgement. Holland ends his article with this paragraph:

> As a matter of fact I find it hard to imagine a saint's having any theoretical ethics whatever: at least if he had one I do not suppose it would contribute to his saintliness. On the other hand if he did have one, it is clear that it would have to be an ethics of absolute conceptions. I brought in the idea of the saint because for all the difference between them there is this significant point of contact between the position of a saint and the position of an ordinary person who has absolute conceptions if he is true to them. Neither could shoot the Indian. The impossibility here is the impossibility of politics.

If one is talking about a *Christian* saint, then I do not think one can entirely agree. A Christian saint *will* need a morality of absolute conceptions, in the sense of absolute standards of good and evil, because he needs to be absolutely clear about what *is* good. Moreover there is no way of defining what one means by 'a good man' except in general and apparently universalizable terms: a good man does not lie; a good man is faithful to his wife. Nevertheless, Holland is surely right in suggesting that these principles, whatever their general and universal force, are only general principles. What is significant about the saint is his different, his surprising, *judgement* on what is to be done in a given situation.

Holland is reluctant to speculate about what Jim would do if he happened to be a saint. This is not surprising because the saint himself would probably not know what he would do, until he was in the situation, and then his decision would very likely be formed by those very complexities of detail whose absence makes hypothetical examples so unsatisfactory. The most important thing, as Holland implies, is that he would not make his decision on the basis of the immoral dilemma with which Pedro is presenting him. This, as it seems to me, is the distinctive thing about Jesus's own attitude to moral decisions as the gospels represent it. Again and again, when he is asked to judge what is right he disconcerts his questioners by refusing to accept the dilemma in the terms or on the premises presented to him: 'In the resurrection there is no marraige or giving in marriage'; 'Let him who is without sin among you cast the first stone'; or even 'Who made *me* a judge over you?' It is this that makes his perceptions so penetrating as well as so disconcerting. And, if Christ is both the source of the Church's holiness and the pattern of the Christian's saintliness – as I have argued in previous chapters – then this refusal to accept the dilemma in the terms presented is of primary significance.

This is not to say that the Christian can always expect Christ's kind of unerring judgement or his power to provide right answers. Jim, if he were a saint, might arrange to be shot by Pedro in exchange for the Indians, or he might convert Pedro by his very offer or by the manner in which he accepted death. But he might talk to the Indians and discover that one of them was also a saint, willing to be shot for the sake of the others. Under those circumstances Jim might conceivably shoot his fellow saint. Or, on being handed the gun, he might even shoot Pedro. In any or all of those decisions he might be acting less than perfectly. Even in accepting his own death he might be failing in his duty to care for and protect his wife. And here we are back with the points made by Bonhoeffer and Oosthuizen. The saint is still a sinner. Even when he believes that he *has* to behave in a certain way, and is driven by a moral compulsion to do so, he will not have escaped from the human condition.

Holland maintains that those who, like Plato, believe in absolute ethics cannot say, 'It was wrong but I had to do it'. The consequentialist, the true Machiavellian, says, 'I *had* to do it, so I was right to do it.' The Christian may often find himself in the situation where he has to say, 'I had to do it because I could see no alternative, but it was nevertheless sinful'. After all, moral problems are not created simply by the fact that we know what to do but do not want to do it. The really difficult moral problems arise, as Christian moral theologians have always recognized, when it is not clear what we *ought* to do – or, in other words, when two abstract and absolute moral principles seem to conflict. Is it right for a man to steal food for his starving children? The difficult decisions that have to be made, in private no less than in public life, cannot be cut loose from the general principles – but they cannot be bound by them either.

In an earlier chapter I compared fallen humanity with a mosaic. If one has a mosaic with one missing piece it is relatively easy to know what that piece ought to look like: if the mosaic is scattered it will be much more difficult. In fact life is a kaleidoscope rather than a mosaic. The pattern turns and shifts, never repeating itself, constantly moving into new forms. And the pattern is not inherent in the arrangement of the pieces: it is imposed by the mirrors and lenses. So we are constantly faced with complex, shifting situations. The saint is concerned to make patterns out of the bits and pieces, the details of life that inform his judgement.

The Christian, therefore, experiences precisely the same paradox in morality as anyone else, in that he or she will encounter situations in which it seems necessary to do something which is nevertheless wrong. And it will not be wrong simply in some subjective, guilty sense. It will involve 'moral cost'. For the Christian, also, as for anyone else, the only safeguard lies in personal integrity exercised in sensitive judgement. Kenneth Thompson, writing about the contrast between what men do politically and what they believe they ought to do, said:

> Societies discover that the gulf separating norms and behaviour must be kept within limits if life is not to become intolerable. Historically, man has most often tried to cope with this tension and contradiction in one of two ways. Either patterns of conduct are transformed to fit moral standards or standards are trimmed and adjusted to accord with behaviour.[23]

That reads almost like a platitude. It is also altogether too static and over-simplified. The truth is that it is a both-and rather than an either-or solution which is needed. One needs the firm assertion of the ideal *and* the recognition that *sometimes* one may have to be content with less than that. If being content with less wins every time, or even most of the time, one will become the kind of person who does not conform to the ideal and probably the kind of person who no longer even strives to conform to the ideal. If the ideal remains firm and, agonisingly, one recognizes occasions when it is unattainable, one is able to retain one's integrity and to remain the kind of person whose goal is clear.

Transferred to the political sphere, that would mean that one retained one's moral values, not only for oneself but for society. One would not only be reacting to political situations by saying, 'What would the kind of person who has these ideals do when faced by such and such a moral choice?': one would also have to be asking, 'What kind of society presents one with this moral choice? What kind of society would enshrine the moral ideals? What can I do to make it that sort of society?' One would, indeed, need commitment to Christ and the gift of his Spirit, in order to retain and preserve one's moral values. But one would also be working for change and discontinuity, so that society did not remain set in structures which denied moral values. A purely personal morality, which accepts or ignores the structures, is not enough. Nor is it enough to wait for everyone to be converted. There is an obligation to protest, to proclaim the imperfections of society and the need for change in the structures where their effects are immoral and even when one does not see how they can be changed or whether one has the ability to achieve a change. 'For', to quote Stanley Benn again, 'what would it mean to care for freedom and justice if one did not express one's concern?'[24]

It does not seem to me that one can rely simply upon intuition. Not only would that seem to rest a weight upon man's natural moral sense, which Christian theology would regard it as incapable of bearing, but it seems difficult to relate intuition to the needs of society. One may intuit what one can oneself stomach morally. How is one to intuit what would be morally right for society? One can, however, be concerned – at one and the same time – to behave as the kind of person one desires to be *and* to do what is possible to make society be the kind of society one wishes it to be, provided the model for oneself and for society are the same. Accepting that one's own judgements will have a provisional and tentative quality and that one cannot be certain of the consequences of any action – recognizing, in other words, that one's judgement may be wrong – one may attempt to live and act according to the ideals of Christ and by the power of his Spirit.

Politically speaking one would be asking questions about the kind of society in which one lives and trying to make one's judgements for it in terms of what is to become of it. But, again, one's judgements will have a tentativeness which contextualism seems to lack. One will be doing the best one can and one will be doing it in a way which gives wholeness to one's personal and political lives. For, in a sense, the problem of contextualism is the reverse of the problem of intuitionalism. One may feel that one knows, with some certainty, what the context of history means for the future of society but how does one see one's historical context as the guide to one's personal morality in any sphere other than the political. Yet to have a 'different' morality in the political and the personal is itself disintegrative. but to have a unified ideal rooted in Christ himself for one's personal life and for the political life of society may help to overcome that difficulty.

This would mean that there was for society, as for the individual Christian and the Church, a morality of tension between the ideal and the actual. What Aristotle and Aquinas said about man being a political animal seems to imply that, out of society, human beings are less than fully human. And this is something which is a matter of common experience. The importance of society, and the reason why Christians should be concerned to obey and serve and preserve it, is that in isolation we are less than we ought to be. But Christians also have an ideal for judging society – is it a society in which the Christian ideals, such as integrity and love, are both manifest and encouraged? If it is not then it will be a society which fails to allow men and women to be fully human. If it is a society which places positive obstacles in the way of realizing those ideals, if it makes men and women less than human, then the Christian will be forced to recognize that society has become demonic and needs change, even change of a drastic and radical kind.

Notes

1. B. Burnett, 'The Spirit and Social Action' in M. Harper (ed.), *Bishops Move*, Hodder and Stoughton, 1978, p. 31.
2. *Ibid.*, p. 30.
3. K. E. Wright, 'To What Extent Does the Church Today Affirm or Limit Basic Belief?', in E. E. Lester (ed.), *In Search of a Living Faith*, Community of the Cross of Nails publications, p. 48.
4. *Ibid.*
5. *Crucible*, October-December 1980, p. 147.
6. *Ibid.*, p. 146.
7. See p. 42.
8. See p. 31.

9. See pp. 6ff.
10. See e.g. P. Lehmann, *The Transfiguration of Politics*, S.C.M. 1975, pp. 232 and 262. See also Lehmann's *Ethics in a Christian Context*, S.C.M. 1963, for a systematic exposition of his ethics.
11. See e.g. J. Rawls, *A Theory of Justice*, O.U.P. (paperback) 1973, pp. 17ff. and 195ff.; and J. R. Lucas, *On Justice*, O.U.P. 1980, pp. 171ff.
12. J. Rawls, *op. cit.*, p. viii; and cf. Plato, *Republic*, II.396ff.
13. J. Rawls, *op. cit.* p. 12.
14. S. Bok, *Lying: Moral Choice in Public and Private Life*, Harvester Press 1978, p. 175.
15. S. I. Benn, 'The Problematic Rationality of Political Participation', in P. Laslett and J. Fishkin, *Philosophy, Politics and Society* (5th series), Blackwell 1979, p. 310.
16. B. Williams, 'Politics and Moral Character' in S. Hampshire (ed.), *Public and Private Morality*, Cambridge University Press 1978, p. 62.
17. *Ibid.*, p. 64.
18. M. A. Boden, 'Human Values in a Mechanistic Universe', in G. Vesey (ed.), *Human Values*, Harvester Press 1978, p. 157.
19. See p. 36.
20. J. J. C. Smart and B. Williams, *Utilitarianism, For and Against*, Cambridge University Press 1974, p. 98.
21. J. Glover, 'It makes no difference whether or not I do it', in *Aristotelian Society Supplementary Volume XLIX*, pp. 184ff.
22. In G. Vesey (ed.), *op. cit.*, pp. 172ff.
23. K. W. Thompson, *The Moral Issue in Statecraft*, Louisiana State University Press 1966, p. 60.
24. See p. 149.

8

THE SACRAMENT OF POLITICS

I have called this chapter 'The Sacrament of Politics' because someone once called death 'the sacrament of time'. What he meant was that, in death, time takes on an outward and visible form. It may usually slip by unnoticed. Change and decay may be so gradual as not to catch our attention. But death makes these things overt, concrete inescapable.

In the same sort of way war seems to me the sacrament of politics. All that is wrong with human society and the way it organizes and conducts itself, all the necessary expediencies of politics, all the compromising, the clash of interests, the supremacy of ends over means, the justifying of morally disagreeable actions, lies, cruelties and injustices, to which we can normally close our eyes, become outward and visible in war.

That war is an evil hardly needs to be said. Certainly, from a Christian point of view, it is one of *the* great threats that hang over the human race. In the difficult and disturbing thirteenth chapter of Mark's gospel (verses 7 and 8), it is listed, together with famine and natural disaster, as one of the seemingly final terrors:

> And when you hear of wars and rumours of wars, do not be alarmed; this must take place, but the end is not yet. For nation will rise against nation, and kingdom against kingdom; there will be earthquakes in various places, there will be famines; this is but the beginning of the birth-pangs.

However we are to understand the meaning of that passage in an apocalyptic sense, it seems abundantly clear that war figures in it as one of the penultimate horrors. And it is still so today. War, famine and natural disaster are the three kinds of crisis that produce human suffering on a large scale. That they are evils seems inescapable.

When we consider further, the tone of so many sayings attributed to Jesus in the gospels, about turning the other cheek and loving one's enemies, war begins to seem not only a crisis of an unquestionably evil kind but clearly also something contrary to the spirit of Christianity. It is hardly surprising, then, that as far back as one can trace Christian moral teaching, war seems usually to have been treated (at least in theory) as something that can only be justified as a desperate last resort – if at all.

There have, of course, been exceptions. Crusades fought for religious causes against the heathen or the heretics have been enthusiastically sponsored by the Church. Secular wars have been categorized as noble by preachers and ecclestiastical leaders. The concept of a *just* war has occupied the attention of moral theologians and has been used to justify every kind of aggression.

There just is not time here to go into the whole field of Christian writing about the morality of war, with its vast secondary literature.[1] Perhaps, in a sense, that does not matter because much of it seems no longer applicable. Moreover I find it difficult to believe that someone like Aquinas, defining a just war as one which is declared by the lawful ruler, for a just cause, and fought with the right intention,[2] meant these as rules which would actually enable X to decide whether he should fight a specific war or not. As a former Principal of Heythrop College has argued, the conditions are 'aimed not at commending war but at controlling and containing destruction of lives'.[3] Such later refinements as that there should be a reasonable hope of success, or that every other means should have been attempted, or that war should be waged in a proper manner, make it more difficult still to use these conditions as an actual test applicable to a particular war. For war itself is now so final a crisis that it is difficult to think beyond it about better or worse states to follow. It is also itself a great catalyst for change so that its own conditions are continually altering. Aquinas recognizes that 'intention' may alter drastically during the course of war and that what has been undertaken 'to promote some good or avoid some evil' may come to be pursued for vengeance or the thirst for power. The rate of change, moreover, is more rapid now than it was when the means or manner of war was first used as a criterion in the early sixteenth century. People entering upon war in 1939 could not have foreseen that it would end in the atomic holocaust of Hiroshima and Nagasaki. It can also happen that what seems a reasonable hope of success at one time may soon turn out to be vain. But it is seldom possible to end a war at will: one's now victorious enemies may be demanding an unconditional and potentially unjust surrender.

One thing, however, is pointed up very sharply by the concept of the just war – the need for logic and consistency in the arguments employed to justify war. Very few people are prepared to say that no war, no force, no violence is ever justified: they will almost always say that under certain circumstances they see no alternative to fighting. But, almost as often, they will condemn violence and acts of war if committed by those whose aims they do not share – and will do so simply on the grounds that violence is wrong. 'The men of violence are the enemies of society,' they will say, forgetting that some societies deserve to have enemies and that they themselves would be perfectly willing to justify acts of violence against certain kinds of society. In other words, they ought really to be defining what is meant by a good society, what are the circumstances that justify acts of violence against society, and what kind of aims are sufficiently important to be worth fighting for.

One Remembrance Sunday not long ago the preacher of the university sermon in Oxford used Aquinas's first principle of the just war to condemn African guerrillas in what was then Rhodesia because they were fighting without the backing of 'lawful authority'. He did this without further qualification, consideration or argument as though it were self-evident that anyone taking up arms against *any* government must be wrong. A little later in his sermon, however, he praised those Germans of the 1940s who engaged in armed resistance against Hitler. Once again, apparently, he saw no need to specify the reasons why they had been right. It was treated as simply self-evident. Yet precisely the same arguments would have been used by the guerrillas as by those Germans – that the government they were opposing was tyrannical, of doubtful legality and threatened to destroy the whole nation. What was required was a rigorous specification of the conditions under which the preacher was prepared to regard the German resistance as justifiable: what kind of society, what kind of government, what methods of resistance, what aims behind the violence? Then it might have been possible for him to define precisely in what way he thought the Rhodesian Africans were different and unjustified. Merely to condemn violence as *per se* immoral in one context, while praising it in another, as though one's own sympathies were a sufficient guide, is illogical.

Yet we all do this. One frequently hears people say, perhaps of the I.R.A. or perhaps of the World Council of Churches' Programme to Combat Racism, 'How can clergymen condone violence?' If one persuades them to clarify what they mean, it usually appears that they are appalled that 'men of God' should seem to approve of bombings and shooting, torture and brutality. The logical implication of such a belief ought to be that all violence is immoral. One cannot seriously maintain that what is immoral for a clergyman is moral for anyone else (though it may be less shocking). Logically that would mean that God himself might approve of something that the 'men of God' ought not to approve. But, in fact, such protesters do not usually mean that all violence is *per se* immoral. They will often argue just as vigorously that Britain must retain a strong military force. They actually believe that there are circumstances in which violence is not improper but they are vague about what those circumstances are and so, when they do not like what is done, they talk rather dishonestly as though they believed that all violence was wrong. They are also unclear as to just how exactly the exceptions ought to be described. Is it that violence is usually wrong but sometimes right, depending on the circumstances? Or is it that it is usually immoral but sometimes morally justifiable? Or is it (as I would say myself) that it is always evil but sometimes unavoidable?

The important thing is to avoid the trap of assuming automatically that violence is right and good when one's own side (or the side with which one sympathizes) uses it but not when the other side does. The radical left will howl about police brutality but insist that only violent methods have any hope of defeating the National Front. Someone who is moved to tears by the tragic courage of the Czechoslovakian student who killed himself in protest against Russian intervention in 1969 will condemn the hunger strikes in the H-blocks of Northern Ireland as acts calculated to provoke violence. People who sympathize with acts of sabotage committed by South African blacks object to the same acts when committed by Welsh nationalists. The list could be endless. If the objecters were honest they would be compelled to admit that they are not condemning violence as such. What they object to are the *aims* of those who use violence, or the use of violence against a state or society which does not seem bad enough to justify it.

To call violence illegal or criminal is also inadequate, for that is merely to say that it is done against the law of one's own society and that society does not like it. Parking on double yellow lines is also illegal; so is smuggling a bottle of gin through customs. It is not the *illegality* of violence that really matters, for that would mean that legalized violence was unobjectionable. What was done by the bully-boys of Amin's Uganda would then be acceptable. But clearly most of the world did not regard them as morally tolerable.

A prejudiced view is obviously very difficult to avoid. We react emotionally in this area. And it is, therefore, all the more important to remember the principle of universalizability whenever war and violence are discussed. If I say that it is wrong for someone to steal from me, it must be equally wrong for me to steal from him. If I am justified in stealing under certain very special circumstances, then someone else, in the same circumstances, would be justified in stealing from me. If I am not prepared to universalize in this way then what I am enunciating is not a moral principle. It is a biased statement of my own self-interest. And the same is true of war and violence. If one nation or group is justified, under certain circumstances, in resorting to them, then so are other nations or groups in the same circumstances.

I have coupled war and violence like this because, for reasons set out at earlier points in this book, I do not believe that something which would be immoral in an individual can automatically become moral because it is approved by a government.[4] This may seem to conflict with Aquinas's first condition of a just war – that it shall be authorized by lawful authority. There are two things to be said about this. In the first place, if Aquinas was not providing criteria intended to determine when wars are moral – as if he were saying, 'Adultery is permissible provided that . . .' – but was concerned to limit the destructive effect of of war, then it made sense to restrict the right to declare war to those relatively few people who were rulers and who had the most to lose from the collapse of political stability. Secondly, if one were specifying the conditions under which it is possible to make a universalizable statement about the exceptional circumstances in which war would be (not wholly moral but) possibly justifiable, then the actions of government would be a factor which one would *have* to consider. It would not mean that one thought that violent actions of government were right. One would be saying that there were certain circumstances in which the immoral was unavoidable. And one such circumstance would be if one's lawful ruler initiated it.

In any case, it would seem that the kinds of war in which Britain is at all likely to become involved are not the kinds in which formal declarations of war are appropriate. There is the kind of fighting in which British forces are engaged at present in what is *de facto* a civil war in Northern Ireland, whatever the legalities of the situation may be. In so far as that war has been 'declared' at all, it was done not by government but by individuals. That makes it no less real, in terms of suffering and brutality. Nor is it the fact that it has not been authorized by lawful government which makes it immoral. British Christians ought to be asking themselves all those heart-searching questions which they would wish, for instance, the Czech government to ask themselves in relation to dissident movements in that country. This is what it means to universalize the issue. And even if one is convinced that British society is just and fair and that the fault lies entirely with Irish extremists, it is still essential to ask the question, 'Is there anything about the nature of British society in Northern Ireland which contributes to the violence there?' For no human society is perfect and it may be possible to improve upon it. It is very much to the credit of successive British governments that, in spite of the obvious temptation to adopt a rigid attitude on the criminality of I.R.A. activities, they have not ceased to look for what are called 'political initiatives' which might effect an improvement in the kind of society that exists in Northern Ireland. As I actually write this there has appeared a statement prepared by the Irish Roman Catholic bishops at a meeting in Maynooth in June 1981 which is a model of what an official ecclesiastical comment on a political issue ought to be. By implication the statement asks all the penetrating questions about the nature of society and does so with complete credibility precisely because it also has firm, clear and uncompromising things to say about Christian moral ideals and the ways in which members of the I.R.A. have departed from them. It is a courageous refusal to be biased in favour of one's 'own side'.

The second kind of war in which European nations are likely to become involved is also one in which formal declarations of war would be out of place. When the advocates of nuclear deterrence proudly say that that policy has preserved peace for nearly forty years, what they really mean is that there have been no wars in *Europe* in that period, apart from internal conflicts of one kind and another, two of which have led to Russian intervention in the affairs of another communist country. But in the same period it is reckoned that there have been about 150 wars, mostly in the countries of the Third World. In some of these the nuclear powers of both East and West have been present as 'advisers' or have sent 'volunteer' troops or have supplied the protagonists with arms. They have seldom been formally at war. Their involvement has been at second hand. One is tempted to say that the cost of peace in Europe has, at least partly, been the way in which rivalries between East and West have been played out through other and less powerful nations.

In such a situation the danger is that, because the involvement is at second hand, there is no formal declaration of war and, therefore, the government does not have to account for its actions with the same thoroughness. It can slip into war, justifying what it is doing inch by inch. It is true, of course, that Vietnam demonstrated that a people which has ceased to trust its government and has deep-seated doubts about both the morality and the practicality of war, can make the prosecution of that war impossible. But it took a very long time for questions about the nature of a society which acts in such a manner to take effect. And in Russia those questions are hardly asked at all. No sensitive person can fail to be aware of and sympathize with the difficulties faced by the Orthodox Church in Russia. One can understand why ecclesiastical leaders may feel that it is more important to secure the existence of the Church and its ability to worship publicly and to seek to influence affairs, if at all, in an unobtrusive way.[5] But history, if there is any, is almost bound to ask why the Russian Church has so seldom been willing to make any statement about the morality of what its government does. It is true, of course, that a state which claims to be Marxist and atheist will feel that there is no particular reason why it should behave in a manner which conforms to Christian ideals. It could be said that the very existence of a Church within such a society constitutes a critique of it. But what can it mean to claim that one is committed to truth, love, mercy and justice if one never protests against political acts which express untruth, hatred, revenge and injustice?

The principle of universalisability still applies, however, and if one expects Russian Christians to be open in their criticism of their own society, then one must expect Christians to be equally critical in and of the West. It is not enough simply to say that everything is to be left in the hands of government. The peculiarly difficult position of a Christian in a Western democracy forbids that sort of evasion of responsibility.

It might be argued that if a society is involved in fighting a war, that war is a 'given' and is, therefore, part of the givenness, the providential character of government which we saw to be so marked a feature of the New Testament view of things. And it may be that war has sometimes to be accepted as the best that we can manage. Providence is not, however, an easy matter to deal with theologically. Calvin was able to make a distinction between special providence and general or universal providence, which is God's rule over the universe not in the sense of 'some blind ambiguous motion' but a watching over each of his creatures. To the latter belong the alternation of day and night, winter and summer. To the former, God's direction of events in the lives of men and nations.[6]

Such a theory is not always easy to maintain in practice, even on its own terms. When modern historians draw attention to the apparent contradictions between William Wilberforce's unremitting fight against the slave-trade and his acceptance of a great many obvious inequities in the social structure of eighteenth- and early nineteenth-century England,[7] they are really drawing attention to the latent difficulties in his theology of providence. Wilberforce, of course, believed in original sin and, therefore, in the imperfectibility of society. He also knew very well that many social ills were the direct result of actual and particular sins. While the first may have to be, in a sense, accepted, the second must always be condemned. But in dealing with imperfectible society, if one believes in special providence, it is almost impossible to determine with any certainty when society is as it is because God has made it so and when it is so because God has not yet made it anything else.

In the context of nineteenth-century developments in the understanding both of the causal network of the natural order of things and of the nature of history, it is not surprising that even deeply committed Christians, concerned with the condition of society, should come to think of providence, as a whole, much more in terms which Calvin would have thought appropriate to general rather than to special providence. Even William Temple often wrote of the way in which the British Empire had been given peculiar responsibilities by providence.[8] But he seems to mean by this that *that* was the way in which history had turned out. He did not mean that God had intervened to determine the contents of the treaty of Utrecht, when France resigned her sovereignty in Newfoundland in 1713, or the outcome of the battle of Omdurman, which led to the Sudan becoming an Anglo-Egyptian dependency in 1898. Indeed, provided one does not take a determinist view of history and makes room for the contribution of individuals to the course of events, there seems to be no real alternative to some such general view of providence. Maintaining a belief in God as a God concerned in history (which seems so clearly a part of the biblical concept of God) appears to necessitate something like the kaleidoscope model proposed in an earlier chapter. God acts through the perpetual subtle shifts of events, themselves the consequence of human freedom, creating the pattern through the lenses and mirrors of meaning which he adds to the raw material of historical contingency.

We may legitimately side with the contextualists, then, in regarding war (however much we may be appalled by it) as part of the givenness of history, like the givenness of government itself. We might even say that the New Testament teaching about obedience to the given authority constitutes a *prima facie* case for our acceptance of an obligation (conscription, say) which government may lay upon us as a consequence of war. But this does not exhaust the Christian response to the given context. For we should have to say, as Tertullian would have insisted, that that obligation was not absolute. Conscience might require us to criticize or even disobey – easier said than defined in practice, hence the fascination of the concept of a just war.

In deciding when one ought to embark upon conscientious criticism and objection, there seem to be three considerations particularly to be borne in mind in the light of the way in which the argument of these lectures has developed up to this point.

If law and morality are different kinds of obligation – if sin and crime are not, that is to say, the same thing – then, though I may use an appeal to morality to explain why I cannot obey the law, I cannot use it to evade the sanction which the law attaches to crime. Obedience to conscience is not a reason for pleading that I should not be punished for refusing to obey the law. The furthest I can go, in fact, in fulfilling my lawful responsibility to society is to go to prison as society requires. That is the simple and obvious corollary of Tertullian's argument and explains why martyrdom figures so prominently in it.

Secondly, there is Bonhoeffer's point that our role in modern society (itself part of the givenness of history) is a peculiarly difficult one. Government is no longer simply a given: we have a responsibility for it. When one has a share, however, small, in the genesis and perpetuation of a law, simple obedience to that law does not exhaust one's responsibility towards it. One has an obligation not only to attempt to change it but to refuse to condone it, if one believes it to be immoral. And the same general point can be made in regard to government as a whole. Not only does one have an obligation to attempt to change government policies and actions which are morally wrong but there is something peculiarly immoral in requiring, encouraging or even permitting, other people to do immoral things on our behalf, even if they enjoy doing them. This we saw in connection with the hypothetical Home Secretary in chapter 2 – and, of course, the argument would apply not only to government but to those other citizens whom I would, in effect, be allowing to fight the war on my behalf if I became a conscientious objector.

One also has to make a careful distinction, in considering one's own role and one's own givenness, between one's conscience and one's sensibilities. It is one thing to say that I cannot fight because I believe I should be behaving immorally and quite another thing to say that I cannot fight because, temperamentally, I do not like the idea.

In the 1870s the Church of Scotland established a mission station at Blantyre in east Africa. Through the influence of a Dr MacRae, its early leaders regarded themselves as 'a Christian colony exercising a civil jurisdiction'. They did so because no 'civilized' power at that time claimed sovereignty over the area and they argued that local African authority was uncertain. Misguided and implicitly arrogant though their attitude now seems, the system worked well enough until a murder was committed on the mission station. After much agonising the missionaries decided that the murderer must be executed – not just to maintain discipline but because they believed that morality required it. The story is littered with what Bernard Williams would call 'morally disagreeable' features, and the execution itself was an appallingly horrible occasion. The leading missionaries were determined that the mission station as a whole should accept responsibility for what was done. How far they actually took part in the killing of the murderer themselves is not certain, but they were present and directed the whole thing. In effect the man was gradually shot to death because no one had the nerve or the competence to do it quickly and effectively. We may recognize that the missionaries were correct in their perception that the responsibility was theirs – whoever actually fired the shot. We may also wish that, however distorted their moral sense, they had employed an efficient executioner with a steadier nerve for the task.[9] In that sense, alone, I may sometimes have to leave the task to someone else.

One has an obligation to be sure that it is conscience and not merely temperamental distaste that leads one to conclude that war, so far from being an unavoidable necessity nor an inescapable 'given', is simply an unqualified evil. But if it is such an evil, then one would be obliged to do everything one could – however little effect that might have – to oppose it.

In the third kind of war – possible, but unlikely to be formally declared by lawful authority – the opposing will have to be done in advance if it is to be done at all. For the third kind of war is nuclear war and it is extremely unlikely that we shall have any opportunity to register dissent effectively once such a war begins. The whole strategy of nuclear armaments depends upon a kind of poker-playing. It is argued that the only hope of persuading other nations not to destroy us is, not that we could beat them in the long run, but that we possess the capacity to devastate them, in our own dying spasm, with an equally savage reprisal. One super-power might launch an attack, and the other an almost instantaneous counter-attack, capable of wiping out the other forty times over – or (if a limitations agreement is accepted) perhaps only twenty times over. We are no longer talking of war as a process but as a momentary and cataclysmic thing in which there will be no time to ask whether justice is on our side. Measured arguments from defence experts seem to assume that it will be possible for there to be a gentleman's agreement not to escalate from conventional to nuclear warfare or from tactical to global use of nuclear weapons. Perhaps in the middle ages, when the Church had the moral authority to act as a sort of Test and County Cricket Board and outlaw certain forms of warfare, such an agreement might have been possible. There seems now to be no such authority, except the fear of reprisals. So one has this sense, whether justified or not, of bluff and double-bluff in which the continual intensification of deterrents, in itself, takes the world nearer potential disaster, total and instantaneous. And this makes the concept of war something qualitatively different from what it was half a century ago.

If nuclear war comes, then, it will come without our being consulted. Because bluff (that is, lying) is such an essential part of the system, we shall not know whether the truth is available to us. We are called upon, in effect, to trust the government. And we are in no position to know whether we are justified in doing so – except that government, any government, has a record. For that reason we have very good grounds for knowing whether government is, in general, trustworthy. A government which has been open and honest, concerned for the good of all sections of society and for the general peace and welfare of the international community, is more likely to earn our trust than a government which has stridently advocated chauvinist policies, rattled the sabre, obscured itself behind unnecessary secrecy and mystification and earned a reputation for manipulation and trickery. Even if there were not other good reasons, this fact alone ought to convince Christians that they must be concerned about political affairs and the morality of the political actions performed in their name. When the crisis comes, it will be too late for moral judgements.

In this connection Britain's possession of an independent nuclear deterrent is obviously one of the issues that everyone concerned about political morality is compelled to consider. To possess nuclear weapons is to accept that they may be used, however much one may hope that they will not. The need to examine moral issues in advance, therefore, requires one to consider the moral implications of nuclear weaponry now.

Unfortunately the British tradition that defence and foreign policy are non-partisan issues makes it very difficult for an informed and serious public discussion of the issue to take place. It would plainly be silly to expect there to be an open discussion of the weapons themselves. Military secrets are necessary. Nor could one expect, in the field of foreign policy, that British *intentions* in specific circumstances should be made public. But *objectives* in foreign policy are a different matter. It was wholly understandable, in the nineteenth century and the first part of the twentieth, that foreign policy should be taken out of the area of party political debate. War was then still an extension of diplomacy. One could use it to achieve the objectives which negotiation failed to achieve. This still happens in certain kinds of war. It took a decade of civil war in Rhodesia before the white inhabitants of the country were willing to accept the necessity for serious negotiation at all. But nuclear war cannot be an extension of diplomacy in that sense. It is most likely to happen in circumstances where force or the threat of force is used in the hope of obtaining an international objective and the bluff is called (that is to say, the lie is not believed). It will be the end of diplomacy as well as the result of its failure. Under those circumstances the objectives of foreign policy are of vital concern to the whole country, yet it is a curious fact that, though economic policies loom large in party manifestos on the ground that they are vital to the country's future, foreign policy has so far largely remained outside the party debate. The result of this bi-partisan approach to foreign policy and defence has been that the debate tends to be conducted by, on the one hand, those who are associated with what might be called the establishment and, on the other, by those who can be dismissed as the lunatic fringe. Accusations of Blimp-like insensitivity or fellow-travelling naivety prevent the discussion from becoming serious and respectable. Almost the only foreign policy objective in recent years which has been the subject of informed, vigorous and public debate has been Britain's membership of the Common Market. Foreign policy as a whole may need the same kind of official framework if it is to be given the serious attention it deserves.

Under present circumstances it is extremely difficult to know how to assess the situation. On the one hand those who press for unilateral nuclear disarmament can very easily be made to seem to be naive and well-intentioned dupes of Communist propaganda. It does seem naive to imagine that to render oneself defenceless is the realistic way to meet the threat of nuclear destruction. But to the impartial observer, the arguments of the establishment seem to have become equally naive. There is something redolent of John Buchan, Dornford Yates and *The Boy's Own Paper* in a simplistic division of the world into bad Russians and decent Englishmen and in a patriotism that over-rides everything else, glorifies courage for its own sake and asserts that we have to be powerful in our own defence even if it leads eventually to a total destruction. It is to escape from this opposition of caricatures that serious discussion is so necessary.

Questions need to be asked, not only about whether it *is* clear that the Russian objective is world domination, but also about why that objective must be resisted at all costs. That is a question that is seldom asked and, when asked, the answer is assumed to be self-evident. An open discussion of the issue might bring other possible answers to light but – as it seems to me – there are three reasons which one might give for asserting that, if Russia is seeking world domination, one ought to resist that objective at the risk of a nuclear war. One is that communism threatens our present partly-capitalist economy and that the grey drab society and the lack of individual opportunity, which seems such a feature of eastern bloc countries, is far less desirable than our present way of life. That leads to two further areas in which we need to be informed: what is life really like behind the 'iron curtain' and what is life really like for other sections of our own society? And then the crucial question we have to be willing to face up to is whether a preference for the kind of economy and society we have is a sufficiently powerful reason for accepting the possibility of almost total destruction rather than allow it to be replaced by a communist system.

The second possible reason is sheer patriotism. Britain is entitled to remain British and not be over-run by any foreign power and, for that reason alone, has a moral right and duty to defend herself. But, if we are talking of moral duties, the principle of universalizability applies and Britain has not always been so certain of the rights of other peoples to their own independence. A hundred years ago it was Britain which seemed to be acquiring, if not blatantly seeking, world domination. It was argued, of course, that she governed other people for their own good and, in fact, a case can be made for saying that many of them did benefit considerably from being part of a British empire. But they did not always *wish* to be ruled by Britain. In 1879, for instance, Britain manufactured a patently dishonest reason for invading and eventually, after a notoriously disastrous defeat at Isandhlwana, conquering independent Zululand which was a threat to the stability of her hegemony in southern Africa.[10] Flowing from that naked act of aggression came the series of events which have led to the Zulu nation's present existence within South Africa. There is a Zulu 'homeland' created by the policy of *apartheid* but, under chief minister Buthelezi, it rejects even the semblance of self-government offered by South Africa because, consisting of a cluster of tiny territorial enclaves within the republic, she could not hope to be administratively (much less economically) viable. Supposing that in 1879 the Zulu people had possessed a nuclear device, would they have been justified in arguing that it was better to be dead than British? Would their present descendants – even knowing that British rule had brought them to their present condition of subservience – prefer never to have been born? The argument that it is better to be dead than red, implies a willingness to take decisions on behalf of one's great-grand-children (who may never exist if the holocaust comes). That is plainly a grave moral issue not to be treated lightly. The Zulu nation still hopes that the time may come when things will improve for them. It is at least possible to argue that for our descendants' sake it would be better to accept Russian domination, in the hope that eventually an over-stretched communist empire would be bound to collapse, than to accept immediate casualties of the order of 20,000,000 in a nuclear war.

It will be said, of course, that this is an argument for appeasement. Munich in 1938 still has a powerful emotive echo. What was wrong with appeasement in the thirties was that it allowed a powerful country to over-run small ones, one after the other, each victory feeding the ambition for others. In the light of what has happened in Afghanistan and elsewhere, the possession of nuclear weapons does not seem to provide any safeguard against precisely the same thing happening again. It only protects, at most, the countries that possess it. No one dare use such weapons to protect anyone else, a point to which we shall have to return.

The third reason for resisting Russian domination is the important one (though, of course, the reasons are not mutually exclusive: the real reason may be a combination of all three). We may believe that communism, in practice if not in theory, produces an inhuman and immoral system which subordinates persons to the state machine, and uses propaganda, lies and subterfuge, brutalities and 'dirty tricks' to maintain that subordination. If that is the case, then it may be true that anything is better than to allow such a system to spread to one's own country. One would be talking about human values and, as someone who has deliberately chosen to live in Britain, I am bound to say that the values displayed by British society are very well worth defending. Even those things that the rest of the western world tends to deride as British weaknesses, seem to me to reflect important values. That there has not been a British 'economic miracle' in the second half of the twentieth century, for instance, may be partly the result of a national feeling that there are more important things in life than productivity, growth and the drive to material success. But values cannot be defended by military force as though they were territorial boundaries. One cannot defend truth by telling lies or freedom by means of oppression. If it is the moral or human values of our present society which we wish to maintain against the encroachments of another system, that cannot be done by adopting the very methods which that system employs. It simply would not be worth destroying half Europe to defend a society which had become only marginally better than that of the enemy. A serious, vigilant concern for the condition of our own society, the values it stands for and the methods it employs is the responsibility which citizenship thrusts upon the Christian in a democracy.

I have to confess that there are least two aspects of the policy of nuclear deterrence whose moral implications disturb me.

The first draws together several issues which have already been raised in this chapter and can best be illustrated by means of a series of letters published in *The Times* in 1981. On 28 May Lord Gladwyn wrote a long letter arguing against Britain's possessing an independent strategic nuclear deterrent, particularly the Trident missile. On the following day Lord Boyd-Carpenter replied with what was later described[11] as a 'very succinct and imaginative' question: 'If Poland or Afghanistan possessed an independent and effective nuclear weapon would the one be in danger of invasion and the other suffering from it?' It took a surprisingly long time for anyone to point out the obvious weakness in Lord Boyd-Carpenter's implicit argument, but on 8 June Lieutenant-General Sir John Cowley wrote, 'This question appears to mean that the best (or only) way for small countries to avoid invasion or the danger of invasion is for each of them to possess an independent and effective nuclear weapon. This is a strange way to ensure a peaceful future for the world.'

It would, indeed, be a strange way to attempt to ensure peace and the logic of the general's riposte is really that the only way to do so would be for no one to possess nuclear weapons. Yet the nuclear powers are at present committed to the illogical and inconsistent view that the need for defence and safety justifies *them* in the possession of nuclear weapons but does not do so for other countries. This is the clear meaning of the non-proliferation treaty of 1968. That treaty, of course, did not claim to embody either a logical consistency or a moral principle. It simply tried to freeze the nuclear situation as it then was, presumably on the simple assumption that the probability of the outbreak of a nuclear war would become greater in direct proportion to the number of countries which possessed these weapons. No one was in a position to force the nuclear powers to abandon the weapons they already possessed, though they undertook to seek the end of the nuclear arms race – an undertaking that does not seem to have had any very notable effect. The treaty, in other words, attempted to maintain the *status quo* and recognized the realities of actual political power.

It is, however, very difficult for Britain to claim a *moral right and duty* to defend herself with an independent deterrent if she is not willing to grant the same moral right and duty to other nations. And there are practical difficulties in the situation, too. Small countries are not necessarily less responsible than large ones and the real danger of nuclear war is posed, not by corrupt or incompetent banana republics or excitable foreigners, but by countries with a relatively high degree of technical competence and a vigorous determination to assert their national identity. Two such countries are not signatories to the 1968 treaty – Israel and South Africa. Both are beleaguered, both almost certainly possess the ability to manufacture nuclear weapons if they do not actually possess them already, both have demonstrated their willingness to make preemptive strikes with conventional weapons against their enemies, and both have vigorously asserted a no-holds-barred determination to preserve themselves in spite of world opinion. It is even possible that the real reason why neither country has so far used nuclear weapons is that in neither case is the enemy one with large urban centres of population whose destruction would have a paralysing effect. The invention of tactical nuclear weapons may create a totally different situation.

As Lord Carver, former Chief of Defence Staff, has repeatedly said, it would be an irresponsible British government that would use nuclear weapons if the United States had not done so. But Britain's determination to retain an independent deterrent must inevitably appear to be, at least in part, a determination to retain the right to *use* the weapons independently also. It is, in other words, an assertion that no one else can really be relied upon to put themselves in jeopardy in order to defend or revenge us. Yet that is precisely what the non-proliferation treaty asks signatories who do not possess nuclear weapons to accept. If Britain has a moral right to possess an independent deterrent, the principle of universalizability would seem to suggest that other nations have similar moral rights. If Britain is morally justified in claiming to decide for herself when the moment has come in which the threat to her national identity is so great that nuclear weapons ought to be used, are not Israel and South Africa justified in making a similar claim? Is Britain in a qualitatively different position or is it just that she already has the power and no one else (except possibly Russia and America in alliance) could compel her to surrender it? It would seem to be self-interest and an appeal to the brute facts of existing power rather than any real moral principle which is being invoked. It could be said that Britain is, in fact, happy for smaller, poorer or weaker nations to be deprived of weapons which she herself is determined to retain but cannot actually use, and is not prepared to threaten to use, when war or aggression looms over countries outside Europe. It is a position which it is very difficult to defend on moral grounds.

The other disturbing moral implication of nuclear deterrents does not apply quite so particularly to Britain. It seems to me to be undoubtedly immoral for any nation which has been attacked and paralysed by nuclear weapons to retaliate with an equally destructive counter-attack when that counter-attack could neither prevent defeat nor obviate further damage. It would be revenge, pure and simple, and be indefensible in terms of any system of morality whatsoever. Yet this is precisely the basis of the policy of Mutually Assured Destruction (with the sardonic acronym MAD) which since the early 1960s has been one of the principal features of peace through deterrence. A widely distributed official publication of the British Ministry of Defence says that, once Russia acquired nuclear missiles which could reach the United States, each side

> . . . has the ability to survive a surprise 'first strike' nuclear attack and be able afterwards to hit back with a 'second strike' capability. It is in this second strike role that missiles launched from nuclear submarines are particularly important, since submarines can hide in the depths of the sea and avoid the effects of surprise nuclear attack. Accordingly it became clear to both sides that if either of them used nuclear weapons against the other massive retaliation could follow.[12]

Indeed the first Strategic Arms Limitation Treaty between Russia and America of 1972 (SALT 1) specifically provided that each of the signatories should have one nuclear weapon site which was protected from nuclear attack by anti-ballistic missiles so as to ensure that it would be able to retaliate after a first strike attack.

Mutually assured destruction, itself an immoral concept by any standards, is therefore one of the implications of accepting the idea that deterrence is the only way in which peace can be preserved. It may be, of course, that no government would actually be so immoral as to put it into practice. But the only alternative to doing so is to persuade not only one's enemies but one's own people that one would. The only way to avoid having to indulge in a grossly immoral act is to lie convincingly about one's willingness to do so. That is, in itself, immoral. One will need to back it up with other acts of ruthlessness and belligerence if one is to be convincing and those acts may be immoral. One will also inevitably raise doubts in the minds of one's own people and one's allies that, if one is prepared to lie in this matter, one may already be lying to them in a whole range of others – for their own good, of course. This seems clearly the end of the road along which power politics without morality has been travelling. Either one has to accept that an appallingly immoral action must be performed or to accept, as the only alternative, a world of dishonesty where even one's friends are not to be trusted. On such a choice between two evils the future peace of the world depends.

What ought the response of the Christian to be to such a situation? He or she may not be in very much doubt about which is actually the lesser of those two particular evils but, as I have already argued,[13] there is all the difference in the world between the reluctant acceptance of a necessary evil in an imperfectible world and the willingness to embrace that evil as an acceptable way of life. The current insistence of many Germans that the stationing of nuclear weapons upon their territory is only tolerable if it is accompanied by an open and determined commitment to negotiate arms limitations, is wholly right. There have been Christian moralists who have sought to use the so-called 'doctrine of necessity' to argue that 'a state which renounced [nuclear weapons] would be failing in its duty to the people it was bound to defend'.[14] But not only would this imply, as I have tried to show, that every non-nuclear nation was failing in its duty by signing the non-proliferation treaty and renouncing nuclear weapons, but the 'doctrine of necessity' means just what its name implies. It means that something which is *prima facie* wrong can be justified *if there is absolutely no alternative*. I should not be justified in stealing bread to feed my children (which is my duty) unless there was no other choice open to me. Merely to say that I had lost my job would not provide me with moral justification unless I had also tried to obtain money or food from friends, social security or organized charity.

There is, moreover, a sense of the interim about any attempt to plead necessity. I may have to steal today because my children are really starving and I have tried every possible alternative source of food or money. But I would not be justified in continuing to steal tomorrow and the next day and every day thereafter for ten or twenty years unless I continued to search rigorously every day for another way of feeding them. Those of us who have lived under a regime which we regarded as immoral and oppressive know very well what a burden this sense of the interim places upon the conscience. One of the traditional conditions of the just war is that one shall have tried every other alternative first. If one attempts to transfer this requirement to the question whether one is justified in using force against an immoral regime, one quickly discovers that it is a test which is less easy to apply than it sounds. At first sight one imagines that what one needs is a check-list of alternatives – negotiation, protest, civil and passive disobedience and so on. Then one could try each in turn and when one has crossed them all off the list one would be left with violence as the only alternative. But one quickly discovers that it does not work like this. To have negotiated for six months and found that conversation to end in deadlock, does not mean that a new discussion begun the next day, is hopeless. I have never, myself, reached a position in which I could honestly say there was no alternative. One may talk, protest and disobey for years without reaching a point where there is no possibility that one more meeting, one more placard might do the trick. If the doctrine of necessity is invoked to justify the retention of nuclear weapons it is only morally tolerable if it is accompanied by a *continued and persistent* search for alternatives.

As a Christian I believe that the central significance of the cross and resurrection means that the right thing to do in our present situation is to hold fast to truth and forgiveness rather than to the lies and vengefulness upon which Mutually Assured Destruction seems to depend. Victory, I am convinced, is not to be found by being more powerful than anyone else but by being true to the values and ideals of Christ. But because most of the other inhabitants of this country do not share that conviction I cannot require them to follow that path and accept the undoubted suffering that would be involved. This is not only because I might be wrong or because I lack the courage to press my convictions upon them. The problem is that they must themselves be convinced. One cannot, as I shall argue in the final chapter, compel morality. Nor can one be forgiving or generous on someone else's behalf. One can crucify someone else without their willing co-operation; one cannot bring them through the suffering of the cross to the joy of the resurrection if they do not believe in the reality of that resurrection. However sure I may be, then, of the right course of action, I am in the position of the writers whom I quoted at the beginning of the previous chapter. Until the whole of society is converted, I cannot expect it to accept my understanding of the right course to take. Nor can I, however, just be content to say that necessity compels me to accept that disaster to which force, vengefulness and lying rapidly seem to be bringing the world. I have to go on looking for alternatives and, since I hold no position of political power, I have to use such influence as I have to persuade governments and potential governments to look for alternatives also. That means encouraging discussion and debate, insisting on being informed so far as I can, asking disturbing questions and compelling other people to face up to the implications of the position we are in. For it seems to me that Christian moral values quite simply forbid one to accept complacently that there *is* no alternative. Meanwhile I have to accept upon my conscience the burden of the knowledge that there is a right way and that I have not been able to follow it.

That seems to me to be my role as an individual Christian through whom the body of Christ is 'earthed' in the world, in the sense described in chapter 6. Other Christians may see their role rather differently. In so far as their responsibilities are different from mine, perhaps they are bound to do so. The actual Church – using the term to mean those ecclesiastical leaders, those organs of denominational institutions and those local congregations of faithful Christians, who in some sense claim to speak for, and approximate to, the true body of Christ – has again a different role. That role, referring back once more to chapter 6, is primarily one of speaking, of teaching, of enunciating what are the true moral values. Inevitably that will force the Church into a negative and critical role. It has to say that this or that feature of current policy is clearly immoral – if it is. The Church ought not, as I have argued, to allow itself to be bullied out of that critical stance by demands that it shall propose alternative policies. That is not its business *qua* Church. Governments alone are in a position to formulate specific policies. But, as the previous chapter maintained in the case of Mr Jenkin and the British Churches, what the Church does have a duty to do is to spell out the cost of present policy and of alternative policies – not just financial cost but cost in terms of human suffering and of the destruction of human values, so that society can make decisions with its eyes open.

Neither the individual Christian nor 'the Church' is likely to make itself popular by adopting these roles. No one likes either the prophet of doom or the perpetual critic. But the amoral politics of power has shown itself bankrupt by bringing the world to the position in which the only way in which peace can be preserved, precariously and at best for one continent alone, is by a policy of guaranteeing that each side can destroy the other several times over. In the face of that bankruptcy it may be time for those who believe in absolute moral values to say so uncompromisingly.

Notes

1. A recent book which I have found particularly useful is B. Paskins and M. Dockrill, *The Ethics of War*, Duckworth 1979; and also M. Walzer, *Just and Unjust Wars*, Allen Lane 1978.
2. *Summa Theologica*, II–II. qu.40, art.1.
3. J. Mahoney, 'The Difficulties of Defining a "Just War" in the Nuclear Age', *The Times*, 21 February 1981.
4. See p. 87.
5. For an essentially sympathetic but critical account of co-operation between one influential Russian ecclesiastic and the state see W. C. Fletcher, *Nikolai: Portrait of a Dilemma*, Collier-MacMillan 1968, particularly pp. 98ff. and 110ff.
6. *Institutes*, I, xvi, 4 and 5.

7. E.g. R. Furneaux, *William Wilberforce*, Hamish Hamilton 1974, p. 194.
8. He seems to have believed that the very existence of nations, like families, was part of providence – see W. Temple, *Christianity and the Social Order*, S.P.C.K. (new edition) 1976, p. 64.
9. Brief accounts of the incident may be found in R. Oliver, *The Missionary Factor in East Africa*, Longmans (2nd edn) 1965, p. 95 and (a more journalistic account) G. Moorhouse, *The Missionaries*, Eyre Methuen 1973, pp. 259ff. I have myself seen the papers relating to the episode (not apparently used by either of the authors cited) in the Scottish National Library.
10. See A. Lloyd, *The Zulu War*, Hart-Davis MacGibbon 1973, pp. 16ff.; and cf. W. Rees, *Colenso Letters from Natal*, Shuter and Shooter 1958, pp. 326ff.
11. In a letter by Air Chief Marshal Sir Nigel Maynard published on 6 June 1981.
12. *Deterrence*, Defence Fact Sheet 3, April 1981.
13. See p. 66.
14. Canon E. C. Bentley in a letter to *The Times*, 8 January 1980.

9

CHRISTIANS, CHURCH AND POLITICS

In the first chapter of this book I cited Tertullian's interpretation of the famous verse (Matthew 22:21) which says, 'Render unto Caesar the things which are Caesar's'.[1] 'Render' is the word used by the Authorized Version to translate the Greek ἀπόδοτε. The New English Bible has 'pay what is due' and the Jerusalem Bible says 'give back'. This last is a perfectly straightforward translation of the Greek word. It captures the sense which the New English Bible seeks also to express – the proper payment of what is due – but it adds the hint that due payment is a matter of returning something to the source from which it came. We have seen how Tertullian thought that we were under an over-riding obligation to give ourselves back to God, because we are coins bearing the image of the coiner. With that it is difficult for any Christian to disagree. However we may interpret it, the only absolute claim upon us is God's.

But there is also, surely, a sense in which it is proper for us to 'give back' to society. 'Give back' is the right term to use for, just as we owe the whole of ourselves to God because he has made us as we are, so we might be said to owe much of what we are to society and thus to have a duty to give back part of ourselves to society. Moreover, the way in which God has created us what we are, has included placing us in society. Society has been one of the means he has used in the process. It is not a separate sphere. He is the Lord also of society. So it may be true that we partly give ourselves back to God by giving ourselves to society. Provided, then, that we remember that society's claim is not an absolute one, there is an obligation to give back what we owe to society for our education, our protection, our medical treatment, our transport and all the other less obvious, less tangible ways in which it plays a part in making us what we are. And putting it like that reminds us that society's part in the making of us is far more obvious now than it was when the New Testament was written.

But, as soon as one says it, it is clear that this is far too simple a statement of the position. For, if we are partly created through the medium of society and if human society is imperfectible, then it will have made us in *its* image, too – an imperfect one. It is necessary for us to be critical of society, to measure it against standards and values, and not simply accept it on its own terms. A vision of a nice, kind, motherly society which looks after us and deserves our devoted service is a little too good to be true. And, if it were true, it might be a little too much like the society of Huxley's *Brave New World*. Reality is more difficult to capture and the difficulty arises precisely because we are so much a part of society that talking about ourselves over against society in itself distorts what ought to be said. If society is imperfect, we are imperfect. Therefore it is true that we are corrupted by society, in one sense. But this does not imply that, detached from society, we could be uncorrupted. Detached from society we should actually be inhuman. In another sense we are society and are no more corrupted by it than we are corrupted by being born. It is we who make society what it is just as much as it makes us what we are.

So there can be no question of our giving an uncritical service to society. We, as society, have done some terrible things to ourselves. One has only to walk through a partly-derelict inner-city area where unemployment is high and boredom and fear are the prevalent features of life to appreciate that. We have to insist upon asking questions and rejecting some of the answers that we have been happy to accept in the past. Being critical is, in fact, one of the ways in which we give ourselves back to society, not grudgingly but positively as part of the giving back of ourselves to God. Loving our neighbours is, after all, part of, not separate from, loving God. A degree of political seriousness, a concern for what is happening to society, an involvement with the way it develops, is the very least we can give. Niebuhr was plainly right. A Christian who does not care about what actually happens in the political sphere, who does not lift a finger to do anything practical about it, is not really a Christian at all. But the problem is still as Niebuhr saw it to be. The very evils of society demand that Christians shall act; political problems require real, political solutions; political solutions seldom if ever measure up to Christian ideals; what can be done for imperfectible society must never be absolutized. Or, to put this in another way, if Christians are motivated in their concern for society by their sense that society is or ought to be, not a separate sphere, but part of God's realm, then they will judge what they ought to give back to society in terms of their Christian vision of good. That will make them critical of society but they will also quickly find that the practicalities seem to demand continual compromise over what they believe to be the absolute standards of goodness.

On the basis of the argument already set out in this book, there are two points to be made about this restatement of the central problem. Firstly, the ideal (if stated as a general principle) will be incapable of defining the conditions under which it may itself be abrogated: the general principle is nevertheless, and must continue to be regarded as, the statement of what is right. When compromise cannot be avoided, I ought to say not 'I have to do it, so it is right', nor 'It is wrong so I cannot do it under any circumstances', but 'It is, in principle, wrong but I may nevertheless have to do it.'

Secondly, we are often not even presented with a clear choice between obeying God and obeying men. Our responsibility to society derives from both our concern for our neighbour and from that sense of providence which regards history as a given to be used in the service of God. A responsibility to society is, at least in part, subsumed under a responsibility to God. We are often, therefore, in precisely the position defined in what has classically been called the doctrine of the perplexed conscience, when it is not even at all clear which *is* the lesser of two evils. We are not able to tell where our primary duty lies.

With those two considerations in mind, one needs to return next to the givenness or providentiality of history. That idea applies in two different ways.

First: it is no good wishing that history had been other than it is. It has happened. It is there. Christians are not required to come up with some blueprint of the perfect society, worked out in terms of abstract moral principles and their doctrinaire political application. The very imperfectibility of societies composed of fallen human beings forbids that. The problems faced by society are given by history and so, at least to some extent, are the possible solutions. History has no real beginnings. Nor, therefore, does politics. A degree of contextualism is wholly proper. What one can say is that, of the apparent solutions on offer, this one or that seems better. But one's assessment of what is 'better' will, if one is a Christian, be determined not simply by the contextualists' (actually impossible) criterion of what is demanded by the facts. It will be determined by the values of Christianity. And here compromise, in David Owen's sense of moving society in the right direction,[2] may be all we can hope to achieve.

Secondly: part of the givenness of history is one's own role in society; and one's actual role is, as we have seen, of primary importance in determining the moral obligations which one has to shoulder. We have a role, as we have also seen, which is peculiarly difficult. Since we are voters, obedience to the law does not exhaust our responsibilities as citizens. Moreover, the fact that, as Christians, selfishness is forbidden to us also compels us *not* to ask what would suit our own purposes best. The real question is what would help to move society in the direction suggested, at that moment, by Christian values. We have no business asking other and more selfish questions, in spite of the fact that every political party will be trying to tempt our allegiance by means of a package designed to appeal to self-interest. Even the fact that no party may seem in the least concerned about the real good of society does not excuse political apathy. Sloth is a deadly sin, in politics as elsewhere, because it may allow evil to win at the polls.

There is another aspect of our own givenness: for some Christians being a voter and a citizen is not enough. Their own gifts, abilities and natural interests will move them to a far greater degree of involvement in public service or political action as professionals. I have no intention of elaborating on the question of how a Christian responds to this vocation. I have never experienced the particular pressures: it would be impossible to talk sensibly about how one tries to live a Christian life when subject to them. It must be both difficult and demanding and I am intensely grateful that there are Christians willing to accept what seems to me to be an appallingly costly but vital role. If they are – and wish to remain – committed Christians, selfishness, pride, ambition and the desire for power are things which they must find themselves wrestling with every day. Moreover, if what one believes and one's morality are as directly related as I have argued in chapter 3 then Christian engagement in political life is possible only on the basis of a convinced understanding of the atonement and what it says about the necessity of suffering and failure – of passion, in effect. For political importance does not excuse sin, as Ambrose told Theodosius, and in the last resort the Christian cannot be committed to party, economic or social class, or even the nation, but to the values expressed in the life, teaching and death of Jesus Christ. The Christian politician's role, like that of the Christian voter, is a vehicle for those values.

This does not mean that as voters, politicians or public servants our duty is to enforce a 'Christian' moral code by law. I have already implied in chapter 3 that one cannot actually compel anyone to *be* moral.[3] One can only stop him *doing* things one regards as immoral. Many of those actions one will seek to forbid, anyway, as damaging to others and some of them one may wish to prevent as damaging to himself. There are those who hold that there are certain things – like abortion, euthanasia and duelling – which no one would wish to make illegal if they did not object to them on purely moral or religious grounds. But even here, it seems to me, there are good reasons (quite apart from religious or moral convictions) for laws on these matters. The quite practical need to protect the weaker from the stronger seems, in some degree or other, to apply to them all.

Basil Mitchell, while arguing with some force that no one can be made moral by law, has argued that laws forbidding immoral behaviour may be useful in an educational sense.[4] People grow up in a context in which certain things are regarded as wrong because the law frowns on them. They are less likely to do them and thus grow into a better kind of person. This seems to me a more forceful argument. But there are two problems. One is that examples of this kind of thing – laws against drunken driving, for instance, which Mitchell cites – are usually justifiable on very practical grounds irrespective of moral or religious convictions. The other is that Christian moral education is much more concerned – as the parable of the sheep and goats shows[5] – with positives than negatives. Could one have a law compelling every citizen to visit prisoners or feed the hungry? The real work of moral education has to be done in some other way.

The Christian has to be concerned with 'moving' society in a much deeper and more positive sense. Since it is with the corporate that politics is concerned, the Christian in politics will not use the law to enforce private moral standards upon private individuals. Rather the aim will be to create a society in which the weak are protected, the casualties are cared for, everyone has some say in what happens to him, no one is denied justice or the necessities of life, and everyone feels that he has the opportunity to contribute. In the creation of that sort of society the Christian politician has the crucial role and the real responsibility. As a member of a party which hopes to provide the country's government and which has, therefore, a potential opportunity to formulate actual policies, he or she has chosen that role and responsibility. No one else can actually make that kind of concrete change in real political terms.

The burden of Christian moral education, on the other hand, is to be borne by the Church rather than by the political legal system. Of course, when the two were indistinguishable it probably was the duty of the state to assert Christian moral truths. There is something peculiarly distasteful about the promulgation of laws which contradict a specific moral character consciously *claimed* by the nation. Thus John X. Merriman, premier of the Cape Colony in the period immediately before the creation of the Union of South Africa, protested bitterly against the constitutional bill which, in its first clause, claimed that the new state would be a Christian state and then proceeded to enshrine the colour bar in subsequent clauses.[6] But most modern states claim to be no more than secular, neutral and pluralist (and Britain must be regarded as one of these in spite of the existence of established churches in some parts of it). Such a state is unlikely to claim a duty to teach its citizens Christian moral truths.

I have argued in earlier chapters that it is the function of the actual Church to assert the absolute claims of holiness. I have also argued that it may not always be possible to say that there is, even in principle, a wholly right course of action in a difficult situation. This is not the same thing as saying that there is no such thing as right and wrong. It is possible both to say that there is such a thing as absolute truth and also that in given circumstances one has no alternative but to lie. Formulating rules, however, about when to lie, is virtually the same thing as saying that one ought to lie and that cannot be a desirable moral principle. The exception must not prove to *be* the rule.

This, I think, is why the churches have such intractable problems about divorce. Christian morality differs from most ethical systems in that it is concerned to assert ideals. The ideal in marriage is the life-long, loving, caring faithfulness of one man and one woman. But no marriage is perfect. Every husband and wife are sometimes desperately unloving. Equally, some divorces are followed by second marriages which are recognisably good, Christian marriages. No one has yet found a way of including the exceptions within a formal assertion of the ideal, without appearing to deny it. The best anyone can do is to provide pastoral ways of dealing with the exceptions and even those involve implicitly (or in some cases explicitly, as in the Eastern Churches) an admission of sin, that is of one's departure from the ideal. In the sphere of politics when the institutional church speaks officially, and thus implicitly claims to speak *qua* Church, its business is to teach the ideal, to assert the truth. It may have to deal pastorally with the problems and the exceptions, advising and providing help in making the difficult personal judgements that general principles cannot cope with. But it cannot proclaim these exceptions as part of the ideal: it can only recognize them as unavoidable departures from it.

The problems raised by divorce also provide a useful analogy in another area of political morality. The question of whether politics really is a dirty game which Christians and the Church had better steer clear of is one we have looked at, in various ways, from time to time. I have argued that politics is not necessarily more corrupt or corrupting than any other aspect of life. I believe that to be true. There is, however, a special difficulty for those professionally involved in it which arises from a point made a little earlier in this chapter. If society is to be moved towards the ideal, that can only be done through policies devised by a government. If Christians are to involve themselves in this work, they have to accept the restraints of party organization and party policy. Since no policy can be perfect, they have to commit themselves to a less-than-ideal. There is a sense in which they must strive, and strive vigorously, for that which is not wholly good. It must become for them a way of life not a temporary aberration. This is where there is a parallel with remarriage after divorce. The Church, in a sense, finds it easier to deal with an adulterer who sleeps with hundreds of other people than with a divorced person, whose first marriage having failed, tries honestly and devotedly to create a good Christian second marriage. This is not because the latter seems more wicked than the former – rather the reverse, in fact. The first person is obviously simply a sinner who can be told to come back to the ideal. What ought to be done is easily stated. The problem with the second case is that the less-than-ideal in this particular instance has had to become a way of life, a permanent state. And this is also the problem with the professional politician, the public servant or even the party member. They are honestly trying to do what they can within the given framework. Doing so involves committing themselves to what is necessarily less than perfect. The Church is bound to seem uncaring and even hypocritical when it points out the imperfections of parties. But the truth is that both Church and party have a role to play and (as in the case of the Church and the remarried divorcee) what is needed is not a new principle which will somehow manage to include its own opposite but a new, more honest and clearer way of seeing how the two relate to each other.

In the first chapter I said that if the Church was not prepared to go beyond negative criticism it looked as if it had no real solutions to offer to real political problems: 'We have no solutions and you mustn't have any either.'[7] That was really a false statement of the problem. The official ecclesiastical pronouncements *must* be largely content with making apparently negative criticisms of political actions and policies. That is forced upon them by theological as well as sociological considerations. No political solution can be absolute, yet the assertion of the ideal must be concerned with absolutes. And the actual Church is not sociologically or structurally equipped, as we saw when we were considering the proposal to launch a confessing Church in South Africa, to take *political* action.

The ecclesiastical leaders are admittedly in a peculiarly difficult situation for they are both official organs or agents of the Church and must assert ideals, and also individual Christians who must take conscientious political action. They usually also have a pastoral role and duty to those caught in political problems of conscience. And it is when *they* speak or act that the cry goes up that the Church should keep out of politics.

In the West German elections of 1980, Chancellor Schmidt was provoked to fury by a pastoral from the Roman Catholic bishops which seemed to be lending support to his opponents in their attack upon the mounting indebtedness of the state. Against the background of German history – the traditional alliance between the Church and the Christian Democrats and the fearful memories of the total collapse of the economy after World War 1 – the bishops were understandably suspected of prostituting ecclesiastical authority for party political advantage. But this did not seem, at least in English newspaper reports, to be what the Chancellor criticized. Instead he attacked the bishops for pretending to a theologically-guaranteed infallibility in economic affairs. And *The Times*, at that stage edging towards a muted support for Ronald Reagan and the 'moral majority' in the American election, sanctimoniously said what a pity it was that the bishops did not confine themselves to moral issues – like abortion.[8]

Since my own political views are more like those of Chancellor Schmidt than of the German bishops, I can the more vigorously assert that this is nonsense. Morality is not, as *The Times* implied, concerned only with one's private (and chiefly sexual) activities. Indebtedness (whether public or private) is a matter with many moral implications and, provided the bishops were not motivated by purely party loyalties, there was no reason at all why they should have kept silence. What would have been wrong was to have used the influence deriving from their spiritual office to manipulate their flock from motives which had nothing to do with morality. For a German bishop to tell his flock to vote for the Christian Democrats because that was where his own selfish political preference lay, would be as improper as to preach a hellfire sermon in the expectation of a bumper collection.

The real obligations resting upon Church leaders was much more fairly spelled out in another article in *The Times*[9] about the English Roman Catholic bishops and their opposition to the 1981 Nationality Bill. Though very critical of the bishops' views, the article said:

> . . . if the bishops choose to come down into the political arena with detailed political argument, they must face the same sort of criticism that can properly be levelled at politicians. [But] Of course, there are always moral and religious questions underlying

the law as it affects the behaviour of human beings to each other. . . .

That seems to me to capture very nicely the mixed status of the ecclesiastical leadership. It does not attempt to make a false distinction between the private (or moral) and the public (or political). Rather it recognizes that the moral issues require the bishops (as pastors and teachers) to take political actions and policies seriously. But the bishops are also citizens: practical and necessary expediencies are things which they have to consider, too. They must, therefore, also expect to be criticized when they act politically, not for being political but because their proposals are politically framed and therefore open to political debate.

Taking the Nationality Bill as an example, in so far as the bishops were acting as spokesmen for the Church, their job was to assert an ideal. The ideal is that all men should treat each other as neighbours, to be loved. In a sense, the whole idea of a Nationality Bill is inappropriate in the context of the Gospel. But in an imperfectible society one has to accept that there will be some degree of national exclusiveness and identity. One ought to teach the ideal relationship between man and man but an actual political policy, falling short of that ideal, need not provoke one into outright condemnation unless it openly obstructs the ideal and is plainly unjust or cruel. If it is, then one ought to condemn it. The moment, however, that one begins to say how a nationality bill *ought* to be framed, one has ceased to talk of perfection (undiscriminating love): one has accepted that a less-than-ideal is what will happen. One has ceased to play the role of 'the Church' and accepted the role of Christian citizen involved in the necessary expediencies of politics. And that is the *right* role to play in the circumstances. One must argue for the best and fairest law that can be devised and be prepared for hard knocks of criticism in the process. What one cannot do is to *commend* the less than ideal (that is, virtually any policy) uncritically.

But any Christian individual or group actively pursuing a political goal, in some degree accepts the less-than-ideal. One has to see oneself (as Augustine hinted that Theodosius ought to see himself and as Bonhoeffer plainly saw himself) as a sinner trying to do what seems best in the circumstances and continually needing forgiveness all the same. One is not looking for an ethic which will justify one's actions: one is living under the judgement of an ideal.

It is easy, of course, to dismiss this as a cheap way out. In a series of television programmes on medical ethics, a year or two ago, the participants were presented with the case of a woman who admitted to a 'mercy-killing' of her senile and incurably ill mother.

The doctors present tried to find ways of justifying the turning of a blind eye. A moral philosopher cut through the evasions with some blunt consequentialist insistence on facing the truth and accepting it as good. A clergyman said, 'I would forgive her,' and provoked a scathing sneer from the moderator of the discussion.

In fact the clergyman was both asserting the moral absolute, that one has no right to end another human life, and, at the same time, meeting the very real human needs of the woman concerned. It is something like that, it seems to me, that a Christian can offer in the world of politics. It may, indeed, be impossible to use the actual word in so direct and simple a way. The reality it represents is as practical as it is far from easy. Being forgiven requires (as we recognize whenever we say the Lord's Prayer) the willingness to forgive others. And that is neither easy nor cheap. In terms of a political career in Northern Ireland, for instance, it would almost certainly be costly and sacrificial. Nor is it out of touch with reality, as we ought to have learnt from the disastrous consequences of two world wars which ended in vindictive peace terms or an insistence on unconditional surrender.

A politics of forgiveness may not, then, be as foolish as it sounds.[10] It might be the ultimate realism, the recognition of the inevitable imperfection of society. Sin is the failure to be the ideal and we are all sinners. To those who object that it is meaningless for a man to say that X or Y is right, if he does not do it, my reply would be that *that* is only true if he *never* does it or does not *try* to do it. What is essential is the firm grasp on the ideal, the recognition that good actually is good, and a striving towards it. Without a clear sense of what is good one begins the long slow slide into corruption. One ceases to be the kind of person who will preserve his integrity, recognize the moral cost of his actions or strive to minimize it, in the practicalities of political necessity.

Yet we have to be very careful not to talk about *society* as if it sinned. In so far as what is wrong with society is the result of human sin, it is as the result of the sins of particular people. In fact the more appropriate category for discussing the failings of human society, as a whole, is original sin which is not something done but something we *are* – sinful, imperfectible. At one stroke that reminds us of the limitations set upon political action. That is one reason why I have spent these lectures talking about political morality and not about what is called political theology. Political theology is vital. It reminds us that theology and religion are public rather than private. It ought always to go with political action because individuals and groups, engaging with society as they must, need to see that their action is grounded in Christian believing. But even political theology is, in a sense, secondary to Christian living. It is also appropriate to particular people in particular situations. Beneath it lies the more fundamental problem, a permanent problem, of relating the ideal to the social.

'Political theology' is usually associated with revolutionary politics and particularly with *violent* revolutionary politics.[11] Though there is no reason why that should be the only kind of political theology, it ought not to surprise us that it is sometimes so. Christianity is a revolutionary faith – in the broad sense of the term. It is also a liberating faith – in the same broad sense. While it may be a distortion of Christianity to substitute political for spiritual goals, there are circumstances in which a down-to-earth, world-affirming religion like Christianity cannot deny the close relationship between the two, without a distortion at least as severe. Christianity is about changing people: it is impossible to change people without changing societies. Attack polygamy, for instance, which is not thought of as a politicizing move, and you attack the whole structure of a society.

Christianity also demands a kind of relationship between people which threatens the accepted patterns of social behaviour. Young men and women in Oxford have created and built Simon House, in their desire to care for those who have dropped out of our own society. Oxford is not very happy about that. 'All the undesirables are attracted here,' we are told. 'It ought to have been built in a less obvious site.' The conventional compromises we have accustomed ourselves to – 'Help the outcast provided you don't upset the respectable' – have been disconcerted. And, in really unjust and exploitative societies, it may be necessary to be more radical than that. It is seldom, I think, that radicals I have known have embraced violence for violence sake. But when a *society* is violent – when the powerful maintain themselves by force and human beings are actually suffering and dying in consequence – it is not surprising that some Christians feel themselves *driven* to fight, as well as to suffer, alongside the oppressed. Unless one is convinced that Christian teaching requires absolute pacifism at all times – and few of the critics of liberation theology are prepared to say that – it is difficult to condemn such radicals out of hand. Certainly one cannot condemn them unless one is equally prepared to judge professional politicians by the same absolute standards. Of course it cannot be *good* to kill even the tyrant and the oppressor. The crucial question is whether there really is no alternative. It is the job of political theology in such circumstances to say why no alternative is available.

It can do so in various ways, some of which involve a radical questioning of the nature of theology itself.[12] Since we are very markedly conditioned in all our thinking by the nature of the society in which we live, we may imagine ourselves to be neutral when in fact 'neutrality' is really an acceptance of the attitudes of dominant social groups. A politically neutral theology will be only too likely, then, to be a politically conditioned and prejudiced theology. The only way out of such a conditioning, it can be argued, is by being committed to the human beings who are actually made to suffer by the way in which society is organized. They are the casualties, the people who need. They, therefore, are the proper objects of a Christ-derived concern and to be committed to them, and to the struggle to obtain justice for them, is to take the first step away from socially conditioned theology.

It is to be noted that even in this most radical kind of political theology (what is called 'liberation theology') the argument is that there is no alternative available, though it takes a rather different form from the usual argument from necessity. Essentially the argument is saying that there is no alternative to radical political action because no genuine politically neutral theology is possible. It does not seek neutrality. It seeks commitment. If one is to be committed, it argues, there can be little doubt as to where one's commitment ought to be.

It is easy to sympathize with much of this thinking. One has only to remember the insipid archiepiscopal 'Call to the Nation' of the mid-seventies, with its assumption that middle-class ideals and aspirations were identifiable with the kind of society that Christians ought to seek, to recognize that 'neutrality' is all too often an unquestioning acceptance of an existing social system and its values. This is, indeed, why I have been concerned to assert repeatedly that the prime function of the Church is to ask critical questions about the nature of our society. Critical questioning is important, not because of some liberal assumption that what authority does must necessarily be wrong,[13] but because we are products of what is actually there and we will inevitably tend to assume that what exists is natural and therefore proper. Radical political theology is better than that kind of complacency.

As Kenneth Leech has recently pointed out, the crucial division is really about how one understands the kingdom of God.[14] How is it related to actual political societies? If one believes that the kingdom of God has nothing to do with any society likely to exist within history, one will be inclined to the view that it does not greatly matter what one's own society is like. And this, of course, tends to political conservatism because one need not ask many questions about the existing state of affairs: what really matters is the eternal realm. If one believes that one of the purposes for which the Church exists is to work for the coming of the kingdom on earth, then one will be concerned with political and social action in order to bring that about. And that will make one critical of society and impatient with things as they are.

No doubt, since we are all conditioned by society, my own views may be the product of conditioning. I have been largely concerned to make two points: there is a close and real connection between the kingdom of God and the actual societies in which human beings live; but the kingdom will not be wholly realized within any society. Obviously a belief of that kind will make me hesitate to take extreme (some would say 'whole-hearted') measures to bring about a change in society, for there will always be the feeling at the back of my mind that the end-product may be as much open to criticism as the society that exists now. So I am very willing to criticize but less willing to act – precisely the kind of 'neutrality' that the liberation theologians dislike. It is no accident, they would say, that I was born, brought up and lived for twenty years of my adult life in a society which seemed to me to offend blatantly and deliberately against the ideals of love, justice and truth which were taught me by my Christian faith yet was never able to convince myself that violent revolution was the only real alternative. It genuinely *seemed* to me that not only the facts of history but the doctrine of original sin made it unlikely that there would ever be a wholly good political society. But my understanding of history and of original sin may have been no more than a product of conditioning.

The assertion that we are all conditioned is one whose truth is very difficult to assess. If we are all conditioned, then so are those who say that we are all conditioned. It may be that society even creates the kind of thinking which reacts against itself, just as over-protective or very strict parents may produce rebellious children. On the other hand over-liberal parents may produce children who do not know what to rebel against and become middle-aged at seventeen. It cannot be assumed, therefore, that a refusal to conform is proof that one is escaping from conditioning. One can believe oneself to have broken free from accepted ways of thought by a great effort of the will and a rigorous intellectual analysis when all one has really done is to react emotionally. Having broken free from one kind of conformity, one is particularly vulnerable to other kinds. When one belongs to a small minority of critical dissidents, under very considerable pressure from those in power, possibly very frightened at times, always conscious of being disliked for one's opinions, the temptation to be accepted *somewhere* can be almost overwhelming. Daniel Oosthuizen, whom I have quoted elsewhere, once described it in conversation as being like the pressure exerted by an invitation to join the most exclusive club in the world. When other dissidents urge one to express solidarity (the very word is emotionally charged) with those who have taken up the armed struggle, it seems the most difficult thing in the world to dissent even from the dissidents. Hence my mistrust of small groups, basic communities, isolated from the wider Church.

All one can do is to try and be honest with oneself and clear and rigorous in one's thinking. The truth seems to me to be represented not by a divide but by a tension. The kingdom of God and the way society is organized have much to do with one another. Christians and the Church *are* to work for the coming of the kingdom on earth. but it will never be wholly realized within the framework of history as we know it. The resulting tension is very hard to live with, for human nature can commit itself most enthusiastically when it believes that the objective is within its reach. To strive for the unattainable seems demoralizing – and sometimes it seems simply to be not an available option. There seems to me to be a kind of parallel between the theoretical truth that the kingdom is to be striven for in human society but is not wholly attainable and the practical reality that when one is doing what seems to be the best one can, one is still a sinner. And that makes me suspicious of anyone – of the left, right or centre – who is absolutely certain that there is only one political goal and only one way to reach it.

The fact that it may not be possible to devise perfect policies or final solutions or ideal blue-prints, is not to say that one political programme is as good as another or that the shape of society is neither here nor there. Nor does the fact that one is a sinner mean that all the options are equally evil. Christian morality may not be able to tell one whether one ought to be a plumber or a doctor but it can tell one not to be a brothel-keeper or a paid assassin. It can also tell one what sort of plumber or doctor one ought to be. In an analogous way Christian morality makes it clear that society ought not to be cruel or unjust. It may not be able to tell one whether capitalism or socialism is the better kind of *economic* system but it can tell one what sort of capitalism or socialism one ought to aim at.

In fact, I believe, Christians really choose between capitalism and socialism on the basis of their, often unconscious, understanding of the fallenness of man (original sin, again). And this can be seen in how they treat the morality of the profit motive. If one believes that man is fallen, in a sense which sees little hope for any real goodness at all, then it is proper to make use of the very shortcomings of humanity to keep society going[15] – to appeal to the acquisitive instincts, hoping that natural checks and balances will prevent their getting out of hand. Unfettered, ruthless selfishness can hardly be disguised as moral or desirable. Nineteenth century Christians feared Darwin's evolutionary hypothesis because it seemed to sanctify just such a ruthlessness, making it appear that a morality of competition accorded with the laws of nature. But even if one believes that man is capable of responding to something other than self-interest, one needs to take account (as Secretary of State John Foster Dulles argued) of 'what men are, not what the Church thinks they ought to be'.[16] An appeal to idealism is not enough and therefore one will attempt, by legislation, to gather into the hands of the state more and more control over the means of production and distribution.

There has not been much recent British interest in political theology nor even in attempts to examine the social dimension of the Christian gospel. Radical political theology emanating from the Americas has attracted some attention, chiefly of a critical kind, but it has remained somewhat exotic. The one attempt at a self-conscious and deliberate application of liberation theology to the British scene[17] has caused little stir. Because *Agenda for Prophets* is a collection of essays it does not bear much resemblance to the closely worked liberation theology of Latin America, a coherent system backed by a clear, if controversial, hermeneutic method and a Marxian analysis of society, deployed in support of a particular *praxis*, The contributors to the volume share a general outlook, anti-capitalist, well left of centre, influenced by and sympathetic to Marxism – though some are more sympathetic than others. Their point of view is clearly enough expressed. They exhibit a fierce anger and impatience with contemporary British society, which one feels is often justified by their experience. But they have not yet set out their arguments, either political or theological, with sufficient coherence and detail for the argument to be tested or even for the objectives to be wholly clear. One feels that one is being exhorted rather than convinced.

I have the impression that there is another reason, besides its collective authorship, why the volume is different from the systematic liberation theologies which have emerged elsewhere. Those radical political theologies have almost always been wrought out of situations in which violence has become an inescapable way of life rather than an occasional happening – whether it is the violence of society or the violence of the oppressed. Hence the liberation theologian's insistence that theology is something *done*. It begins with *praxis* in a society where the choices are both inescapable and agonizing. This does not mean that it can be lightly dismissed as rationalizing after the event, as though any theology which is produced by serious reflection upon reality must be unsatisfactory theology. It would be absurd to suppose, for instance, that Hooker's writings owed nothing to a desire to present an apologia for the political events of the sixteenth century.

It seems to me, however, that even the contributors to *Agenda for Prophets* do not, as yet, believe that Britain is in the condition in which those final, agonizing but inescapable choices have to be made. There is a rubicon which they have not crossed. They plainly believe that radical upheaval is necessary if the present economic system and the power structures built upon it are to give way to something more akin to justice and equality. But it does not seem to me that they have actually reached the point where they are prepared to say that there is violence, oppression or exploitation in British society of such a kind as to represent what is normally meant by tyranny. I am sure that they believe that the powerless suffer at the hands of the powerful, live in conditions which amount to grave injustice and at times are subjected to actual violence by the agents of society. It is not clear, however, that they are convinced that the final choice has to be made. For all that they reject reformism, the over-all impression they give is that British society is not quite beyond hope of being changed by methods other than actual violent revolution.

In part of Britain, in Northern Ireland, violence is a fact of everybody's lives. In other parts of the country, in the inner cities, the cool, damp early summer of 1981 saw violence become a fact of life for some people. It may be that there are those who see these events as the beginning of the violent confrontation between an oppressing society and the oppressed. It may be that there are Christians who analyse the situation in this way, find themselves caught up in the confrontation and are making the final, agonizing choices. The logic of radical liberation itself – and the stress it lays upon the primacy of *praxis* – suggests that until the choices are made and the confrontation comes, the theology will not be completely done. And it does not seem to me that the authors of *Agenda for Prophets*, at least when they wrote their essays, judge that that moment has yet been reached.

It is the insistence of the liberation theologians that theology is something *done*, the consequence of *praxis*, that has convinced me that a consideration of political morality must take precedence over those other issues which, in the first chapter, I set aside. If *real* theology can only follow action, then how one acts (morality) becomes the primary issue. Liberation theologians do not appear to be much concerned to examine the moral issues raised by political action, though obviously their whole theology springs from a moral concern for justice. They do not believe it possible to construct a Christian ethic. Theirs is, on the whole, a contextual morality – the situation is such that one really has no option but to act, as God acts, to liberate the poor and the oppressed. This seems to me to suffer from the weakness of all contextual approaches: it is impossible to apply the principle to one's personal life in any context other than the political. One has to say that one's behaviour in every other sphere is governed by some wholly 'different' morality.

It is also unsatisfactory to imply that one can judge, and act against, the immorality of the oppressors unless one is prepared to apply the standards of morality to one's own behaviour. Simply to argue that one must choose for those who have justice on their side is not enough if it implies that any action that will further that cause is acceptable. This is precisely the kind of pragmatism which has been used to immoral effect by some of those who hold power now and it ignores the need to assert that good is good. Liberation theology is, in fact, the reverse of the provisional and tentative. It asserts the primacy of a single biblical theme, the liberation of the oppressed, as the basis for all hermeneutics; the Marxian analysis of history and society which makes a contextual morality possible; and the importance of the basic community, the group of Christians engaged in political action, as the place where the actual Church is most authoritatively to be found. None of those assertions is beyond question but any modification of them casts doubt upon the whole system. Liberation theology appears to be saying that what matters is that the just cause must be made to succeed. One is bound to ask whether an interpretation of the Bible which makes that the *controlling* principle is compatible with the cross. For it is at least arguable that the two most obvious features of the death of Christ are a determination to die rather than to triumph by *any* means and to forgive at *whatever* cost.

But, if one is to be critical of liberation theology, it is important to take note of it also. It will not do to be complacent and say that those who are militantly opposed to our society (within or without) are obviously wicked and that we may use any means that may come to hand in order to deal with them. This is simply to accept uncritically our society and its laws and to lose sight of the fact that society, law and order are only good when they encourage men and women to be fully human. The mere existence of a liberation theology ought to be enough to make us ask searching and difficult questions about society as it now exists. It may be naive to work on the assumption that the critics of society are always right but it must be even more naive to assume that society is above criticism. The crucial thing is to know why one is asking questions. Why is injustice immoral? By what standard does one determine whether society is less just than it ought to be? One needs, in other words, to be sure what demands Christian morality makes upon citizens and society and why it does so. I realize that there is some circularity in the argument, for I have also maintained that morality is essentially a part of believing and therefore requires a theological basis. Recognizing that most varieties of ethics are inadequate because they are too static, in that they treat the human beings involved as though they were not themselves changed by the moral choices they make, I accept the contention of political theologians that theology cannot be a purely academic study detached from social experience. But I am uneasy about claims for the absolute priority of action over every other consideration.

In the last essay in *Agenda for Prophets* Herbert McCabe deals with the twin questions of violence and the class struggle. He believes that the class struggle is inevitable. Violence he regards as not quite inevitable nor absolutely incompatible with Christian love. Since the class struggle will inevitably evoke oppressive action from those who at present possess power, and their violence will necessitate the use of violence by the oppressed, the hope of a peaceful solution is not very great. 'It will be the Christian's aim', say the editors, commenting on McCabe's essay, 'to transform society without such bitterness and pain but, as McCabe suggests, that hope is likely to be a vain one.'[18] Here, as it seems to me, there is an instinctively Christian hesitation about pressing directly for the use of violence in the reform of society. It is what led me earlier in this chapter to say both that it is not surprising that, *when society is violent*, some Christians should feel driven to fight as well as suffer alongside the oppressed, and also that even the most radical of political theologies will tend to regard violence as justifiable only when no other alternative is left. It is one thing to feel compelled by Christian love and justice to side with the oppressed when open conflict exists: it is quite another to advocate the *initiation* of violent conflict.

It is also significant that Father McCabe discusses violence in the context of forgiveness. It will be obvious by this time that I am convinced that a theology of forgiveness is the only thing that makes political (or any other kind of) morality possible. But I have to recognize that there is one area in which forgiveness seems to lose its power. This is a point which I made in the last chapter about the cross and the resurrection. One cannot do other people's forgiving for them. One cannot say to a party of Jews on the way to the Nazi gas chamber, or to the relatives of South African blacks who have 'fallen' from a fourth-storey window while being questioned by the police, 'The way to solve this problem is for you to forgive those who persecute you'. I do not think I could even say it to an innocent citizen of Brixton whose house had been smashed by police looking for petrol bombs. What I might *do* would depend upon the degree to which I understood the situation (which is why naivety is so dangerous), the degree of real brutality and oppression involved, and the resources available to me.

Moreover the three examples I have given are not on the same level and it is absurd to talk as though they were. A society in which some policemen can behave brutally on infrequent occasions is different from a society in which several million people are systematically destroyed. One cannot condone either case but the level of response appropriate in one would be totally inappropriate in the other. Everyone involved in such a situation, including myself, might need to forgive or to be forgiven. No doubt it would be important for the victims to learn to forgive, but I do not think I could insist that that was the answer for them or refuse to help if they were unable to forgive. If, unable to forgive, they were to use violence against violence, then there would be a new situation. I could not always expect to be a peace-maker because reconciliation is not the same thing as compromise. That option might not be available. I might *have* to choose sides. Perhaps the liberation theologians are giving notice that they would have to choose a particular side if and when the moment comes. I suppose that if one were absolutely convinced that the Marxist analysis of society were correct and applicable, one could take up that position. It would still not be clear precisely when one would have to say that there was no longer any alternative to the use of violence. And, if it is presumptuous to decide that the oppressed must forgive the oppressors, it is equally presumptuous to decide, on behalf of the oppressed, that the moment has come when no forgiveness is possible and that they ought to kill and be killed in the class struggle.

The contributors to *Agenda for Prophets* make no bones about, and little attempt to defend, their left-wing views. For the most part they simply assert that a socialist society is the only kind of society consonant with Christianity. There is a surprisingly widespread assumption, even among those who dislike the implications, that if Christianity is to be given political expression it is likely to be socialist. When it first became known that I was preparing these lectures people would ask what my topic was. If I said, 'Christianity and Politics', their response very often was to smile and say, 'Ah, my own views are more like Dr Norman's' – Dr Norman[19] being the person who is even-handedly opposed to both politics and the left. The assumptions seemed to be (a) that they were going to disagree with *whatever* conclusion I came to; and (b) that that would be because my conclusions would inevitably be too far to the left. And that would apply, they seemed to say, to anyone who was interested in the relationship between Christianity and politics.

Equally widespread is the belief that support for the Social Democratic Party is somehow the 'respectable' political attitude for a Christian to adopt.[20] In fact, the vast majority of Christians whom I actually meet seem to belong neither to the radical left nor to the marginally left of centre. Perhaps because they are inevitably mostly middle-class and Anglican like myself, they appear to vote Conservative. It ought to be apparent by this time that I do not believe that there is *any* political programme or blue-print which will be true for all time or produce a society which will permanently embody a Christian ideal. It is possible to say that at this particular time this particular society needs to be changed in this particular way to make it conform more closely to that ideal. But if I were a Polish Christian the political programme I would most ardently support would be very different from the programme I thought most desirable in Britain.

But no Christian, whatever his view of fallen men – *because* of his view of fallen man – can ever allow the pursuit of a political programme (revolutionary, monetarist or collectivist) to become an absolute good. For human society *will not* become perfect. Those committed to the most idealistic programme will either be crushed by an intolerable burden of guilt for the corporate sinfulness of society – in which they share but which they cannot eradicate – or they will project their guilt, in the form of hatred, upon those whom they identify as the enemies of justice, freedom or brotherhood.[21] That is always the danger in political theology, of whatever kind.

In spite of the limitations I have already recognized, it remains true that, if society is imperfectible because man is sinful, then forgiveness is the primary way to deal with it. For forgiveness is the Christian, because it is Christ's, way of dealing with sin. Christian commitment to political programmes has to be accompanied by forgiveness for society, for groups and individuals within it, and for oneself. That is the heart of what saintliness is. The saint is not the impeccably pure human being, but the forgiven sinner. And saintliness, as I have argued, is what the Christian has to strive for in politics as in every other aspect of life.

I am not pleading that Christians should seek to create or to occupy some kind of formalized role of 'saint-in-politics'. Indian politics seems to have known such a figure from time to time, though even there it has not always been successful and can be out-manoeuvred by the politicians of expediency – as the history of the Janata government demonstrated. Contemporary Iran also has such figures. Their saintliness does not always seem very appealing. But, in any case, it is not a publicly acknowledged holy wisdom or a religious fanaticism which is the real mark of the Christian saint. He or she is, rather, the forgiven and forgiving sinner, possessing an inner integrity and a firm grasp upon what is good; striving to live by ideals but willing to face the agonizing and costly business of grappling with human imperfection (including his own); trying nevertheless to serve society and to move it towards what it ought to be; challenging accepted consequentialist pragmatism by the unexpectedness of his vision.

The fact that, in the moral dilemmas which politics continually creates, the saint may do surprising things is very important. In the end a logical analysis of the problem is not enough in itself because reasoning about what one ought to do *is* qualitatively different from reasoning about matters of fact. There cannot be more than one right answer to a problem in logic. That may not be true of a problem in morals.

To illustrate what I mean, the human race seems to me to be divided into two classes of shopper. One class, to which my wife belongs, believes that there is, in principle, the precise article for which she is looking, somewhere, in some as yet undiscovered shop round some unexplored corner. The other class, and I am one of them, goes to the obvious shop and buys the best he can find. The difference between theoretical and practical reasoning may be rather like that. There *may* not be one single solution to the moral problem. In any case there is not all the time in the world to devote to finding it. One may have to do the best one can, making one's analysis, facing the dilemma and admitting one is a sinner. One has also to be like Holland's saintly version of Williams's Jim, examining the dilemma to see whether it ought not to be rejected altogether.[22] And, even if there seems to be no right thing to do, one still has to refuse to be paralysed into inaction. It is being a certain kind of person in a given context that really matters.

That will, of course, sound terrifying to the non-Christian for it will awaken memories of those well-meaning people who have been responsible for some of the great disasters of history. It will seem to drive a potentially dangerous distinction between what it is right to do and what is good – a distinction which, moreover, encourages hypocrisy. It will also seem to go back on the point made several times in this book and even in this chapter, that clear, rigorous and informed thought is necessary in making moral judgements.

No contradiction is intended. What I am concerned to urge is the necessity for extremely careful and thorough thinking precisely because integrity depends upon it. And when those situations arise in which there seems to be no single, wholly good course of action open to one, or when there is little time for rigorous thinking, it is integrity which will enable one to come to the best judgement possible. The 'surprising' actions of the saint derive from the kind of person he is and that person is formed by his own continuing endeavour to live a life that expresses the ideals of Christ. And that involves continuous concern for and wrestling with moral questions.

John Finnis, arguing against consequentialism and for the principles of natural law, has reminded us that even every good course of action may have consequences that are incalculable and may prevent other equally good actions – that to choose to save lives as a doctor will mean that I cannot serve the community by producing material goods or making new scientific discoveries.[23] That is the nature of choice and of history. He also argues that one ought never for consequentialist reasons to choose to do anything '*which of itself does nothing but* damage or impede . . . basic forms of human good'.[24] This looks like a clear assertion that the good and the right thing to do must be the same, so that (in what seems to be another version of Williams's Jim) one ought not to shoot an innocent person to secure the release of hostages. But even Finnis is willing, in the end, to say that there are many cases which, because of their complexity and tragic implications, call not so much for strict application of principles but for the judgement of 'wisely-good persons'. 'In abstract discussions', he says, 'we ought not to expect more precision than the subject matter will bear.'[25] So he, too, while preferring principle to consequentialism, seems to be saying that personal judgement is not simply a matter of applying absolute standards. Even to choose what is good may involve not choosing something else which is also good.

The really intractable problem remains the case where the choice appears to be not between goods but between evils. And it is here that the kind of person one has become is of crucial importance. The integrity and acuteness of one's moral judgement is tested as in no other situation. In a novel called *Lion's Ransom* Philip Loraine makes one of his characters seek the advice of a priest in the confessional. The priest says: 'Since you must do one thing or the other, and to you both seem wrong, you can only choose and go through with that choice, and count this time as a dark valley out of which you will emerge somehow or other, as we all do; and on the other side of it, waiting for you in a way you can't begin to understand now, will be the love of God; and though what you have done will still have been wrong, you will be forgiven as we are all forgiven.'

That may be too simply put – missing much of the agony of choice, omitting the provisos, suggesting that God's forgiveness is automatic. But it is what a Christian priest would have to say to someone who had really tried to find a good answer and had failed. The best thing to do in a particular situation may not always be the wholly good, the ideal thing to do. There is no way of laying down in advance the precise conditions in which it will be right to do something which is itself wrong. What makes it wrong is not whatever feelings of guilt one may or may not have, but the damage it does, the moral cost. The decision that, nevertheless, something wrong is the thing to be done is always a matter of last rather than first resort, when one has wrestled with the options and thought rigorously about them. And then it is only to be chosen in the spirit which the priest in the novel described – as a kind of going down into a darkness. It is to be arrived at, not by weighing facts against principles, but by weighing the moral implications of one set of facts, actions and probable consequences against another. One may be wrong in one's judgement. One will be doing, whatever one decides, something which is less than good. One is a sinner who needs forgivensss. But that does not mean that one need not act at all or that it does not matter what one does. One has to do the best one can and the only safeguard is one's own integrity which depends above all upon a clear sense of what is good and what is evil. Recognizing that the only course open is nevertheless wrong goes some way to preserve integrity for its prevents that dangerously arrogant conviction that whatever one does must be the right thing to do. It has, therefore, both a practical and a moral value.

I do not believe there is a necessary incompatibility between the moral and the practical in politics more than there is in any other aspect of human life. Such disconsonance as there is ought not to be thought of as arising from the demands of absolute moral rules, on the one hand, and of expediency on the other.Nor is it due to an incompatibility between pure and holy men and women and corrupt politics. Christian morality is about being a kind of person and that kind of person is an ideal derived from knowledge of God revealed in Christ. It is a goal not a state from which one starts. What makes politics a difficult sphere in which to struggle towards that goal is the fact that violence, manipulation and other invasions of the dignity and worth of men and women seem to be unavoidable. But there is, nevertheless, a real difference between a reluctant acceptance of them when they are unavoidable and a willing embracing of them as if they were desirable. That difference is real and recognizable, even if it cannot be precisely defined.

When the imperfectibility of human nature creates a situation in which the choice between evils appears to be unavoidable, the kind of person one is becomes of paramount importance because at that point rules become inadequate if not actually impossible. What is to be done is a matter for the agonizing judgement of the man or woman concerned. This does not mean that general principles have no significance: they will have played a large part in determining the kind of person that man or that woman has become. They also provide the framework for all the difficult questions that have to be asked before one can be certain that a choice between evils is all that remains.

Because 'the Church', in any of the institutional or organizational forms in which we know it, stands between the true Body of Christ and its earthing in the lives of Christian individuals or groups, it is 'the Church' which has the obligation to maintain the absolute ideals of holiness to which the Christian moves. It delimits the framework, demands that the critical questions are asked, asserts the uncompromising standards, educates and assists and cares for the Christian along the way. Or it should do so. If it appears to be negative and critical, that is no more than a symptom of its fulfilling its proper role over against society.

Upon Christians, as members of society, there falls the obligation of actually shaping the political community. This is not a matter of choice, for even to do nothing will still have an effect. But if action is forced upon us so is humility: there will never be a perfect blueprint for society. Faced with the imperfection of human life we are to remember that even to choose a *lesser* evil is to proclaim oneself a sinner, dependent on the forgiveness of God and of those whom we harm. It follows, then, that to be generous in our willingness to bear the cost of other people's actions, because we perceive that they have to bear the moral cost of ours, is part of a general purpose to minimize damage to, or devaluation of, human beings. In this there is little difference between the way a Christian copes with political and with personal moral decisions. The cynical and the superficial will say that this is not a practical recipe for politics. Let them consider what are the most intractable problem areas in British society – class, race, Northern Ireland, the inner cities, unemployment. All these are problems in which a deeply ingrained and bitter sense of having been *wronged* plays a tremendously important part. Policies which increase that sense of wrong must exacerbate the situation. For instance, to urge the importance of, and promise rewards to, those who work hardest, while accepting massive growth in unemployment, is inevitably to increase the number of people who are made to feel that they are failures, scroungers and unwanted by society.

If people are the proper interface between Christianity and politics, and if forgiveness is the one practical means of making the interface feasible, one has also to remember that forgiveness is not easily come by. The very fact that makes it necessary – the imperfectibility of human beings and human society – is the thing that also makes forgiveness hard to achieve. Christians, therefore, have two reasons for always choosing the generous, caring, unselfish political course. Not only is it an expression of their own sense of what it is to be forgiving and forgiven. It is also a recognition of the fact that one ought not to ask other people to bear a more difficult burden of forgiveness than human nature can bear. The prophets of violence will prove to be right unless society recognizes that the deep and bitter sense of having been wronged arises because the burden of forgiving is all too often placed solely upon the minorities or the powerless, whom we thought could be compelled to accept it.

Notes

1. See pp. 3ff.
2. See p. 35.
3. See p. 57.
4. B. Mitchell, *Law, Morality and Religion in a Secular Society*, O.U.P. (reprint) 1978, p. 72.
5. Matthew 25:31ff.
6. L. M. Thompson, *The Unification of South Africa*, O.U.P. 1960. pp. 116–26.
7. See p. 13.
8. See the leading article 'Pastoral Politics', *The Times*, 16 September 1980.
9. By Ronald Butt, 12 February 1981.
10. Haddon Willmer has attempted to develop a politics of forgiveness in a series of articles – 'The Politics of Forgiveness – A New Dynamic', in *The Furrow*, April 1979; 'The Politics of Forgiveness' in *Third Way*, May 1979; 'Forgiveness and Politics' in *Crucible*, July-September 1979.
11. There is now an extensive literature on the subject of political theology. In view of the use made of Niebuhr in the first chapter of this book an interesting recent work is D. P. McCann, *Christian Realism and Liberation Theology*, Orbis Books 1981.
12. See e. g. J. L. Segundo, *The Liberation of Theology*, Orbis Books 1976.
13. As is assumed by C. H. Sisson, 'The Church's Abdication' in *The Spectator*, 7 March 1981.
14. K. Leech, 'Liberating Theology: the Thought of Juan Luis Segundo', *Theology*, vol. LXXXIV, p. 259.
15. See e. g. R. Preston, *Religion and the Persistence of Capitalism*, S.C.M. 1979, p. 105.
16. K. W. Thompson, *The Moral Issue in Statecraft*, Louisiana State University Press 1966, p. 48.

17. R. Ambler and D. Haslam (eds.), *Agenda for Prophets*, Bowerdean Press 1980.
18. *Ibid.*, p. 174.
19. See p. 4.
20. See e.g. Clifford Longley, 'The growing "social democrat" face of British Christianity' in *The Times*, 2 February 1981.
21. This is a near-quotation of words from *The Time is Now* (Report of the first meeting of the Anglican Consultative Council) S.P.C.K. 1971, p. 43. I was a member of the preparatory committee for this section and was responsible for suggesting these particular words.
22. See p. 155.
23. J. Finnis, *Natural Law and Natural Rights*, O.U.P. 1980, p. 120.
24. *Ibid.*, p. 118.
25. *Ibid.*, p. 124.

INDEX